STUDY GUIDE TO ACCOMPANY

NATION

OF NATIONS

A NARRATIVE HISTORY
OF THE AMERICAN REPUBLIC

Volume II: Since 1865

SECOND EDITION

JAMES WEST DAVIDSON

WILLIAM E. GIENAPP
Harvard University

CHRISTINE LEIGH HEYRMAN
University of Delaware

MARK H. LYTLE
Bard College

MICHAEL B. STOFF
University of Texas, Austin

McGRAW-HILL, INC.

New York   St. Louis   San Francisco   Auckland   Bogotá   Caracas
Lisbon   London   Madrid   Mexico City   Milan   Montreal   New Delhi
San Juan   Singapore   Sydney   Tokyo   Toronto

Study Guide to Accompany NATION OF NATIONS
A Narrative History of the American Republic, Volume II: Since 1865

 This book is printed on recycled, acid-free paper containing a minimum
of 50% total recycled fiber with 10% postconsumer de-inked fiber.

1 2 3 4 5 6 7 8 9 0 DOH DOH 9 0 9 8 7 6 5 4

ISBN 0-07-015637-9

The editors were Peter M. Labella and Lisa V. Calberg;
the production supervisor was Annette Mayeski.
The cover was designed by Katharine Hulse.
R. R. Donnelley & Sons Company was printer and binder.

Reproduced on the cover: *Armistice Day Parade*, 1919, by Theresa Bernstein. Oil on canvas, 30" x 40".
Courtesy, Janet Marqusee Fine Arts, Ltd..

CONTENTS

INTRODUCTION

This Study Guide is designed to accompany the second edition of *Nation of Nations: A Narrative History of the American Republic.* In it, we try to help you organize more clearly the facts and themes presented in the text and to present that material more cogently in exams and papers. Ultimately, we hope, the guide may even help you come to grips with the history of a nation that has shaped us all in countless ways. To quote from the preface of the text itself, "History supplies our very identity--a sense of the social groups to which we belong, whether family, ethnic group, race, class, or gender. It reveals to us the foundations of our deepest religious beliefs and traces the roots of our economic and political systems. It explores how we celebrate or grieve, sing the songs we sing, weather the illnesses to which time and chance subject us. It commands our attention for all these good reasons and for no good reason at all, other than a fascination with the way the myriad tales play out."

A CRITICAL APPROACH TO READING HISTORY

Before providing more information about the study guide, a word may be in order about the textbook itself. In the days before the consumer movement dictated that warnings be affixed to hazardous products, the traditional attitude of most sellers was summed up in the Latin motto, *caveat emptor:* let the buyer beware. We have not affixed warning labels to our text, but we would like to make it clear that buyers should be more than a little wary when reading *any* history--including our own.

Why? All history is presented in a way that is slightly seductive. Textbooks come dressed out in the full trappings of authority. They present the printed word on crisp white pages, provide a host of detailed maps, charts, and appendices, plus a list of authors with university affiliations after their names. The subliminal message behind all these trappings is, *This book is authoritative. This is history the way it* really *happened. Read and believe.* When, of course, the truth is much more complicated.

Look, for example, at the following paragraph, taken from Chapter 20 of *Nation of Nations*. It discusses conditions in the South after the Civil War.

> In 1860 slaves accounted for nearly 60 percent of the agricultural wealth in the cotton states stretching from South Carolina to Louisiana. The value of farm lands and buildings amounted to less than a third. Emancipation changed all that. With slaves no longer "property" that could be controlled or moved at will, land itself became an important measure of worth. Southern planters and farmers who had once been "labor lords"

became landlords to whom property now meant land. This shift was reflected in the geography of the postwar South.

On the face of it, the paragraph seems straightforward. It is not an impassioned argument
filled with value judgments about whether Andrew Carnegie was a hero or a villain,
whether Franklin Roosevelt was an inspired political leader, or whether the Vietnam War
could have been avoided or won with honor. It merely describes the nature of agricultural
wealth after the Civil War.

But the word *merely* is misleading. The paragraph lists statistics about the percentage
of wealth as measured in slaves and in farm lands and buildings. How accurate are the statistics? Even when historians discuss such "factual" topics as agricultural wealth or the mortality rates among immigrants or the size of middle-class families, the computations can be
full of uncertainty. Often, years of research lie behind such what seem to be simple statements about numbers. And in most cases, the numbers are being placed in a text to make a
more complicated point. The paragraph quoted makes a distinction between wealth based
on land and wealth based on slaves. It argues that after the Civil War, cotton planters came
to value land much more strongly than they did before the war. Suddenly, we are talking
less about "simple facts" and more about interpretations that depend on many different
sources of information. Is this an accurate portrayal of the way planters thought after the
Civil War?

There is no way, of course, for readers to skeptically check the research behind this
particular assertion--or to check the evidence supporting a multitude of other assertions in
any history text. Yet it is worth understanding, right at the start, that to compress an account of American history even into an ample 1000 pages means leaving out most of the
uncertainties behind any statement of "facts."

Beyond those doubts lie even larger uncertainties in the matter of interpretation. In
composing a narrative like this, the authors have had to make hard choices about presenting
American history. These decisions must be made chapter by chapter, paragraph by paragraph, and even sentence by sentence. How much biographical information should one include of pivotal figures like Lincoln, Franklin Roosevelt or Martin Luther King? How much
should one discuss anonymous Americans like the Okies heading for California after the
dust storms of the 1930s? To what degree should we cover topics like abortion or the history
of American writers and artists? Such decisions are not merely questions of space. They in-
volve larger issues of interpretation. Do individual actions shape history more than broad
social forces and trends? Is it more important to talk about the rise of a consumer-driven
economy or the rise of the modern presidency? Putting words to paper involves making
choices about a host of different issues, both large and small.

In the limited space available to a textbook, it is impossible to explore in any detail so many differences of interpretation. But as alert readers, you should be aware that those differences remain, always lurking below the narrative's confident surface. One goal of this study guide is to help students become more sensitive to the choices historians must inevitably make.

HOW TO USE THIS STUDY GUIDE

The guide proceeds chapter by chapter, providing both **Review Questions** that are designed to help you review for exams as well as a **Critical Thinking** section designed to hone skills that are crucial for analyzing historical problems and writing concise, coherent essays, research papers and examinations. Within each chapter, the material is presented as follows:

The Chapter in Perspective opens with a paragraph or two placing the chapter under review within the larger context of the American history. These paragraphs underline links to materials discussed in previous chapters. Sometimes, they identify trends that will become increasingly important in future chapters.

Overview. This provides a summary of the chapter's major themes, using the same headings that appear in the chapter itself. It may be useful to read the overview before beginning your reading, as a preview of the material. Or read afterward, the Overview serves as a tool for review. Summaries like these, of course, cannot include all the facts and interpretive material you will need to discuss key themes and topics. But they should serve to focus attention on those areas you would naturally elaborate upon in an exam.

Key Events are time line chronologies. Use them as a checklist of important occurrences and trends, but also consider how they relate to each other in sequence, in order to develop a sense of the pacing of history. How long were the Pilgrims in Massachusetts before John Winthrop's Puritans arrived? (Chapter 3) Was it years or decades between the time that William Lloyd Garrison established his radical abolitionist newspaper *The Liberator* and his split with the more moderate antislavery forces? (Chapter 12) Thus time lines allow you to better sense the progression of events and the matter of historical timing.

Learning Objectives. These list the chapter's five or six most important themes. Like the Overview, they serve as a means of reviewing key material that is likely to be covered, especially in essay questions. In fact, they could be treated as just as easily as exam questions: if you find you can't answer each of them coherently, you need additional preparation.

Multiple Choice Questions include ten per chapter. Although they cover a representative range of topics, they are not meant to be exhaustive in coverage--only to provide a general feel for the *type* of factual questions that may be asked on an exam. Following each item is a page reference to the text, indicating where the correct answer may be found.

Identification Questions. These include both terms and concepts as well as individuals and places. They are fairly comprehensive for each chapter: that is, if you can explain the significance of all of them, you should be well prepared to handle the factual aspects of the chapter material. In addition, each chapter includes an outline map and asks you to locate significant places or other geographic information central to the period.

Essay Questions. These cover a range of topics of the sort that might be encountered on an exam. In using the questions for review, it may not be necessary to write out an entire sample essay, although putting something to paper is always a superior way to organize your thoughts. (It is remarkable how many ideas that seem brilliant when floating around in one's brain, end up looking vague and imprecise when actually committed to paper.) An alternate way to review would be to jot down a brief outline of the points that the essay would cover, and talk them through orally, perhaps with a friend. In any case, jotting an outline down before beginning an essay is always a good practice.

Evaluating Evidence (Maps, Illustrations and Charts). Each Critical Thinking section begins with questions asking for evaluation or analysis of the text's illustrative material. As authors, we feel strongly that students, professors and even the writers of many textbooks do not pay close enough attention to the materials that accompany the core narrative. We have included the maps, graphs and illustrations not merely as window dressing, but as ways to make clearer the points in the text. Thus these questions can be seen as ways to help you understand more clearly the main point of a map or chart, and to notice details in paintings or photographs that might not have been so obvious at first glance.

Critical Analysis. On the face of it, this section of the Study Guide would seem the most easily skippable. It merely reprints a section of the text itself--usually two or three paragraphs--that you have already encountered. But the passage may bear rereading, for two reasons. First, it has often been selected because it is pivotal, making a point that is likely to be encountered on an exam question. Second, the questions that follow the selection are designed to test your skills as a reader. If you can answer them easily, then your reading of other portions of the narrative has most likely been equally sharp. If they prove more difficult to answer, or require a rereading of the passage, then they point up the need to develop the kind of close reading skills indispensable not only for analyzing *Nation of Nations*, but any historical narrative or argument.

Primary Source. Each chapter concludes with a primary source excerpt that illustrates one of the chapter's themes. A *primary source* is one that has been written (or made, or left behind in some way) by historical subjects themselves, not by later historians studying or analyzing the period. It could be a diary, a song, a last will and testament, an official record of laws passed, or the sketch on the back of an envelope. Primary sources are the raw materials of history: those pieces of the puzzle from which the narrative in this and all history books are pieced together. We include a selection of them in order to underline the point we made about: that is, what a chancy business interpreting history is. The "lessons" history provides are usually not so evident in the primary sources as they are in a textbook. To understand a subject in depth, we must all become our own historians, going to the primary sources to put together the story for ourselves.

Obviously, in such a short space we can provide only a hint of what that process involves, just as in *Nation of Nations*, we can only sketch the major outlines of American history. But in the text and Study Guide, we hope we have provided enough of both the sinews and the savor of the historian's task so that you may wish to continue your own explorations of history. Like it or not, the events shaping this teeming nation of nations have also defined and shaped us, and we can look to our future more intelligently the better we understand the contours of our past.

James West Davidson

William E. Gienapp

Christine Leigh Heyrman

Mark H. Lytle

Michael B. Stoff

17

RECONSTRUCTING THE UNION

THE CHAPTER IN PERSPECTIVE

T he Civil War resolved several longstanding problems in the Republic. For one, the threat of secession had been laid to rest; the Union was perpetual, as Andrew Jackson had proclaimed in 1832. Slavery had also been destroyed, and with it the most "peculiar" feature of the culture of the Old South. With the agrarian South vanquished and impoverished, the industrial North was now the dominant section politically and economically, and the nation's course toward full industrialization established. But the war had also created new problems. What rights the former slaves would have, and what their place would be in American society was unclear. Similarly, the process by which the former states of the Confederacy would regain their previous rights was uncertain.

Yet if the potential for far reaching change existed at the end of the war, key elements of the American political tradition continued to hold sway and exerted a restraining influence. For example, Americans remained committed to the federal system. Although the federal government exercised greater power after the war than before, most Americans continued to believe that protecting individual rights was the responsibility of the states. In addition, the fear of a standing army, a heritage of the Revolution, remained undiminished. Not only had the Union army been quickly demobilized, but Northerners were uncomfortable at the thought of a prolonged military occupation of the South or the active intervention of the army in domestic affairs. Finally, bolstered by the market revolution, Americans remained wedded to the doctrines of private property, self-reliance, and individual achievement, values that worked against any program of government assistance to the freed people. It was within this mix of change and tradition--of the possibility to overthrow the past and the desire to conserve it--that Reconstruction would take shape and eventually unravel.

OVERVIEW

The chapter begins by examining the saga of Benjamin Montgomery, an extraordinary ex-slave who after the war purchased the plantation of Confederate president Jefferson Davis. Through energy and hard work, Montgomery became a leading planter in the postwar South during the period of Reconstruction, when the South was in the process of resuming its place in the Union. Montgomery's hopes and aspirations, as well as his ultimate failure, symbolized both the possibilities for radical change in the South and the ultimate tragedy of Reconstruction for black Americans.

Presidential Reconstruction

The problem of Reconstruction forced consideration even during the war, as Lincoln formulated plans for the restoration of the Union once the fighting was over. Lincoln favored a less stringent plan than Congress did, since he was eager to bring states back into the Union and wanted to build up a Republican party in the South. Radical Republicans in Congress doubted southern whites' loyalty, wanted to punish the South, and saw blacks as the only sizable loyal group in the region. Lincoln vetoed the Radicals' plan in 1864, but by war's end he seemed to be moving in the direction of the Radicals.

Lincoln's assassination elevated Andrew Johnson, a War Democrat from Tennessee, to the presidency. It was crucial in this critical moment, with southerners bewildered and looking for guidance, that the president make clear what was required of them. Johnson moved in the summer of 1865 to enact Lincoln's program, but in so doing he changed its terms and lessened its requirements. Under Johnson's guidelines, all the former states of the Confederacy established new state governments in 1865. Yet southern whites refused to give blacks many civil rights enjoyed by whites, instead passing a series of black codes. These laws applied only to blacks, and were designed to keep them an uneducated, propertyless, agricultural laboring class. Equally disturbing to northerners, white southerners defiantly elected prominent former Confederates to office.

Congress repudiated Johnson's program in December 1865 and refused to seat the senators and members of Congress from the former Confederate states. Instead, it extended the life of the Freedmen's Bureau over Johnson's veto in order to provide assistance to freed people (former slaves) and passed the Fourteenth Amendment, sending it to the states for ratification. This amendment made blacks citizens, extended basic civil rights to all citizens, required prominent Confederates to be pardoned by Congress, and by indirection provided for black male suffrage in the South. Only Tennessee of the Confederate states ratified the amendment. It was promptly readmitted to the Union. The remaining 10 states still lacked congressional representation and were under military rule. Breaking with Congress, Johnson took his case to the northern people in the fall elections of 1866. To his dismay, Republicans won a sweeping victory, including more than a two-thirds majority in both houses of Congress (thus allowing them to override any presidential veto).

Congressional Reconstruction

Given a popular mandate, Republicans in Congress proceeded to enact their own program of Reconstruction, requiring the unreconstructed states to ratify the Fourteenth Amendment and adopt black suffrage. States that delayed the process were required to ratify the Fifteenth Amendment, which also forbid racial tests for voting. Congress refused, however, to redistribute land to the freedmen, believing that giving blacks the ballot and civil rights was sufficient.

Johnson remained at odds with Congress and tried to obstruct the will of the legislative branch by interpreting laws as narrowly as possible and removing army generals in the South who sympathized with Congress on Reconstruction. When the president attempted to remove Secretary of War Edwin Stanton, a Radical, in violation of the new Tenure of Office Act, the House finally impeached Johnson. Despite his obstructionism, he was acquitted in the Senate by one vote. Those Republican Senators who voted for acquittal believed that Johnson had not committed any crime, only political errors, and they were uneasy about using the impeachment process to resolve a political dispute between the two branches of government. Johnson served out the remainder of his term, but the power of the Radicals had peaked.

The Supreme Court refused to intervene in the dispute between Johnson and Congress, and it declined to rule on the constitutionality of Reconstruction. It adopted the position that Reconstruction was an extraordinary situation and essentially a political matter.

Reconstruction in the South

Under Congress' program, radical governments assumed power in the South. Despite the complaints and allegations of unreconstructed southerners, none of these governments was controlled by black southerners. Only in South Carolina, where a majority of the voters were African-Americans, did black officeholders approximate their proportion of the population. Black officeholders, who ranged widely in ability, generally came from the top rungs of African-American society.

In most southern states, black voters were not sufficient to form a majority. The party needed white support as well. Native white southerners who joined the Republican party were called scalawags; they were often Unionists from the hill counties or former Whigs attracted by the party's economic nationalism. Northerners who came to the South after the war and held public office were derisively referred to as Carpetbaggers. Contrary to their image, they were not all poor and self-interested. They were much more sympathetic to black rights than were southern-born white Republicans and disproportionately held office, and especially the highest offices, in the Republican regimes.

The new southern state constitutions adopted some important reforms, most notably the establishment of public schools. But they were cautious on the issue of racial equality and did not forbid segregation.

The southern Republican governments confronted the problem of rebuilding the war-ravaged South. They sought to encourage industrialization and expand the railroad network. Taxes went up with expenditures, and these governments came under heavy attack for corruption. Corruption certainly existed--indeed, it was a nationwide problem--but opponents exaggerated its extent for partisan purposes. In truth, the major objection of opponents to these governments was that they shared power with blacks.

Black Aspirations

Initially, black southerners thought of freedom largely as a contrast to slavery: the freedom to move about, the right to choose their employer, and freedom from physical punishment and the breakup of families. In freedom, blacks moved to protect the black family and gain educational rights. The Freedmen's Bureau initially established black schools in the South, and thousands of adults as well as children enrolled, even though they were not free. Blacks also left the white-controlled churches and established their own churches with black ministers. They negotiated new working conditions with white landlords, refusing to live in the old slave quarters or work in gangs under the supervision of an overseer. Eventually the system of sharecropping evolved as the way to organize black agricultural labor. The Freedmen's Bureau supervised the contracts between white landlords and black workers and special Freedmen's Courts adjudicated disputes. The Bureau's record in protecting blacks varied considerably, but in general it had only limited success in getting them fair compensation for their labor.

Planters responded to emancipation seeking physical and psychological separation from former slaves. They discarded the old paternalist ideal in favor of segregation. Less prosperous than before the war, they developed a new way of life based on segregation and sharecropping.

The Abandonment of Reconstruction

In 1868 the Republicans rejected all their experienced leaders and nominated Ulysses S. Grant for president, who was elected. The enforcement and maintenance of Reconstruction thus rested in Grant's hands. Republicans tried to make Reconstruction more secure by passing the Fifteenth Amendment, which forbade a state from denying the right to vote on grounds of race. Efforts to include women's suffrage by forbidding discrimination based on gender failed.

Grant lacked the skill or commitment to make Reconstruction succeed. A series of scandals rocked his administration, creating widespread popular disenchantment and fostering the Liberal Republican revolt in 1872. As charges of corruption swelled and public disorder continued unabated in the South, northern public opinion, which never had much faith in the abilities of former slaves, became increasingly disillusioned with Reconstruction. Many decided that erecting the program on black suffrage was a mistake. In addition, the beginning of a severe depression in 1874 directed public attention closer to home and gave Democrats control of the House for the first time since 1861.

With the northern commitment weakening, white southerners stepped up their assault on the radical governments in the South. They used social ostracism, economic pressure, and racist appeals to undermine Republican support. Their most effective weapon, however, was terror and violence directed against Republican leaders and black voters. The constant violence in the South during elections further weakened the northern commitment to Reconstruction. Grant acted decisively to suppress the Ku Klux Klan, a leading terrorist organization, but the tide of violence could not be stemmed.

In the end, a combination of southern white terror and northern white indifference combined to end Reconstruction. The 1876 election failed to produce a clear winner, as both parties claimed to have carried South Carolina, Florida, and Louisiana, the three southern states still under Republican control. In the end, a special electoral commission by a straight party vote declared Republican Rutherford B. Hayes the winner. In private negotiations Republicans had already agreed to restore home rule in the South in exchange for Hayes' election. This deal became known as the Compromise of 1877. Once in office, Hayes withdrew support for the remaining radical governments in the South and they collapsed. Every southern state had been "redeemed" by 1877 and Reconstruction was at an end. Thus the dreams of so many African-Americans for equal rights were bitterly disappointed. The courts soon overturned the racial legacy of Reconstruction. By both weakening northern resolve and stimulating southern white resistance, racism played a major role in failure of Reconstruction.

KEY EVENTS

1863   *Lincoln outlines Reconstruction program:* moves to establish loyal governments based on loyal white population

1864   *Lincoln vetoes Wade-Davis bill:* Radicals bitterly denounce the president

                  Louisiana, Arkansas, and Tennessee establish governments under Lincoln's plan: none grant suffrage to blacks

1865   *Freedmen's Bureau established:* to provide temporary assistance in the South

Johnson becomes president: puts his program of Reconstruction in place in the summer of 1865

Congress excludes representatives of Johnson's governments: southern defiance, Johnson's lenient program disturbs Republicans in Congress

Thirteenth Amendment ratified: slavery abolished in the United States without compensation

Joint Committee on Reconstruction established: Congress demands say in shaping Reconstruction policy

1865-1866   *Black codes enacted:* southern states limit rights of former slaves

1866   *Civil Rights bill passed over Johnson's veto:* Congress extends basic civil rights to former slaves

Memphis and New Orleans riots: anti-black and anti-Republican violence alarms northern public opinion

Fourteenth Amendment passes Congress: indirectly provides for black suffrage in southern states

Freedmen's Bureau extended: granted stronger powers to protect black rights

Tennessee readmitted to Congress: first Confederate state to regain representation after ratifying the Fourteenth Amendment

Republicans victorious in congressional elections: northern voters repudiate Johnson and his program of Reconstruction

1867   *Congressional Reconstruction:* Congress enacts program of Reconstruction based on black suffrage

Tenure of Office Act: Congress tries to prevent Johnson from removing Secretary of War Edwin Stanton from the cabinet

Ku Klux Klan organized: southern white resistance to Reconstruction turns to violence

1867-1868   *Constitutional conventions in the South:* new, progressive state constitutions adopted

African-Americans vote in southern elections

1868   *Johnson impeached but acquitted:* Radical power peaks in Republican party

Fourteenth Amendment ratified

Grant elected president: Republicans shocked at closeness of the election

1869   *Fifteenth Amendment passes Congress:* Republicans seek to make black suffrage constitutionally secure

1870   *Last southern states readmitted to Congress:* remaining states required to ratify both the Fourteenth and the Fifteenth Amendment

1871   *Ku Klux Klan Act:* government moves to break up the Ku Klux Klan

1872   *General Amnesty Act:* all but a handful of prominent Confederate leaders pardoned

Freedmen's Bureau dismantled: protection of black rights in the South undermined

Liberal Republican revolt: scandals weaken Grant's hold on party

1873-1877   *Panic and depression:* Republican party hurt by hard times

1874   *Democrats win control of the House:* Republicans increasingly concerned about maintaining support in the North

1875   *Civil Rights Act:* Congress seeks to protect black rights, but the Supreme Court eventually strikes down most of its provisions

Mississippi Plan: Democrats resort to violence to carry the state

1876   *Disputed Hayes-Tilden election:* outcome in three southern states in doubt

1877   *Compromise of 1877:* Hayes declared winner of electoral vote, last Republican governments in South fall

LEARNING OBJECTIVES

When you have finished studying this chapter, you should be able to:

1. Discuss the general problem of Reconstruction following the defeat of the Confederacy.

2. Describe Lincoln's and Johnson's plans of Reconstruction, and the failure of Johnson's program.

3. Describe the growing conflict between Johnson and Congress over Reconstruction.

4. Discuss the nature of Congressional Reconstruction, including the principal laws and amendments passed as part of this program.

5. Discuss the course of Reconstruction in the southern states, including the aspirations and experiences of black southerners.

6. Describe the abandonment of Reconstruction, and the causes for its failure.

7. Discuss the importance of the question of race for Reconstruction, and the racial legacy of Reconstruction.

Review Questions

MULTIPLE CHOICE

1. The chapter introduction tells the story of Benjamin Montgomery to make the point that
   a. former slaves who really tried could achieve a measure of prosperity in the postwar South.
   b. Reconstruction clearly hinged on northern rather than southern actions after the war.
   c. Reconstruction was an impossible task, for neither northerners or southerners wanted African-Americans to gain political and economic opportunity.
   d. for former slaves to attain meaningful lives as free citizens, they would need economic power which in turn required political power.
   (pp. 606-608)

2. According to your text, what two issues lay at the heart of Reconstruction?
   a. Whether the federal or state government was ultimately sovereign, and whether African-Americans or Native Americans were the most oppressed minority group.
   b. Which party would gain the ascendancy, and how the government could regulate the economy.
   c. The future of political and economic power for freed slaves, and the future of North -South economic and political relations.
   d. Rebuilding the North's shattered economy and restoring the South's shattered society.
   (p. 608)

3. Under new President Andrew Johnson, presidential reconstruction
   a. would implement a harsher program on the South than Lincoln had called for.
   b. adhered substantially to the views of Congressional leaders.
   c. made it possible for former high-ranking Confederates to assume positions of power in the reconstructed southern governments.
   d. never was implemented because Congress passed its own program before Johnson's could go into effect.
   (pp. 610-614)

4. The North interpreted Black Codes as
   a. evidence that the South sought to keep freedmen in an economically dependent and legally inferior status
   b. evidence that the South, by granting limited rights such as allowing jury service, was slowly accommodating to an improved status for former slaves.
   c. a realistic solution by the South to the problems created by sudden emancipation.
   d. a dangerous experiment by the South that could lead to social equality for blacks in the North.

   (p. 612)

5. Andrew Johnson narrowly avoided conviction on impeachment charges because:
   a. of his earlier cooperative attitude toward Congress.
   b. Radical Republicans were beginning to support his policies.
   c. some Republicans feared that removal would set a bad precedent for using impeachment as a political weapon against the Presidency.
   d. only a minority of the Senate voted to convict.

   (pp. 619-620)

6. What was the role of the Supreme Court during Reconstruction?
   a. It mediated between the President and Congress.
   b. It upheld the position of President that the impeachment charges were invalid.
   c. It prudently exercised restraint, basing its occasional rulings on narrow grounds.
   d. It took the lead in protecting the civil rights of African-Americans.

   (p. 620)

7. One measure of black efforts to strengthen the family unit was
   a. that males would rather work for wages than live the rough life of a sharecropper.
   b. the small but tidy homes built by hand in villages separate from the land they farmed.
   c. the tendency for husbands to insist that their wives and children work alongside them in the fields.
   d. adoption of a surname.

   (pp. 625-627)

8. The Freedmen's Bureau
    a. had as its main purpose to prevent armed clashes between former masters and former slaves.
    b. enforced working conditions for former slaves primarily through Freedmen's Courts.
    c. was criticized bitterly by southerners, but consistently praised by the former slaves.
    d. was canceled by Congress over the opposition of Radicals who saw the need for a permanent welfare agency for African-Americans.

    (pp. 630-631)

9. Among the causes of the success of "redemption" in the mid-1870s were all EXCEPT:
    a. Northern weariness and disillusion with Reconstruction
    b. the distraction of economic boom times
    c. Southern Democratic efforts to win back white votes
    d. terror and violence to prevent blacks from voting

    (pp. 637-639)

10. Reconstruction should be understood in all of the following ways EXCEPT:
    a. as a radical, vengeful program, imposing Northern values on Southerners.
    b. as a program of political and economic adjustment they failed because of racism.
    c. as a time of failure to bring blacks into the American mainstream.
    d. as a time of Congressional dominance that ended in corruption and disillusionment.

    (pp. 608, 634-637, 640-643)

IDENTIFICATION QUESTIONS

You should be able to describe the following key terms, concepts, individuals and places, and explain their significance:

Terms and Concepts

Fourteenth Amendment
sharecropping
Mississippi plan
Freedmen's Bureau

Fifteenth Amendment
Ku Klux Klan
redemption
Electoral Commission

General Amnesty Act
black codes
scalawag
freedmen
Civil Rights Act of 1875
Wade-Davis Manifesto
Texas v. White

Tenure of Office act
Wade-Davis bill
carpetbagger
Liberal Republicans
Civil rights Act of 1866
Radical Republicans
Compromise of 1877

Individuals and Places

Andrew Johnson
Thaddeus Stevens
Rutherford B. Hayes
Edwin Stanton
Susan B. Anthony
Lucy Stone
Memphis riot

Ulysses S. Grant
Benjamin F. Wade
Samuel Tilden
Horace Greeley
Elizabeth Cady Stanton
New Orleans riot

MAP IDENTIFICATION

On the map on the next page, label or shade in the following places. In a sentence, note their significance to the chapter. (For reference, consult the map in *Nation of Nations* on page 617.)

1. southern states where Reconstruction ended before 1872
2. southern states where Reconstruction ended between 1872 and 1876
3. southern states where Reconstruction ended after 1876

ESSAY QUESTIONS

1. Contrast the terms of Lincoln's program of Reconstruction with Johnson's program.

2. What were the black codes? What role did they play in the early stages of Reconstruction?

3. Explain why four of the following issues were important to freed people after the Civil War: marriages, family, names, travel, labor contracts, work done by women and children.

4. Why did Republicans in Congress impeach Johnson? Was this action justified?

5. What were the advantages and disadvantages of sharecropping to black laborers? to white landowners?

6. "The persistence of racism, in both the North and the South, lay at the heart of Reconstruction's failure." Agree or disagree and explain why.

7. List three major achievements of the radical governments in the South. Which do you think was the most important?

Critical Thinking

EVALUATING EVIDENCE (MAPS)

1. How had the Georgia plantation shown on page 629 changed since 1861? What new buildings are there? Why are they there?

2. Are the changes in the Georgia plantation (page 629) significant? Are the changes more apparent than real? What has not changed on the plantation?

3. What does the layout of the plantation in 1881 (page 629) tell us about the social and economic dimensions of Reconstruction?

4. Does the election map for 1876 (page 639) indicate that the Republican party is still a sectional party? Does this mean Reconstruction has failed?

5. How is the party's strength different in 1876 than 1860 (pages 639 and 556)?

EVALUATING EVIDENCE (ILLUSTRATIONS AND CHARTS)

1. What does Winslow Homer's painting opening the chapter (page 607) indicate about race relations after emancipation? What are the attitudes of the white mistress and the black woman? Do either seem comfortable?

2. What does the picture of Andrew Johnson's tailor shop (page 611) indicate about his origins? What clues does this provide for his behavior as president?

3. What does the picture on page 627 of the black sharecropper's cabin indicate about sharecroppers' lifestyle? What does it tell us about their standard of living?

4. Why would the picture on page 613 alarm many Northerners? How would this activity violate their understanding of freedom? Why wouldn't they be equally bothered by the system of sharecropping?

5. How does the drawing on page 633 convey a negative view of women voting? What about this scene would have been disturbing to many males? Why are children included in the picture?

6. Is the cartoon on page 635 an anti-Grant cartoon? What is the significance of Grant's location? Why is he placed where he is? What is its message about his role in the scandals of his administration?

CRITICAL ANALYSIS

Read carefully the following excerpt from the text and then answer the questions that follow:

> The old ideal of a paternalistic planter, which required a facade of black subservience and affection, gave way to an emphasis on strictly economic relationships. Mary Jones, a Georgia slaveholder before the war who did more for her workers than the law required, complained of their disrespectful language and poor work. But her patience snapped when two workers accused her of trickery and hauled her before a Freedmen's Bureau agent, with whom she won her case. Upon returning home, she announced to the assembled freedmen that "in doubting my word they offered me the greatest insult I ever received in my life; that I have considered them friends and treated them as such but now they were only laborers under contract, and only the law would rule between us." The subservience that slaveholders had demanded and taken for granted-- touching one's hat, the obsequious, smiling demeanor, the fawning guise of gratitude--now melted away in freedom. Only with time did planters develop new norms and standards to judge black behavior. What in 1865 had seemed insolence was viewed by the 1870s as the normal attitude of freedom.

> Slavery had been a complex institution that welded black and white southerners together in intimate relationships. Under the new system, however, planters increasingly embraced the ideology of segregation, or the legal separation of the races. Since emancipation significantly reduced the social distance between the races, white southerners sought psychological separation. Planters kept dealings with African-Americans to a minimum. By the time Reconstruction ended, white planters had developed a new set of values to replace those of slavery. Their new way of life was based on the institutions of sharecropping and segregation and undergirded by a militant white supremacy. Planters endured, but with emancipation, they lost their pride, confidence, and the essence of their identity.

Questions

1. What type of behavior did the ideal of paternalism impose on slaves?

2. What did planters resent about black behavior in freedom?

3. How did planters' values change after emancipation? Why did they adopt new values after slavery ended?

4. What do the authors mean when they assert that "emancipation significantly reduced the social distance between the races"? How did whites seek "psychological separation" to replace it?

5. Given the analysis put forth in this excerpt, how would you explain the fact that, before strict segregation began to develop in the South after the war, the North was much more strictly segregated than the South?

PRIMARY SOURCE: A Freedman Writes to His Former Master[*]

After the war, Jourdon Anderson, like other former slaves, had to decide for whom he would work and on what terms. In Anderson's case, this decision was especially difficult because his former master wrote and asked him and his family to return to their home in Tennessee. In his response, Anderson, who had fled slavery during the war, voiced his new attitudes in freedom.

Dayton, Ohio, August 7, 1865. To My Old Master, Colonel P. H. Anderson, Big Spring, Tennessee.

SIR: I got your letter and was glad to find that you had not forgotten Jourdon, and that you wanted me to come back and live with you again, promising to do better for me than anybody else can. I have often felt uneasy about you. I thought the Yankees would have hung you long before this for harboring Rebs they found at your house. I suppose they never heard about your going to Col. Martin's to kill the Union soldier that was left by his company in their stable. Although you shot at me twice before I left you, I did not want to hear of your being hurt, and am glad you are still living. It would do me good to go back to the dear old home again and see Miss Mary and Miss Martha and Allen, Esther,

[*] From the New York *Tribune*, August 22, 1865. The punctuation has been slightly modified for clarity.

Green, and Lee. Give my love to them all, and tell them I hope we will meet in the better world, if not in this. I would have gone back to see you all when I was working in the Nashville Hospital, but one of the neighbors told me Henry intended to shoot me if he ever got a chance.

I want to know particularly what the good chance is you propose to give me. I am doing tolerably well here; I get $25 a month, with victuals and clothing; have a comfortable home for Mandy (the folks here call her Mrs. Anderson), and the children, Milly, Jane and Grundy, go to school and are learning well; the teacher says Grundy has a head for a preacher. They go to Sunday-School, and Mandy and me attend church regularly. We are kindly treated; sometimes we overhear others saying, "Them colored people were slaves" down in Tennessee. The children feel hurt when they hear such remarks, but I tell them it was no disgrace in Tennessee to belong to Col. Anderson. Many darkies would have been proud, as I used to was, to call you master. Now, if you will write and say what wages you will give me, I will be better able to decide whether it would be to my advantage to move back again.

As to my freedom, which you say I can have, there is nothing to be gained on that score, as I got my free-papers in 1864 from the Provost-Marshal-General of the Department at Nashville. Mandy says she would be afraid to go back without some proof that you are sincerely disposed to treat us justly and kindly--and we have concluded to test your sincerity by asking you to send us our wages for the time we served you. This will make us forget and forgive old s[c]ores, and rely on your justice and friendship in the future. I served you faithfully for thirty-two years, and Mandy twenty years. At $25 a month for me, and $2 a week for Mandy, our earnings would amount to $11,680. Add to this the interest for the time our wages has been kept back and deduct what you paid for our clothing and three doctor's visits to me, and pulling a tooth for Mandy, and the balance will show what we are in justice entitled to. Please send the money by Adams Express, in care of V. Winters, esq., Dayton, Ohio. If you fail to pay us for faithful labors in the past we can have little faith in your promises in the future. We trust the good Maker has opened your eyes to the wrongs which you and your fathers have done to me and my fathers, in making us toil for you for generations without recompense. Here I draw my wages every Saturday night, but in Tennessee there was never any pay day for the negroes any more than for the horses and cows. Surely there will be a day of reckoning for those who defraud the laborer of his hire.

In answering this letter please state if there would be any safety for my Milly and Jane, who are now grown up and both good looking girls. You know how it was with poor Malida and Catherine. I would rather stay here and starve and die if it comes to that than have my girls brought to shame by the violence and wickedness of their young masters. You will also please state if there has been any schools opened for the colored children in your neighborhood, the great desire of my life now is to give my children an education, and have them form virtuous habits.

From your old servant,

Jourdan Anderson.

P.S.--Say howdy to George Carter, and thank him for taking the pistol from you when you were shooting at me.

Questions

1. What is Anderson's attitude toward his former master? Are his feelings entirely clear?

2. How has Anderson's life changed in freedom? Do you think he has developed new attitudes as a result?

3. What does freedom mean to Anderson? Does he articulate the meaning of freedom clearly and precisely? Does he think of freedom primarily in terms of its contrast with slavery?

4. Why does Anderson find the idea of returning to the old plantation attractive? Why is he hesitant to do so? Why is he worried about his daughters Milly and Jane?

5. What are his hopes for the future? Are these aspirations realistic?

6. What does this letter indicate about southern white attitudes after emancipation? How do Colonel Anderson's attitudes differ from those of his former slaves?

7. What is the relevance of this letter to the problem of Reconstruction?

18

THE RISE OF A NEW INDUSTRIAL ORDER

THE CHAPTER IN PERSPECTIVE

A new industrial order arose in the late nineteenth century. Machine-driven productivity, mass manufacturing, nationwide marketing, and factory workers replaced the old market economy of farmers, local merchants, and small factory owners. A new network of industrial systems linked the economy as never before. New business strategies and structures coordinated and controlled it. And workers struggled to adjust. In a pattern that would mark the twentieth century, they, too, began to organize. The new industrial order changed life in America and launched the United States as a major world power.

OVERVIEW

This chapter begins, appropriately enough, with railroads. They are America's first big business and a key to the new nationwide industrial order. An abortive journey along the "Great Southern Mail Route" from the Mississippi River to Washington, D. C. gives a sense of just how difficult rail travel was in 1866. A scant twenty years later, a more ambitious "scamper across America" takes place in relative comfort from one end of the country to the other. The world of difference between the two trips reflects the changes brought on by a maturing industrial economy. The changes involved not just the comfort afforded passengers. A complex system of transportation was needed to carry people quickly and efficiently across the country, just as a complex network of industrial systems was required to create the new industrial order.

The Development of Industrial Systems

Transportation by rail was only one dimension of the new industrial order, which involved the emergence of interlocking industrial systems. Communication by telegraph and other devices, resource development and new industrial technologies, systematic invention, finance capital, the rise of the corporation, and a growing pool of labor were slowly stitched together. Many processes, all linked, all acting together, forged an industrial nation.

Such development came at a price. Smokestack industries began to foul the environment. The scramble for raw materials grew frantic. More and more workers found themselves in jobs that were monotonous, alienating, and sometimes deadly.

Railroads: America's First Big Business

At the core of the new industrial order were the railroads. They moved people and freight, stimulated economic growth, and, just as important, sparked a managerial revolution that would be copied by other big businesses.

Because they brought together shorter branch or "feeder" lines, "trunk" lines were forced to pioneer new techniques of management to control their growing operations. "Central offices" served as corporate nerve centers, with a new class of "middle managers" heading divisions responsible for purchases, production, transportation, sales, and accounting. Even so, huge fixed costs, together with massive overexpansion and savage competition, led to rate wars and consolidation in the form of cooperative pools, purchases, leases, and outright mergers. Investment bankers such as J. P. Morgan played a prominent role, whether in raising the large amounts of capital required to build and run railroads or in helping to reorganize troubled firms.

The Growth of Big Business

The process of system-building continued to spread as businesses grew bigger and bigger through *combination*--a loose affiliation of enterprises--and *consolidation*--a blend of companies in a single corporate entity. Some industries, like salt producers in Michigan, adopted a horizontal strategy for growth by allying with competitors. Others, such as meat packer Gustavus Swift, adopted a vertical strategy, acquiring both outlets to consumers and sources of raw materials.

Andrew Carnegie moved both horizontally and vertically in building a fully integrated steel empire, while oil-magnate John D. Rockefeller moved beyond integration to develop the trust, a quasi-legal arrangement in which stockholders surrendered their shares "in trust" to a central board of directors. In 1901 J. P. Morgan bought out the Carnegie steel interests to form the United States Steel Corporation, a giant holding company, or corporation of corporations, worth more than $1 billion. Similar holding companies sprang up in the 1890s as a wave of mergers swept through American industry in the wake of the depression of 1893. Bigness helped to reduce competition and bring down prices as "economies of scale" (the reduced price of each item that resulted from the production of many) increased profits. Competition diminished, though scarcely disappeared.

Industrialization helped to create a visible new class of multi-millionaires and subjected the economy to enormous disruptions. A vicious cycle of boom and bust developed, in which precipitous declines were followed by slow recoveries. Corporate apologists justified the system by applying Darwin's theories of evolution to society at large, claiming that "Social Darwinism" dictated the survival of the fittest. Meanwhile critics such as Henry George and Edward Bellamy attacked corporate capitalism as a greedy promoter of poverty and class exploitation. Radicals such as Daniel DeLeon and the Socialist Labor Party tried unsuccessfully to win a sizable political following among working class Americans.

The Workers' World

The new industrial order created a new culture of work. Factories required people to work in novel ways. Unlike the farm, the factory was not governed by the changing seasons or the movement of the sun. Instead, the harsh discipline of productivity dictated the rhythm of work. Wage earners were often on the job for 6 days a week for 10 hours a day. The use of heavy machinery increased the dangers as well as the tedium of factory work. The Taylor system of scientific management, which studied the most efficient ways to get work done, boosted output but added to a growing sense that workers were cogs in the vast industrial system.

Workers struggled to maintain control of their lives and work. They took unauthorized days off or limited their output or simply quit. In these and other ways, they strained to balance their obligations as wage earners, family members, and citizens. Women and children worked at countless factory jobs, generally earning less than men. Overall, however, workers enjoyed modest gains in real wages. Most believed in the American dream of success. Yet it was they who bore the brunt of the new industrial order. Most workers suffered the ravages of unemployment and industrial accidents on their own.

The Systems of Labor

Workers responded to the industrial culture as more and more of them found employment in industry. Often divided by race, gender, and ethnicity, a minority of workers attempted to organize by creating unions. Some were radical like the Knights of Labor. Others, such as the American Federation of Labor, accepted the wage system and tried to improve conditions within it. At the turn of the century, however, less than one worker in ten belonged to a union.

Discontent boiled over in the 1880s and 1890s as a wave of strikes crippled industry. Managers fought back with blacklists, "yellow dog" contracts, strikebreakers, and Pinkerton police. When all else failed, they relied on court injunctions and federal troops to crush strikes and keep order. By 1900, employers had weathered the disruptions to emerge as the masters of the mightiest industrial economy on earth.

KEY EVENTS

1859   *First oil well*: drilled near Titusville, Pennsylvania

1866   *Transatlantic cable*: links United States and Great Britain

                    National Labor Union: first national labor union created

1869   *Knights of Labor:* radical labor union is founded in Philadelphia

1870   *Standard Oil Company:* John D. Rockefeller incorporates the giant oil company in Ohio

1872   *Air brakes:* George Westinghouse perfects air brakes for smooth railroad stops

                    Crédit Mobilier scandal: furor erupts over fraud involving millions of dollars in government funds during building of transcontinental railroad

1873   *Cable cars:* first used, in San Francisco

                    Carnegie Steel Company: steel giant founded in Pittsburgh

                    Panic of 1873: 12 years of frantic financial and industrial expansion plunges the country into a five-year depression

1874   *Protection for working women:* Massachusetts enacts first ten-hour workday law for women

1876   *Telephone:* invented by Alexander Graham Bell

1877   *Great RR Strike:* Railroad wage cuts lead to violent strikes that paralyze nation's rail system

                    Phonograph: invented by Thomas Edison

1879   *Incandescent light bulb:* developed by Edison

                    Progress and Poverty *by Henry George:* details widespread poverty in America

1882	*First trust:* Rockefeller's Standard Oil Company
1883	*Time zones:* Railroads establish standard time zones
1886	*American Federation of Labor:* federation of unions of skilled workers organized
	Haymarket Square bombing: deadly bomb thrown at police at labor rally in Chicago leads to arrest of eight anarchists
1891	*Motion picture camera:* patented by Edison
1892	*Homestead Steel strike:* succession of wage cuts at Carnegie's steel mill triggers a violent strike
1893	*Panic of 1893:* bankruptcy of Philadelphia and Reading Railroad sends overheated economy into a four-year tailspin
1894	*Pullman strike:* lay-offs and wage cuts spark a strike at the Pullman Palace Car Company that is crushed by federal troops
1901	*U.S. Steel Corporation:* the nation's first billion-dollar company created

LEARNING OBJECTIVES

When you have finished studying this chapter, you should be able to:

1. Describe the development of industrial systems, including their constituent parts.

2. Discuss the rise of railroads and explain how they became America's first big business.

3. Explain why and how big business developed.

4. Discuss the justifications for and the criticisms of big business.

5. Describe the lot of industrial workers and their responses to industrialization.

Review Questions

MULTIPLE CHOICE

1. America in the late 1800s was becoming an industrial power. According to your text, what best describes what was going on in the world outside?
   a. An autocratic emperor was threatening to take over Europe.
   b. Revolutionary struggles created upheaval in Europe, Africa, and Latin America.
   c. In a quest for markets and raw materials, European powers vied for colonial dominions overseas.
   d. Stabilized by a balance of power, European nations remained at peace, allowing the U.S. to become an active participant in world affairs.

   (Part 4 Intro, p. 647)

2. The chapter introduction tells the story of the journeys of Robert Ferguson and T.S. Hudson to make the point that
   a. America underwent a transportation and industrial transformation between the 1860s and 1880s.
   b. The railroad was America's first big business.
   c. Travel in the United States was difficult and crude by twentieth century standards, but Americans loved to travel anyway.
   d. Few foreigners toured the United States before 1900.

   (pp. 650-652)

3. The industries of Rockefeller and Carnegie illustrate not only the process of developing an industrial corporation, but also
   a. how new technologies made it possible to use natural resources in new ways and on a grander scale than before.
   b. how the "robber barons" of that era rejected any sense of responsibility to the public.
   c. vertical, though not horizontal, integration.
   d. enlightened labor practices.

   (pp. 653-654, 668-671)

4. It was an essential system undergirding the rise of big business; it was itself big business; it was a cultural symbol of American industrialization; it was a stimulus to other enterprises because it consumed so many natural resources. It was
   a. the railroad system.
   b. the steel industry.
   c. the investment banking industry.
   d. combined national, state and local government.

(p. 662)

5. Although the traditional ideology of capitalism stresses the benefits of free competition, large corporations suffered from the competitive environment. What economic factor made businesses--railroads in particular--seek to minimize competition?
   a. the profit motive
   b. government interference
   c. labor unions
   d. high fixed costs

(p. 664)

6. The wave of corporate mergers after 1893 resulted in all of the following EXCEPT:
   a. Economies of scale both lowered prices and raised profits.
   b. Americans came to resent the corruption and concentration of wealth represented by the giant corporations.
   c. With the stability that came through the rise of big business, Americans enjoyed less extreme cycles of boom and bust.
   d. Though the percentage of wealth concentrated in the hands of the few showed little change, the very rich became more conspicuous.

(pp. 671-673)

7. Who advocated what was called "Social Darwinism"?
   a. Charles Darwin
   b. Herbert Spencer
   c. Henry George
   d. Edward Bellamy

(p. 673)

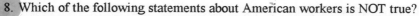

8. Which of the following statements about American workers is NOT true?
   a. Although the Horatio Alger "rags to riches" stereotype hardly matched the experience of most workers, opportunity to rise economically--with higher wages and fewer hours--was enjoyed by most white males.
   b. Samuel Gompers of the AFL succeeded as a union leader because he advocated radical changes in the structure of American capitalism, rather than merely seeking better wages and working conditions.
   c. During the later nineteenth century, labor unions provoked alarm among social and political leaders because of a wave of strikes.
   d. To achieve high productivity, managers tended to treat workers as impersonal cogs in the industrial machinery.

   (pp. 676-684)

9. What does the text mean by asserting that certain jobs were "feminized"?
   a. Lower-paying jobs tended to be held by more females than males.
   b. Males tended no longer to pursue certain professional occupations once women entered them in significant numbers.
   c. Enlightened managers in certain industries raised wages in response to women's protests.
   d. Certain dangerous factories adopted new safety measures in response to protests by the wives of their male workers.

   (pp. 678-679)

10. Which statement about the American Federation of Labor is true?
    a. The AFL, a combine of craft unions, stressed concrete, practical economic gains.
    b. The AFL's approach to labor consolidation paralleled Gustavus Swift's and Andrew Carnegie's primary technique of business consolidation.
    c. The AFL attracted a majority of U.S. skilled workers into its ranks.
    d. The AFL's longtime leader was Eugene V. Debs.

    (p. 681)

IDENTIFICATION QUESTIONS

You should be able to describe the following key terms, concepts, individuals and places, and explain their significance:

Terms and Concepts

"railroad time"
padrones
the Labor Contract Law
Robber Baron
vertical integration
the trust
holding companies
Socialist Labor Party
Social Darwinism
National Labor Union
Haymarket massacre
American Federation of Labor

Bessemer process
Edison Electric Light Company
New York Stock Exchange
Erie Wars
horizontal integration
Standard Oil Company (Ohio)
Michigan Salt Association
Looking Backward
the Homestead Steel Mill
Knights of Labor
the Pullman strike

Individuals and Places

George Eastman
George Westinghouse
Daniel McCallum
Gustavus Swift
John D. Rockefeller
Frederick W. Taylor
Eugene V. Debs

Thomas Alva Edison
Alexander Graham Bell
Jay Gould
Andrew Carnegie
J. Pierpont Morgan
Samuel Gompers

MAP IDENTIFICATIONS

On the map on the next page, label or shade in the following places. In a sentence, note their significance to the chapter. (For reference, consult the map in *Nation of Nations* on page 667.)

1. Areas of track laid before 1876
2. Areas of track laid after 1876
3. Transcontinental railroad line
4. Railroad time zones

ESSAY QUESTIONS

1. What contributions did Thomas Alva Edison, George Eastman, and Alexander Graham Bell make to business and industry? How did their contributions promote the rise of industrial systems?

2. Describe the growth of big business, making sure to distinguish among combination, consolidation, and vertical and horizontal growth.

3. Describe the new pattern of industrial work, and explain how it affected workers.

4. Compare and contrast the Knights of Labor and the American Federation of Labor.

5. How successful were business leaders in overcoming the problems that confronted them in the last third of the nineteenth century?

6. How valid were criticisms raised by corporate critics?

7. Explain why there were so many strikes between 1875 and 1900 if the real wages of workers were rising.

Critical Thinking

EVALUATING EVIDENCE (MAPS)

1. The railroad map on page 667 details the growth of the railroad system after the Civil War. In what direction does growth proceed? Why?

2. How did trunk lines (of the kind illustrated in the inset of the railroad map on page 663) make for more efficient use of rail lines?

EVALUATING EVIDENCE (ILLUSTRATIONS AND CHARTS)

1. According to the chart on page 653, how does American steel production compare to steel production in other countries? How do you account for the differences?

2. A boom-and-bust business cycle afflicted the late nineteenth century (see chart on page 671). At what intervals did the cycles occur, and how deep were the busts? Is there any correlation between busts and political and social protest? If so, why?

3. Thomas Edison systematized inventing but was also a master businessperson. Does the picture of him (on page 654) harken back to an older image of inventors or represent his innovative approach to inventing? Explain.

4. What generalizations can you make about the nature of "women's work" from the picture on page 676? How were women workers affected by the managerial revolution and advances in office technology?

5. The strike (depicted on page 682) arrayed management against labor. When did this one occur? How might the managers be responding? Is there any indication that violence was imminent? What impression did the artist intend to make by including the woman standing with a child in her arms?

6. According to the photograph on page 658, how has the industrial revolution affected the financial world on Wall Street? In what ways might it have changed the way the financial community conducted business?

CRITICAL ANALYSIS

Read carefully the following excerpt from the text and then answer the questions that follow:

> Carnegie succeeded, in part, by taking advantage of the boom-and-bust business cycles of the late nineteenth century. He jumped in during hard times, building and buying when equipment and businesses came cheaply. He also had a knack for finding skilled managers who employed administrative techniques pioneered on the railroads. Carnegie set managers against each other in races to quicken the pace of production. The winners received handsome bonuses, the losers embarrassing telegrams: "Puppy dog Number Two has beaten puppy dog Number One on fuel." Competition was also Carnegie's way of dealing with rival steelmakers. To undercut contenders, he would scrap new machinery, a new mill, even his own workers for the sake of efficiency and low costs.
>
> The final key to Carnegie's success was expansion and still more expansion: horizontally, by purchasing and constructing more and larger steel mills; and vertically, by buying up sources of supply, transportation, and eventually even sales. Beneath his steel mills lay a supporting network of industries: huge furnaces for making pig iron and ovens for making coke; 40,000 acres of coal land; fleets of railway cars and ore-carrying steamers; a shipping company; a docking company; and nearly two-thirds of the Mesabi iron ore range. Controlling such an integrated system, Carnegie could assure a steady flow of materials from mine to mill and market as well as profitable investments at every stage along the way. In 1900 his company turned out more steel than Great Britain and made $40 million in profits....
>
> Integration of the kind Carnegie employed expressed the logic of the new industrial age. More and more, the industrial activities of society were being linked in one giant, interconnected process.

Questions

1. Underline the passages in the excerpt that express the opinions or judgments of the authors rather than a narrative of facts.

2. How was Andrew Carnegie able to "outcompete anyone?"

3. How was Carnegie able to assure a "steady flow of materials" for his steel business, and why did that help to maximize his profits?

4. How did "integration of the kind Carnegie employed" express "the logic of the new industrial age?" Could a man like Carnegie succeed in today's industrial world?

5. Can you tell if the authors approve or disapprove of Carnegie's techniques? What additional information would you need to make a judgment of your own, and where would you go to find it?

PRIMARY SOURCE: Henry George on the Nature of Property*

Henry George, a self-taught social philosopher and one of the most original economists of the late nineteenth century, settled in California in 1868 after traveling in Asia. Seeing rampant speculation in land and want amid plenty, George described America as "the House of Have and the House of Want." He believed wealth was created by applying labor to land and advocated redistribution of wealth promoted by a single tax on land.

> What constitutes the rightful basis of property? What is it that enables a man justly to say of a thing, "It is mine?" From what springs the sentiment which acknowledges his exclusive right as against all the world? Is it not, primarily, the right of a man to himself, to the use of his own powers, to the enjoyment of the fruits of his own exertions? Is it not this individual right, which springs from and is testified to by the natural facts of individual organization--the fact that each particular pair of hands obey a particular brain and are related to a particular stomach; the fact that each man is a definite, coherent, independent whole--which alone justifies individual ownership? As a man belongs to himself, so his labor when put in concrete form belongs to him....
>
> If production give to the producer the right to exclusive possession and enjoyment, there can rightfully be no exclusive possession and enjoyment of anything not the production of labor, and the recognition of private property in land is a wrong.

---

* From Henry George, *Poverty and Progress* (1879).

Questions

1. How does Henry George define the nature of property? What attitudes and assumptions underlay his definition?

2. What does he mean by "the right of a man to himself?"

3. What are the "natural facts of individual organization," and how are they related to the ownership of property?

4. Why does George conclude that "the recognition of private property in land is wrong?" How does such a conclusion vary from more conventional beliefs about ownership and property?

5. George's *Progress and Poverty* became a runaway best-seller. How might his reasoning have affected contemporaries, and why do you suppose one historian concluded that the book was "responsible for starting along new lines of thinking an amazing number of men and women" who became reformers?

19

THE RISE OF AN URBAN ORDER

THE CHAPTER IN PERSPECTIVE

This chapter tells the story of the rise of modern industrial cities and their effect on American life in the late nineteenth century. Cities became the indispensable nodes of the new industrial order. They provided capital, labor, and markets, as they grew and profited from the industries they attracted. They attracted not only industry but people, some from the hinterlands of America, others from abroad. The city-bred mix of cultures soon dominated America life. As you will read in Chapter 23 on the Progressive Era, the problems bred by cities just as quickly came to dominate American reform.

OVERVIEW

The chapter begins in the heart of an industrial city--at a bootblack stand in New York. Here politics intersects grimy city life. Ward boss George Washington Plunkitt sits atop the stand, dispensing favors in return for votes. Born of immigrant parents, Plunkitt is emblematic of the new breed of urban politicians. They are drawn from the common folk and regard politics as a profession like any other, with opportunities to make money. For many Americans, as we will see, the golden door of opportunity opened onto the city.

A New Urban Age

The modern city was the product of industrialization. The vast systems of communication and transportation, of manufacturing, marketing, and finance, of labor and management came together in the industrial city. Cities acted as magnets, pulling people from the American countryside and from overseas.

Cities began to assume their modern shape of ringed residential patterns around central business districts--slum cores, zones of emergence, and suburban fringes. New forms of urban transportation, including horse-drawn railways, cable cars, elevated railroads, and electrified trolleys and subways, helped these segmented cities hold together even as they sprawled outward into growing suburbs. Bridges also helped to join the city. New skyscrapers soared high into the air, revealing the value of urban space. Tenements, smaller and squatter, carried the same message. They crammed hundreds into what soon became over-

crowded, disease-ridden dwellings. Even such innovations as the dumbbell tenement, introduced in early 1880s, failed to improve matters.

Running and Reforming the City

Industries and people presented cities with a host of demands for services. But cities were
hamstrung by political problems: outdated charters, a cumbersome system of checks and
balances, the hostility of state legislatures, and a lack of middle- and upper-class leadership.
In part, boss-dominated political machines developed to resolve those problems. Like the
corporation, the urban machine centralized control and imposed order on the world around
it. It furnished needed goods and services, whether coal for heat, jobs for the unemployed,
or building projects that modernized the urban landscape. In the process, poor immigrants
sometimes found a way out of poverty and into the mainstream of American life. The price
was considerable--graft and corruption, inflated taxes, and election fraud. Ultimately city
politics was transformed into a petty business.

Urban blight and corruption, together with the flood of new immigrants, inspired social as well as political action, especially within churches. Some Protestant ministers continued to look on poverty as the result of individual failure, while others, allied with new
nativist organizations, called for the restriction of immigration to reduce the menace of cities. Still others embarked on urban religious revivals to bridge the gap between the poor and
the middle class. A tiny minority began preaching a "Social Gospel," which advocated the
betterment of society through boys clubs, gymnasiums, libraries, and training programs as a
way to save individual souls. Settlement houses, like Jane Addams' Hull-House in Chicago
(1889), served as community centers to help the working class and immigrant poor.

City Life

Immigrants affected city life as much as their native-born counterparts. They clustered together in ethnic neighborhoods and assimilated slowly. Their mix of old- and new-world
ways added diversity and vitality to American cities that sometimes produced tensions between natives and newcomers.

Urban middle-class life blossomed. By the turn of the century over a third of the middle class owned their homes. More and more middle-class urbanites lived in single-family
dwellings in suburban fringes, with husbands away at the office during the day, wives at
home, and children in school. Victorian morality governed personal conduct and stressed
sobriety, industriousness, self-control, and modesty, all designed to protect against the turbulent life of the industrial city. The middle-class creed of discipline and social control extended beyond the home to society at large in a host of social reforms that included the temperance and anti-obscenity movements. Some women bridled against such rigidity and
moved toward liberalization by advocating greater sexual freedom and female suffrage.

City Culture

Cities also served as centers of culture and education. Enrollment in public schools doubled between 1870 and 1890 under the impact of greater demands for literate and well-trained workers. Education became a powerful tool for social control and assimilation. Colleges and universities increasingly met the needs of an urban industrial society by furnishing a corps of educated leaders and managers. Women's enrollment increased both in coeducational schools and in new all-women's schools, many of which added home economics courses to a more conventional curriculum. By the turn of the century, when only about 5 percent of college-aged Americans pursued it, higher learning extended more and more beyond college to graduate and professional education.

In cities, middle- and working-class urbanites gained access to a new material culture and new forms of mass entertainment that were leveling and homogenizing American society. Ready-made clothing, mass-produced furniture, department stores and chain stores, and a growing mail-order business made consumption a national endeavor and bound up the nation as never before. City people increasingly turned leisure into a consumable commodity. Sports--from the mannered games of tennis and croquet to more "democratic" ones like bicycling, baseball, football, and basketball--grew in popularity. Higher culture, too, was made available in stage plays, symphony concerts, museums, and a growing record industry. Cities, radiating their influence outward, were transforming America, as the political system struggled to find within the traditions of a democratic republic some way to bring order out of the seeming chaos of urban life.

KEY EVENTS

1869   *Professional baseball:* Cincinnati Red Stockings become first professional baseball team

       Collegiate football: Rutgers beats Princeton in first intercollegiate football game

1870   *Elevated railroad:* begins operation in New York City

1871   *Chicago fire:* a fire in the O'Leary's barn sets the city ablaze, killing 250 people

1872   *Boss Tweed convicted:* William "Boss" Tweed convicted of defrauding New York City of millions of dollars

1873   *Comstock Law enacted:* federal government outlaws "pornographic" material (including birth control information) from the U.S. mails

1874   *Prohibition movement:* delegates from 17 states gather to form the Women's Christian Temperance Union

1875   *Urban revivalism:* Dwight Moody begins preaching the Gospel in the cities of the East

1876   *Central Park:* Frederick Law Olmstead completes the country's most famous city park in New York

               Graduate education: Johns Hopkins University opens nation's first graduate school

1882   *Chinese Exclusion Act:* Congress bans the immigration of Chinese laborers

1883   *Brooklyn Bridge:* 14 years in the making, the world's longest suspension bridge opens

1886   *Statue of Liberty:* the statue, a gift from the people of France, is dedicated in New York harbor

1887   *Looking Backward, 2000-1887:* Edward Bellamy's utopian novel about corporatized life in the twentieth century is published

               Rural free delivery: mail service is extended to all communities with 10,000 or more people

1888   *Nation's first electric trolley line:* begins operation in Richmond, Virginia

1889   *Social settlement movement:* Jane Addams opens Hull House in Chicago

1890   *How the Other Half Lives:* Jacob Riis's book about the poor is published

1892   *Ellis Island:* new receiving station for immigrants opens in New York harbor

1893   *World's Columbian Exposition:* a world's fair commemorating the 400th anniversary of Columbus's encounter with America opens in Chicago

1894   *Immigration Restriction League is organized*

1896   *Plessy v. Ferguson:* the Supreme Court sanctions racial segregation

1897   *Nation's first subway system:* opens in Boston

LEARNING OBJECTIVES

When you have finished studying this chapter, you should be able to:

1. Explain why and how industrial cities grew.

2. Explain how modern cities remained integrated, functioning wholes.

2. Describe the urban political machine, including its cost and benefits.

3. Discuss the responses of reformers to urban blight.

4. Describe urban middle class life and the effects of Victorian mores.

5. Explain the importance of mass education, mass entertainment, and mass distribution of goods.

Review Questions

MULTIPLE CHOICE

1. The chapter introduction tells the story of George Washington Plunkitt's "day of helping" to make the point that
   a. city life was becoming especially stressful for many Americans.
   b. while the city was a harsh place, there were some who cared enough to give aid.
   c. politics in the late 19th century at all levels of government was unusually corrupt, failing to serve the people.
   d. people's needs in the exploding cities gave a new breed of politicians a chance to get rich from graft.

   (pp. 688-690)

2. Which one of the following statements about late nineteenth and early twentieth century immigrants is NOT true?
   a. Most settled in ethnic communities centered on church life.
   b. Most married later, but bore more children, than the native-born.
   c. Most were Protestants.
   d. Significant numbers of Americans sought to restrict the immigrant influx.

   (pp. 692-693, 702, 704-706, 724)

3. What was the primary solution to the realization that cities could hardly survive, let alone grow, without improved transportation?
   a. the horse-drawn trolley
   b. the cable car
   c. one way streets
   d. electric streetcars

   (p. 696)

4. The political bosses of turn-of-the-century cities were most often
   a. wealthy businessmen or their hired agents.
   b. descendants of the leading families of a century before.
   c. immigrants or the children of immigrants.
   d. urban reformers.

   (pp. 688-690)

5. Which is NOT true of political machines?
   a. They served as a crude welfare system.
   b. They enriched the bosses.
   c. They convinced city-dwellers that government should not be trusted to help the needy.
   d. They built modern city systems and forced city government to work.

   (pp. 701-702)

6. A new experiment in providing social services to slum-dwellers featured centers where middle-class women lived among the poor, providing amenities and teaching American ways to immigrants. This was called the
   a. social gospel.
   b. vaudeville house.
   c. settlement house.
   d. rescue mission.

   (pp. 703-704)

7. What statement about the urban middle class home and family is NOT true?
   a. It was understood as both a haven and an indicator of social standing.
   b. Birth rates rose as childbirthing became safer and more routine.
   c. Child rearing practices focused on nurture and training more than strict physical discipline.
   d. Courtship and marriage rituals became more romantic and couple-centered, featuring common leisure activities, elaborate weddings and honeymoon trips.

   (pp. 706-707, 722-724)

8. Trends in education in the late 19th century included all EXCEPT:
   a. city girls and boys, as required by laws in most states, attended school together for most of the workday.
   b. many new colleges were established, underwritten by grants from both private philanthropists and government.
   c. marginal groups like blacks and immigrants looked to education as a way to get ahead.
   d. literacy rose sharply.

   (pp. 710-711)

9. New outlets for selling consumer goods included all EXCEPT:
    a. the mail order catalog, for rural residents.
    b. the chain store, for the working class.
    c. the downtown department store, for city dwellers.
    d. the outlying shopping center, for middle class commuters living at the end of the streetcar lines.

(pp. 712-714)

10. With increasing leisure time city dwellers and small town folk alike pursued a variety of entertainments, making _____ into big business, thanks to the likes of John Philip Sousa and Scott Joplin.
    a. popular music
    b. the circus
    c. vaudeville magic acts
    d. serious theater

(p. 718)

IDENTIFICATION QUESTIONS

You should be able to describe the following key terms, concepts, individuals and places, and explain their significance:

Terms and Concepts

ward Boss	Tammany Hall
"boodle"	urbanization
steerage	immigration
"birds of passage"	*The Rise of David Levinsky*
urban ghettos	ethnic communities
"walking" cities	tenements
zones of emergence	suspension bridge
skyscrapers	*How the Other Half Lives*
boss rule	settlement houses
Victorianism	Women's Christian Temperance Union
the Comstock law	*McGuffey's Reader*
Plessy v. Ferguson	corset
National American Woman Suffrage Association	

Individuals and Places

Ellis Island
Louis H. Sullivan
William Tweed
Victoria Woodhull

George Washington Plunkitt
Elisha Graves Otis
Jane Addams
Susan B. Anthony

MAP IDENTIFICATIONS

On the map below, label or shade in the following places. In a sentence, note their significance to the chapter. (For reference, consult the map in *Nation of Nations* on page 695.)

1. Business core (downtown) and Vieux Carre (Old Quarter)
2. Built-up areas as of 1841, 1878, and 1900
3. Trolley lines
4. Upper Protection Levee

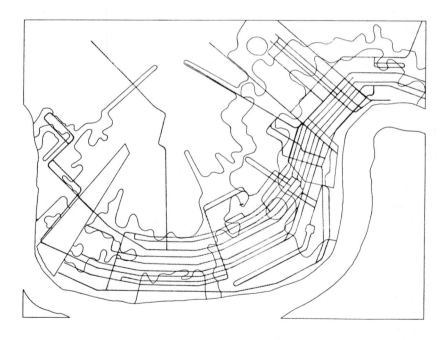

ESSAY QUESTIONS

1. What brought about the modern city, and what factors accounted for the urban explosion of the late nineteenth century?

2. Describe immigrant life in the city.

3. Describe how the following all were responses to the pressures created by developing urban metropolises: streetcars, dumbbell tenements, canned foods, department stores.

4. What was Victorianism, and how did it affect urban middle class life?

5. Why did well-defined ethnic communities develop, and how do you explain the quicker pace of assimilation among the children of immigrants?

6. In what sense did boss rule revolutionize city government? What was the price paid for the boss system? Were the costs worth the benefits?

7. How did mass consumption and mass entertainment help to tie the nation together?

8. What was the impact of city life on women, African-Americans, and homosexuals?

Critical Thinking

EVALUATING EVIDENCE (MAPS)

1. On the map of New Orleans (page 695), does the city seem to have expanded more between 1841 and 1878 or between 1878 and 1900? Approximately how long would it take a person walking three miles an hour to travel from one end of the city to the other in 1841? In 1878? in 1900? How does the trolley system allow the city to grow and still remain integrated?

2. Why do you think New Orleans did not expand more in a northwesterly direction from the Vieux Carré?

3. What is the "Upper Protection Levee"? Why do you think a trolley line runs toward it by 1900, even though the area is marked as undeveloped?

EVALUATING EVIDENCE (ILLUSTRATIONS AND CHARTS)

1. The chart on page 692 illustrates the sources of immigration. Where are immigrants coming from? How does this trend differ from earlier sources?

2. Compare the trolleys in this picture of Canal Street with the map on page 695. What potential traffic problems are visible in the picture that are not so clear from the map?

3. What features of urban life are depicted in George Bellows' *Cliff Dwellers*? What kind of neighborhood is it? How can you tell?

4. Billy Sunday began his urban religious revivals in the 1890s, though the George Bellows painting (page 703) was done later. Which figure is Billy Sunday? How are people reacting to him? What does the painting suggest about the role of religion in people's lives?

CRITICAL ANALYSIS

Read carefully the following excerpt from the text and then answer the questions that follow:

As the nineteenth century drew to a close the city was reshaping the country, just as the industrial system was creating a more specialized, diversified, and interlocking national and even international economy. Most Americans were ambivalent about this process. The old Jeffersonian bias against cities warred with the gospel of material progress and wealth that cities so dramatically embodied. Cities beckoned migrants and immigrants with unparalleled opportunities for work and pleasure. The playwright Israel Zangwill celebrated the city's transforming power in his 1908 Broadway hit, *The Melting Pot*. "The real American," one of his characters explained, "is only in the Crucible, I tell you--he will be the fusion of all the races, the coming superman."

Where Zangwill saw a melting pot with all its promise for a new super race, champions of traditional American values like the widely read Protestant minister Josiah Strong saw "a commingled mass of venomous filth and seething sin, of lust, of drunkenness, of pauperism, and crime of every sort." Both the champions and critics of the late nineteenth century had a point. Corruption, crudeness, and disorder were no more or less a part of the cities than the vibrancy, energy, and opportunities that drew people to them. The gap between rich and poor yawned most widely in cities. As social critic Henry George observed, progress and poverty seemed to go hand in hand.

In the end moral judgments, whether pro or con, missed the point. Cities stood at the nexus of the new industrial order. All Americans, whatever they thought about the new urban world, had to search for ways to make that world work.

Questions

1. How were cities "reshaping the country"?

2. Where did playwright Israel Zangwill find "the real American," and why do you think he believed this creature was "the coming superman"?

3. What was Josiah Strong's view of cities? How did it differ from Zangwill's?

4. Why did contemporary moral judgments about the city "miss the point"? Does the historian have any obligation to make moral judgments about historical events and processes? What place do such judgments have in the study of history?

5. What kind of judgment is implicit in the author's assertion that cities stood at the "nexus of the new industrial order"?

PRIMARY SOURCE: An Anti-Chinese Riot in Los Angeles*

In October 1871, Los Angeles exploded in an anti-Chinese riot. A dispute among rival Chinese clans over the ownership of a Chinese woman led to the death of one white citizen and the wounding of two others, a young Hispanic and a police officer. Marauding gangs of vigilantes entered "Chinatown" seeking revenge. Twenty-three Chinese died.

By this time, Chinatown, wholly surrounded, was in a state of siege. Mounted men came galloping from the country--the vacquero was in his glory, and the cry was: *"Carajo la Chino!"*

---

* From P. S. Downey, "A Prophecy Partly Verified," *Overland Monthly* (1886).

Among the Spaniards whose boldness and vigor attracted attention that night was Vasquez, afterward famous as a bandit, and Jesus Martinez, his chum and relative. Chief among the Americans, plying a Henry rifle until excessive labor clogged its mechanism, the writer observed a certain high official; and in the van of the fight, one of the city fathers--a member of the City Council and a Wells Fargo official--valiantly struck out from the shoulder. A young Israelite, heavy-framed and coarse-featured, and a German known as "Dutch Charley" were prominently active and cruel. "Crazy Johnson" seemed to represent all Ireland; while Jacques, a Frenchman, shirtless and hatless, and armed with a cleaver, reveled in the memory of Pont Neuf and the Sans Culottes. Jacques was the fire-fiend of the occasion--time and again Chinatown was ablaze--and Jacques with his cleaver was always found pictured in the glare....

The condition of the Chinese had now become wretched indeed. The "Quarters," it will be remembered, were an old Spanish hacienda one story high, with an open courtyard in the center. Martinez and his companions, armed with axes as well as firearms, cut holes in the asphaltum roof, through which the cowering creatures below were shot in their hiding places or hunted from room to room out into the open courtyard, where death from the bullets of the roof was certain. Within or without, death was inevitable. The alternative was terrible. As each separate wretch, goaded from his covert, sought in his despair the open space, a volley from the roof brought him down; a chorus of yells telegraphed that fact to the surrounding mob, and the yells were answered by a hoarse roar of savage satisfaction....

Close behind the boy [who had just been hung by the mob] followed the Chinese doctor; a man of extreme age, well known, and reputedly wealthy. The doctor begged piteously for his life, pleading in English and Spanish; but he might as well have pleaded with wolves. At last he attempted to bribe those who were hurrying him to his death. He offered $1,000- $2,000- $3,000- $5,000- $10,000- $15,000! But to no purpose. He was hanged, and his $15,000 spirited away none the less. At his death the old man wore a valuable diamond ring upon his left index finger, but when his corpse was cut down it was found that the left index finger had been wrenched from its socket, and the finger and ring were gone.

Questions

1. What is the ethnic complex of the marauding mob? How do you account for its diversity?

2. How do you suppose city officials reacted to the actions of the mob?

2. How did the Chinese react to the assault? Why were they such easy prey?

3. The riot occurred in 1871; yet the excerpt is taken from an article that did not appear until 1886. How do you account for the disparity in dates? Is there any evidence in the excerpt itself to suggest that it is a trustworthy account? Where might you look to verify this account?

4. Why did the mob attack a defenseless child and an old man? Why did the mob mutilate the body of the old man? What does the old man's profession and wealth suggest about the economic and social make-up of Chinatown?

5. What attitudes might account for the extreme violence of the riot?

20

AGRARIAN DOMAINS: THE SOUTH AND THE WEST

THE CHAPTER IN PERSPECTIVE

A|s Chapters 15 and 16 (on the Civil War and Reconstruction) made clear, sectionalism had long been a source of conflict in American society. The Civil War was fought in part to prevent the forces of sectionalism from dividing the Union. Even so, the regional geographies, economies, and cultures of the South and the West continued to set them apart as distinct sections. In both sections, ethnic and racial conflict led to widespread violence and the development of social caste systems to justify segregation of African Americans, Indians, Hispanics, and Asians. But the West and South cannot be viewed as regions isolated from the increasingly industrialized Northeast and Midwest; far from it. As this chapter will show, the process of industrialization and urbanization described in Chapters 18 and 19 had a powerful impact on the South and West, even though both regions depended heavily on agriculture and the exploitation of natural resources.

OVERVIEW

As its title indicates, this chapter is in some ways two stories in one. That is why the chapter opens with the story of the Exodusters, black southerners who were driven from the South by poverty and violence and drawn to the West by the opportunities of cheap land. Their story links the two regions. Though their history and geography differ in most ways, important similarities link the regions. Both had underdeveloped public sectors, depended on outside human and capital resources, and hence saw themselves as colonial economies. Both provided the nation's industrial centers with vital raw materials and markets for manufactured goods. And both resorted to segregation and violence to maintain racial caste systems.

The Southern Burden

After the Civil War many Southerners saw industrialization as one way to restore prosperity. But the southern economy remained wedded to cotton. The shortage of credit and cash for wages gave rise to tenantry and sharecropping. That system left most poor black and white farmers hopelessly in debt. Even the rapid growth of industries like railroads, textiles, and tobacco could not overcome the poverty of the region. The problem was not so much that the South was a "colony" of the industrial North. Rather, the rapid natural increase in population and low wages in southern agriculture made it difficult to attract skilled labor and enough outside capital to help the South develop a more diversified economy.

Social Life in the New South

Southerners not only rebuilt the region's economy after the Civil War, they constructed a new social system to replace slavery. Once the North adopted a laissez-faire approach to race relations, the South was able to create a "Jim Crow" system of segregation. Newly erected legal codes forbade blacks and whites from mingling in almost any public place. Thus, blacks and whites were socially separated and blacks could not compete for most jobs. The Supreme Court gave segregation constitutional authority in the case of *Plessy v. Ferguson* (1896). The Court would not view separate facilities as discriminatory so long as they were equal, though they seldom were.

Southern social life was separated along gender lines as well as racial ones. Most social activities reflected the rural character of the South and fell into male and female domains. When not working, men loved to hunt, gamble, and court danger. Women socialized around more domestic activities like quilting. Most rural folk looked forward to trips to town. Especially during court week town offered a variety of entertainments and opportunities to do business. More than the town, however, church was at the center of southern life. Here too services were generally divided along gender lines. Besides spiritual uplift church provided a welcome chance to socialize.

The Transformed West

The conflicts of race also affected the changing settlement of lands beyond the Mississippi. That came about partly because Indians and newly arrived white settlers held markedly different attitudes toward the land. Europeans saw nature as something to exploit systematically and were prepared to do so through a system of world markets. Indians exploited the land in their own ways, but their populations were less dense and their religious beliefs encouraged a view of the land as a complex web of animals, plants and other natural elements, all with souls of their own.

The intense development of the West's resources thus threatened the Indian way of life. Beyond Indian resistance, two barriers limited white settlement: the difficulty of transportation over vast distances and the scarcity of water. The Homestead Act of 1862 and the completion of the transcontinental railroad by 1869 made settlement and development more attractive in the West. Visionaries like William Gilpin underestimated the limits imposed on the West by the scarcity of water. John Wesley Powell had a more realistic view of the water problem, but his ideas were too restrictive for those who saw the West as a new garden landscape.

War for the West

To remove the Indians, whites adopted a policy of concentrating them on reservations. When that failed, violence resulted. After the 1862 uprising of the Santee Sioux in Minnesota sporadic guerrilla wars erupted between whites and Indians. One climactic battle occurred when Sioux and Cheyenne forces trapped Colonel George Custer's cavalry along the Little Big Horn River in 1876.

But such victories could not stem the flood of white settlers, the spread of disease, or the slaughter of the buffalo that all undermined Indian cultures. Under the Dawes Act reformers tried to draw Indians out of communal tribal cultures and turn them into independent farmers. That well-intended reform struck as hard a blow to Indian life as did war. Similarly, Hispanos in the southwest saw their way of life challenged by the spread of Anglos to their region. Sometimes with violence, more often by legal and political means, Anglos deprived Hispanos of their land and political influence. A new wave of immigration from Mexico, more urban in character, also changed the character of the Hispanic Southwest.

Boom and Bust in the West

Silver and gold strikes brought the earliest waves of fortune-hunters into the West, particularly in California, Nevada, and parts of the Rockies. Then followed the railroads, which linked the region to urban markets in the East and Europe. The builders of the railroads often resorted to ruthless and corrupt means as they raced to link the West to the East. They exploited both Chinese and Irish laborers. Control over transportation gave the railroad companies enormous influence over the region's economic and political life.

Cattle ranchers soon moved huge herds of steers into the vacated grasslands and drove them along the cattle trails to the new rail heads. As with railroads, large corporations came to dominate the cattle industry. Violence sometimes erupted between sheep and cattle interests. But in the end nature proved even more violent, as blizzard and drought from 1886-1887 took the boom out of the cattle business.

The Final Frontier

The growing demand for food and lure of cheap land under the Homestead Act also brought farmers into the once lightly settled high plains. Conflict often erupted as ranchers and farmers each tried to impose their ways on the land. But the farmers, like the ranchers, eventually ran up against harsh realities. The best lands were far from free and farmers required expensive equipment to meet the conditions of the western environment. Droughts, grasshopper plagues, prairie fires, blizzards and rural isolation were among the difficulties facing farm families in the western plains. Many left defeated, but among those who stayed, the church offered some solace and social life. Eventually the frustrations of western farmers boiled over into an agrarian revolt which will be described in Chapter 21.

KEY EVENTS

1849-1859	*Gold and silver strikes*: discoveries open western mining frontier
1862	*Homestead Act*: provides cheap lands for family farms
	Minnesota Sioux uprising: begins Plains Indian wars
1866	*Drive to Sedalia, Missouri*: launches cattle boom
1869	*Transcontinental railroad completed*: railroads link the West to the East
1874	*Barbed wire patented*: makes possible the fencing of the western range
1876	*Battle of Little Bighorn*: Indian victory over Custer
1880	*Bonsack cigarette rolling machine invented*: leads to boom in cigarette smoking
1885-1887	*Severe winter and drought cycle*: end of cattle boom in the West
1887	*Dawes Severalty Act*: undermines communal tribal culture
1890	*Ghost Dance Indian religious revival*: leads to Wounded Knee massacre
1892	*Wyoming range wars*: battle between small and large ranchers
1896	*Plessy v. Ferguson*: Supreme Court upholds separate but equal doctrine

LEARNING OBJECTIVES

When you have finished studying this chapter, you should be able to:

1. Compare and contrast the similarities and differences in the regional cultures of the South and West

2. Explain why cotton continued to dominate the Southern economy in an era of rapid industrialization and urbanization

3. Describe how the hopes of the Freedmen under Radical Reconstruction gave way to a "Jim Crow" system of biracial caste

4. Explain why unusual environmental conditions played such a central role in the development of the West

5. Describe the source of white-Indian conflicts in the West and explain why white settlement proved so devastating to Indian cultures

6. Analyze how building of the railroads encouraged the development of western resources and tied them to markets in the East and Europe

Review Questions

MULTIPLE CHOICE

1. The chapter introduction tells the story of the "Exodusters" to make the point that
   a. religious imagery was important in the lonely lives of rural folk in the late 19th century.
   b. hopes for the future in the South and West confronted realities of "colonial" economies built on exploited lands and peoples.
   c. while the South suffered from floods and worn out soil, Westerners suffered from locust infestations and the Dust Bowl.
   d. both the South and the Midwest lost population as blacks and whites alike joined the "boomer" land rushes in the Far West.

   (pp. 726-729)

2. What is NOT true about the post-Civil War southern economy?
   a. The South's economy was poor, decentralized and isolated.
   b. Cotton remained the dominant southern product, despite falling prices.
   c. Despite dreams of a New South, industry never took hold in the South before 1900.
   d. A capital shortage made tenant farms the prevailing pattern in southern agriculture.

   (pp. 729-734)

3. "Sharecropping" means
   a. renting land by giving a fraction of the crop to the landowner.
   b. planting two separate crops (e.g. cotton and beans) in the same field.
   c. borrowing against a future crop to obtain seed.
   d. organizing a farm as a corporation to gain tax advantages.

   (pp. 730-731)

4. Wages in southern industries remained low because
   a. of the historic low wage pattern in agriculture.
   b. unions had no success in organizing key industries.
   c. of the close relationship between mill owners and workers.
   d. extremely low wage scales for black workers offset the decent wages whites earned.

   (pp. 720-730, 735, 738)

5. At the center of southern life was
   a. slavery.
   b. the small town.
   c. the saloon.
   d. the church.

   (pp. 738, 741-742)

6. To what does the term "Jim Crow" refer?
   a. a process by which freed slaves established new communities in Kansas
   b. a Supreme Court case that declared that legalized segregation was constitutional
   c. a system of legalized separation of blacks as socially inferior
   d. a technique used by the Ku Klux Klan to intimidate rural African-Americans in the south so they would not try to vote

   (p. 739)

2. What does the picture of baptism (page 742) suggest about the racial make up of church congregations in the South?

3. If a formal portrait reveals a good deal about a family's aspirations and feelings, what qualities does the portrait of sodbusters (page 761) suggest? What significance might be attributed to the table in front of the house? of the cow on the roof? the horses?

4. Examine the graph on school expenditures in the South (page 738). How many dollars per white pupil was being spent by Alabama in 1890? how many dollars per black pupil? What was the ratio of support between white and black pupils?

5. Which state had the most equal amounts of money being spent on white and black education in 1890? Which state had the least equal spending? in whose favor? How do the ratios change between 1890 and 1910? In which state is the difference between spending on black and white pupils greatest?

6. What events occurred in the South after 1890, according to the text, that might account for the sharp change in spending?

7. The Supreme Court ruled in *Plessy v. Ferguson* that separate schools were legal so long as they were equal. In point of fact, were these schools legal under the principles of that decision? If spending *had* remained equal, as in Alabama and North Carolina in 1890, would segregated schools have been equal in your opinion? Why or why not?

CRITICAL ANALYSIS

Read carefully the following excerpt from the text and then answer the questions that follow:

> Some whites--usually those with the least contact with Native Americans--viewed them as "noble savages" whose "natural" way of life remained in harmony with the elements, a myth still too widely held. To be sure, Indians could be remarkably inventive about in using scarce resources around them. The bark of the cottonwood proved good food for horses during the winter, while the buffalo supplied not only meat but bones for tools, fat for cosmetics, and sinews for thread. But Indians had traditionally hunted bison by stampeding them over cliffs, which resulted in a significant waste of food. They irrigated crops, set fires on

the plains to improve the game and vegetation, and in other ways actively altered their environment.

By the mid-nineteenth century, they had also become enmeshed in a web of white trade, supplying furs in return for firearms, cloth, metal tools, and jewelry. Since the environment could sustain only a finite amount of use, Indians suffered, just as white trappers did, when the fur trade led to overtrapping. And the Sioux nation expanded aggressively because its increasing population forced the tribe to enlarge its base of resources. It would be misleading, then, to view native societies in the Great Plains as isolated from white cultures, living as they had from time out of mind. For more than a century, the West had been in dramatic flux, as white, Hispanic, and Indian cultures borrowed and adapted from one another, often clashing in competing for the region's limited resources.

Questions

1. Identify important ways this paragraph claims Indians altered their environment.

2. Identify the passages that assert an opinion. What is the major argument, summed up in a sentence, that the authors are making in these two paragraphs?

3. What do you think is the authors' view of Indian culture? In what ways do they suggest Indians were not "noble savages" leading a "natural" way of life? How does their discussion of trade with whites contribute to this view? How does the example of the Sioux support their argument?

4. If one conclusion of the two paragraphs is that white and Indian cultures had more in common than some scholars have suggested, why were the clashes between them so harsh? What various factors contributed to the conflict between whites and Indians? How would you rank them in importance?

5. Contrast Indians' use of their resources, as described here, with white uses of resources, as exemplified by cattle ranchers, sodbusters, and miners? What are the essential differences? How do differing uses of environmental resources play a role in other conflicts between these groups?

PRIMARY SOURCE: "Recollections of a Black Migrant to Kansas"*

Bill Simms was not, strictly speaking, one of the "Exodusters" described in the introduction, because he came to Kansas earlier. But his recollections, given in the mid-1930s, vividly detail his experience heading west after the Civil War. The following excerpt is the summary of an oral interview collected by the Federal Writers Project during the Great Depression.

My name is Bill Simms. I was born in Osceola, Missouri, March 16, 1839.

I lived on the farm with my mother, and my master, whose name was Simms. I had an older sister, about two years older than I was. My master needed some money so he sold her, and I have never seen her since except just a time or two....I had a good master, most of the masters were good to their slaves. When a slave got too old to work they would give him a small cabin on the plantation and have the other slaves to wait on him. They would furnish him with victuals, and clothes until he died. Slaves were never allowed to talk to white people other than their masters or someone their master knew, as they were afraid the white man might have the slave run away. The masters aimed to keep their slaves in ignorance and the ignorant slaves were all in favor of the Rebel army, only the more intelligent were in favor of the Union army.

When the war started, my master sent me to work for the Confederate army. I worked most of the time for three years off and on, hauling canons, driving mules, hauling ammunition, and provisions....When the Union army came close enough I ran away from home and joined the Union army...until the war ended. Then I returned home to my old master, who had stayed there with my mother. My master owned about four hundred acres of good land, and had had ten slaves. Most of the slaves stayed at home. My master hired me to work for him. He gave my mother forty acres of land with a cabin on it and sold me a [sic] forty acres, for twenty dollars, when I could pay him....My master's wife had been dead for several years and they had no children. The nearest relative being a nephew. They wanted my master's land and was afraid he would give it all away to us slaves, so they killed him, and would have killed us if we had stayed at home. I took my mother and ran into the

_____

* from George P. Rawick, *The American Slave: A Composite Autobiography,* 19 vols. and supplements (1972).

adjoining, [St.] Claire County. We settled there and stayed for sometime, but I wanted to see Kansas, the State I had heard so much about.

I couldn't get nobody to go with me, so I started out afoot across
the prairies for Kansas. After I got some distance from home it was all
prairie. I had to walk all day long following buffalo trail. At night I
would go off a little ways from the trail and lay down and sleep. In the
morning I'd wake up and could see nothing but the sun and prairie. Not
a house, not a tree, no living thing, not even could I hear a bird. I had
little to eat, I had a little bread in my pocket. I didn't even have a pocket
knife, no weapon of any kind. I was not afraid, but I wouldn't start out
that way again. The only shade I could find in the daytime was the rosin
weed on the prairie. I would lay down so it would throw the shade in my
face and rest, then get up and go again. it was in the spring of the year
in June. I came to Lawrence, Kansas, where I stayed two years working
on the farm. In 1874 I went to work for a man by the month at $35 a
month and I made more money than the owner did, because the grasshoppers ate up the crops. I was hired to cut up the corn for him, but the
grasshoppers ate it up first. He could not pay me for sometime. Grasshoppers were so thick you couldn't step on the ground without stepping
on about a dozen at each step. I got my money and came to Ottawa in
December 1874, about Christmas time.

Questions

1. Where did Bill Simms grow up? Where did he journey to in Kansas? On a map, locate these places and estimate the distance between them.

2. What are "victuals"?

3. What was the primary reason Simms decided to leave for Kansas? He also notes
   that he has "heard so much about" Kansas. Based on your reading of the introduction to Chapter 20, what might he have heard?

4. What was Simms' opinion of most masters when slavery was permitted in Missouri? What examples does he give to support his views? Are there other examples
   in the narrative that might suggest that he was not being entirely candid in giving
   his opinion? If he was not being candid, why not?

5. How was Simms' experience similar to that of the Exodusters described in the introduction to Chapter 20? How did it differ? How was it similar to the experience of Benjamin Montgomery, described in Chapter 17?

21

THE FAILURE OF TRADITIONAL POLITICS

THE CHAPTER IN PERSPECTIVE

This chapter deals with the failures of traditional, two-party politics in the Gilded Age. The trends that we have seen in the previous chapters--toward industrialization, urbanization, and a sharply increased immigration--all worked to fracture conventional politics. Cities were gaining in political and cultural strength, while farmers, despite an outburst of political activity, had begun an irreversible decline in numbers that would continue steadily into the next century. The chapter stresses the importance of the period as a precursor to the politics of organization, professionalism, and national vision that also characterize the twentieth century. But those features of political life would not be evident until after the wrenching effects of social change disrupted the politics of the Gilded Age during the 1890s.

OVERVIEW

The introduction picks up Tom Watson and the Populists as they try form a biracial coalition of poor farmers at the end of the century. In doing so, it begins to underscore the deeper problems of American society--the gulf between rich and poor, the divisions of race and class, the growing power of corporations, the poverty of cities and farms, wrenching cycles of boom and bust, the needs of outsiders and the dispossessed. During the late nineteenth century, all those stresses would increase as a function of the social changes transforming the nation.

The Politics of Paralysis

In the last third of the century politics was grinding into a dangerous paralysis, as evenly divided Democrats and Republicans fought to win power. Improved organization, rigid loyalty, and broad ideological similarities left neither party in command. There were, however, distinguishing differences. Democrats, centered in the South and supported too by immigrant political machines in the industrial North, believed in states rights and limited government. Strongest in northern cities and among businesspeople and the middle class, Republicans were the party of national vision and favored industrial development.

Cultural differences also divided the parties. Democrats tended to belong to "ritualistic" religious sects like Catholicism, Judaism, and more formal brands of Protestantism. As such, the party was grounded in tradition and toleration, adopting a hands-off policy toward both the economy and society at large. Republicans were often "pietistic" Protestants who favored a politics of morality, social control, and energetic government. More zealous reformers often fashioned their own political instruments, whether for temperance, woman suffrage, monetary change, or farm issues.

Congress focused on the well-worn and popular issues of regional conflict, patronage, tariffs, and currency. In many instances these had symbolic value for voters, which politicians of the Gilded Age tapped with success. Meanwhile the presidency, weakened by the impeachment of Andrew Johnson (and constrained by traditional limitations on the office), fell into the hands of a near-anonymous run of caretakers: Rutherford B. Hayes, James Garfield, Chester A. Arthur, Grover Cleveland, and Benjamin Harrison. What ferment and innovation there was came from the states and cities. Investigative and regulatory commissions, statutes extending public control over shippers and processors, and municipal leagues to promote clean and effective government marked the era's more successful experiments in public policy.

The Revolt of the Farmers

No one seemed much to have the interests of farmers in mind, so they took matters into their own hands. In the process they challenged the politics of paralysis. A host of problems beset farmers: overproduction; declining prices; discriminatory railroad rates; heavy mortgages; and widespread poverty, promoted by a "crop-lien" system that shackled them to debt.

In response farmers organized, first in local chapters or "granges" of the Patrons of Husbandry, then in the more economically-oriented Farmers' Alliance. In the 1870s Grangers succeeded in enacting state "Granger laws" regulating shippers and processors and pressed Congress to create a federal Interstate Commerce Commission (1887). Southern and northern Alliances developed farmer cooperatives and by 1890 were winning local and state elections with their candidates. In 1892 the Alliances convened a national convention of farmers, laborers, and other reformers and nominated candidates for the presidency and vice-presidency. The frustrations of farmers now had a national political outlet.

The Depression of 1893

The depression of 1893 deepened discontent across the nation. Strikes, protests, and masses of unemployed workers--including a rag-tag army led by Jacob Coxey--were all signs of strain. The approaching presidential election of 1896 (called the "battle of the standards") brought about a decisive political realignment. The Republicans nominated Senator William McKinley of Ohio and staunchly supported gold as the nation's monetary standard. The Democrats were split, with its northern wing in favor of gold and its southern and western wings in favor of adding silver as a basis for coining money.

In the end Democrats supported both silver and gold and nominated Nebraska congressman William Jennings Bryan. Populists, who favored silver to increase the supply of money and so ease the terms of credit, faced a quandary. If they nominated Bryan (and thereby fused with the Democrats), they risked losing their political identity. If they nominated anyone else, they risked splitting the vote of silverites and losing the election to the pro-gold Republicans. In the end they nominated Bryan and lost the election. Thereafter they faded from politics.

The New Realignment

In 1896 the Republicans became dominant, finally breaking the politics of paralysis with a powerful coalition. Centered in northern industrial cities and the Far West, it would dominate national politics for most of the next three and a half decades. Meanwhile African-Americans, the target of some Populist efforts to form a biracial alliance, found themselves the victims of a rising tide of racism. Segregation and disfranchisement undercut black political and social progress. Many poor whites were victimized as well, as conservative Democrats throughout the South fought political insurgence from below. In response, African-American leaders warred over whether to follow a policy of accommodating white discrimination or fighting it in the courts. In the end most followed the path of accommodation.

Once in power, the Republican party became a powerful governing instrument. Well organized, using modern techniques of publicity and management, and relying on an executive with a national agenda, they oversaw economic recovery. At the dawn of the new century, deep divisions of race and class still split the nation but confidence reigned as McKinley guided the country toward a promising future of prosperity at home and empire abroad.

KEY EVENTS

1867   *Patrons of Husbandry:* also called the "Grange," it soon becomes the voice of the farmer

1869   *Prohibition Party:* created to outlaw alcohol

Regulatory commission: first such state commission created in Massachusetts.

1872   *Greenback Party:* organized to promote the use of "greenbacks," paper money not redeemable in gold

1874   *Women's Christian Temperance Union:* formed to combat drinking alcohol

1875   *Farmers' Alliance:* first organized in Texas to unite farmers

1877   *Munn v. Illinois:* in a victory for the Granger movement, Supreme Court upholds power of a state to legislate warehouse and intrastate traffic rates

1878   *Bland-Allison Silver Purchase Act:* Congress orders a limited amount of silver coinage

1881   *Garfield assassinated:* Chester Arthur sworn in as president

Tuskegee Normal and Industrial Institute: Booker T. Washington founds all-black vocational school in Alabama

1887   *Interstate Commerce Commission:* federal agency regulating trade across state lines created

1890   *National Woman Suffrage Association:* formed as a national organization to promote the vote for women

Sherman Anti-Trust Act: Congress outlaws business combinations that restrain trade

Women's suffrage: Wyoming enters the Union as the first state to give women the vote

1892	*Populist Party:* organized by Farmers Alliance and other reform groups
1893	*Panic of 1893:* the overexpanded economy plummets into a 4-year depression
1894	*"Coxey's Army:"* led by Jacob Coxey, 400 people march from Ohio to Washington to demand public works for the unemployed
1896	*League for the Protection of the Family:* organized to promote the interests of families
	William McKinley elected president: defeats Democrats and Populists to usher in three decades of Republican control of the White House
1903	*The Souls of Black Folk:* W. E. B. DuBois publishes his call to black action
1909	*National Association for the Advancement of Colored People:* founded by DuBois and other black and white leaders

LEARNING OBJECTIVES

When you have finished studying this chapter, you should be able to:

1. Describe the political system of the late nineteenth century and explain why it stood in such perilous equilibrium.

2. Describe the dominant issues of the day, including the "bloody shirt," civil service reform, the tariff, and monetary reform.

3. Explain the limits of executive leadership.

4. Explain the revolt of the farmers and the rise and fall of Populism.

5. Describe causes and effects of the depression of 1893, and explain why government failed to take action to resolve it.

6. Explain the significance of the election of 1896 and the political realignment it marked.

7. Explain the rise of Jim Crow politics and discuss African-American responses to it.

8. Discuss the emergence of modern campaign techniques and the early stirrings of the modern activist presidency.

Review Questions

MULTIPLE CHOICE

1. The chapter introduction relates the story of Populist Tom Watson's 1892 campaign to make the point that
    a. the 1890s marked a return to a more stable political and social order after the upheavals of the previous two decades.
    b. a political revolution in the 1890s undermined the longstanding power of the Republican party.
    c. the national political system had failed to function well in the midst of recent social and economic transformations.
    d. by the 1890s politicians from the South and West were winning national office more regularly than Easterners.

    (pp. 768-770)

2. All of the following are terms the text uses to describe the political climate of the quarter century after the Civil War EXCEPT:
    a. the politics of complacency.
    b. the politics of stalemate.
    c. the politics of paralysis.
    d. the politics of efficiency.

    (pp. 771, 780)

3. Which statement is NOT true of Grover Cleveland?
    a. He won on the strength of his campaign slogan blasting the opposition as the party of "Rum, Romanism and Rebellion."
    b. Conservative and business minded, he supported civil service and the Interstate Commerce Commission.
    c. He sought, unsuccessfully, to lower the tariff.
    d. He served two terms, but not consecutively.

    (pp. 778-779, 787-791)

4. The legacy of the Populists included all EXCEPT:
   a. adoption of the subtreasury system.
   b. enactment of many of their proposed political and economic reforms.
   c. a pioneering, if abortive, effort at a biracial political coalition.
   d. a warning that the political parties were failing to meet the needs of many Americans in the new industrial society.

   (pp. 770, 787-788, 795)

5. What is the best explanation of "free silver"?
   a. The U.S. government would promote prosperity by inflating the money supply, through minting all the silver offered to it.
   b. The U.S. government would promote prosperity by distributing cash subsidies to the unemployed, paid for by recent mining bonanzas on public lands.
   c. The U.S. government would support farmers by buying up surplus crops with silver coin ("hard money").
   d. The U.S. government would support investors by allowing the purchase of silver on the open market.

   (pp. 776-777, 792)

6. As a result of the depression of 1893
   a. new attitudes towards poverty and government responsibility emerged.
   b. the federal government adopted a silver standard of currency.
   c. the Populists expanded their following to the urban working classes.
   d. the Democrats and Republicans unified around strong leaders.

   (pp. 790-792)

7. All of the following statements about the Election of 1896 are true EXCEPT:
   a. Republican William McKinley decisively defeated William Jennings Bryan, who ran on both the Democratic and Populist ticket.
   b. Both candidates employed new techniques in their campaigns.
   c. A major political realignment occurred, as Republicans forged a dominating new coalition of voters.
   d. Progressives used the free silver issue to achieve their first success in national politics.

   (pp. 792-794)

8. Disfranchisement of African-Americans
   a. was unsuccessful EXCEPT in a few southern states.
   b. insured whites could pass the tests or pay the taxes that excluded blacks.
   c. was opposed, unsuccessfully, by Populists and other reformers.
   d. targeted whites who might break party ranks no less than blacks.

   (pp. 794-795)

9. Distinguish between the strategies (for improvement of the lives of black Americans) of Booker T. Washington and W.E.B. DuBois:
   a. Washington advocated radical Socialist ideas, while DuBois accepted the Social Darwinist notion that certain races were inferior.
   b. Washington sought political rights, while DuBois emphasized religious experience.
   c. Washington counseled patience, hard work and practical education; DuBois demanded that leading blacks protest inequality.
   d. Washington believed in vertical integration, while DuBois preferred horizontal integration.

(pp. 796-798)

10. William McKinley is notable as
   a. a relatively passive president.
   b. an active chief executive who re-energized the executive branch of government.
   c. a politician swayed by the influence of party bosses.
   d. a typical Republican, in that he wished to restrain the role and reach of the federal government.

(p. 798)

IDENTIFICATION QUESTIONS

You should be able to describe the following key terms, concepts, individuals and places, and explain their significance:

Terms and Concepts

Populism
Mugwumps
Pendleton Act
McKinley Tariff
Bland-Allison Act
Patrons of Husbandry
Granger laws
Ocala Demands
Depression of 1893
free silver
Niagara Movement

crop-lien system
Anti-Saloon League
protective tariff
bimetallism
Sherman Anti-Trust Act
Interstate Commerce Commission
Southern Alliance
Populist platform, 1892
anarchism
disfranchisement

Individuals and Places

Thomas E. Watson   James Garfield
Charles W. Macune   Mary Elizabeth Lease
Ignatius Donnelly   Jacob Coxey
Marcus Hanna   William Jennings Bryan
Booker T. Washington   Tuskegee Institute
W.E.B. DuBois

MAP IDENTIFICATIONS

On the map below, label or shade in the following places. In a sentence, note their significance to the chapter. (For reference, consult the map in *Nation of Nations* on page 795.)

1. States whose electoral votes went for William McKinley in 1896
2. States whose electoral votes went for William Jennings Bryan in 1896
3. States most urbanized
4. States least urbanized

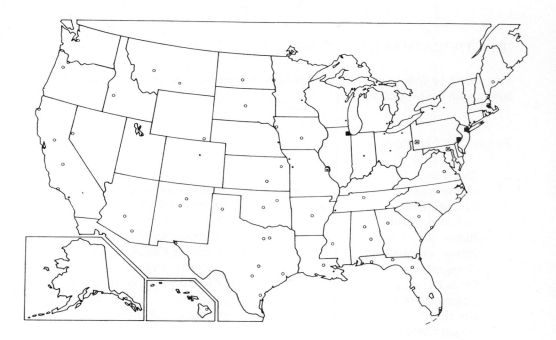

ESSAY QUESTIONS

1. Compare and contrast the Democratic and Republican parties in the last third of the nineteenth century.

2. Why was it so difficult to resolve such issues as the spoils system, the tariff, and bimetallism, that consumed congressional energies in the late nineteenth century?

3. List and defend what you see as the three most important ways the election of 1896 foreshadowed modern presidential campaigns?

4. Compare and contrast the racial policies of Booker T. Washington and W. E. B. DuBois.

5. What do you believe are the three most important reasons for the rise and fall of Populism? What role did the election of 1896 play in its demise?

6. Why did the Republicans emerge as the dominant political party in 1896?

Critical Thinking

EVALUATING EVIDENCE (MAPS)

1. The election of 1896 marked a dramatic realignment in American politics. What does the election map on page 795 indicate about the geographic nature of the new alignment? What does geography tell us about the Republican and Democratic constituencies?

2. Although Democrat William Jennings Bryan and Republican William McKinley were less than a million popular votes apart in the election of 1896, McKinley received nearly twice as many electoral votes. Why?

EVALUATING EVIDENCE (ILLUSTRATIONS AND CHARTS)

1. What features of the political system does the opening picture of New York's Tammany Hall (page 769) decorated for a Democratic national convention in the early 1880s, illustrate?

2. Compare the men "waiting for bread" (in the drawing on page 789) during the depression of 1893. Who might they be? How can you tell? The drawing, by Charles Dana Gibson, is not particularly characteristic of his work. Consult an encyclopedia and explain why.

3. Why is Bryan depicted as a snake swallowing itself in the political cartoon on page 793? What is its message?

4. What kind of class is being taught at the Tuskegee Institute, pictured on page 796? Why is such a class being taught a school whose principal mission is to train students in agriculture and manual trades? How are the students segregated? Why?

CRITICAL ANALYSIS

Read carefully the following excerpt from the text and then answer the questions that follow:

> As the campaign of 1892 heated up, white Populists found themselves barred from their churches by hostile fellow citizens, denied credit at local stores, driven from their homes. Citizens of both races nevertheless worked eagerly for Watson. One young black preacher, the Reverend H. S. Doyle, made over 60 speeches on the candidate's behalf. When a lynch mob threatened Doyle, Watson gave him haven on his own lands and protected him with some 2,000 Populists. They arrived on "buggies and horses foaming and tired with travel." "We are determined," said Watson, "in this free country that the humblest white or black man that wants to talk our doctrine shall do it, and the man doesn't live who shall touch a hair of his head, without fighting every man in the people's party."
>
> Still, upright intentions could not outweigh fraud and violence. As many as 15 blacks died in the Democratic campaign of intimidation. Whiskey was dispensed liberally to persuade citizens to vote Democratic. Blacks were trucked in from across the South Carolina line to vote. Many Democrats stuffed more than one ballot box, and cash bribes routinely changed hands. After winning through such a convincing show of force, Watson's opponents expected that their adversary had learned his lesson--was so badly beaten that he would have to be laid out like a corpse at a funeral. Watson was having none of it. "We decided not to die," he

announced, on behalf of his party. "We unanimously decided to post-pone the funeral."

Questions

1. What evidence is there that Populists were unpopular?

2. How do the authors depict Tom Watson? Can you tell if they are sympathetic or hostile to him? Underline those passages which might provide an indication.

3. How do we know that "citizens of both races...worked eagerly for Watson"?

4. In what way are the intentions of Watson and the Populists "upright"? How were those intentions undermined by Democrats in the election of 1892?

5. Tensions of race and class have always divided America. As much as Watson was trying to forge a biracial coalition, he was also seeking to unite the "have-nots," or those at the bottom of the economic ladder. Which was more threatening to established power? Do you think Watson's campaign might have met with a more successful end if he had concentrated on poor whites alone?

PRIMARY SOURCE: "Tariff on the Brain"*

The tariff was a major source of controversy in the late nineteenth century. Industrialists favored it, claiming that it protected American business from foreign competition and kept workers' wages up. Advocates of free trade, many farmers among them, opposed it with counterclaims that American industry no longer needed protection and consumers no longer needed to pay tariff-inflated prices. The following song appeared in a Populist newspaper in the 1890s.

> Come all you honest people,
> Whoever you may be,
> And help the honest workingmen
> Resist monopoly.
> 'Tis headed by the brokers--
> They deal in bonds and stocks;

---

* From a Populist newspaper, 1890s, reprinted in *Kansas Quarterly* 1 (Fall, 1969).

They cite us to the tariff
While they're getting in their knocks.

CHORUS:
Tariff on the brain! Tariff on the brain!
Look out for politicians
Who have tariff on the brain.

The goldbugs, knowing Grover
To their scheming would agree,
They put him in the White House,
Their agent there to be.
They robbed us of our silver
And grabbed up all our gold--
They cite us to the sheriff
And leave us in the cold.

CHORUS

They've a scheme to throttle labor
And monopolize the land,
To make of us a servile herd
While they are rich and grand.
Their schemes cause want and hunger,
And they may be foiled perhaps;
Or will our fair Columbia
By their greediness collapse.

Questions

1. What is the attitude of the songwriter toward the tariff?

2. What other issues are bound up with the tariff? Why should "honest workingmen resist monopoly"?

3. What are "goldbugs"? Who is "Grover"? Why did they "put him in the White House"?

4. In what ways does the song suggest the need for class solidarity between workers and farmers?

5. What does the songwriter see as the ultimate threats of politicians with "tariff on the brain"?

6. What does this song tell us about feelings toward the tariff in the 1890s?

7. How useful are songs to historians? What problems do they present? What other sources should you consult before coming to final conclusions about such evidence?

22

THE NEW EMPIRE

THE CHAPTER IN PERSPECTIVE

Chapters 18-21 have set forth the impact on American society of industrialization, urbanization, and mass migration. Chapter 20, for example, examined the ways in which the South and West emerged both as internal markets and sources of raw materials. By the late nineteenth century those markets had been well integrated into the American economy. Yet internal and external factors kept the national economy in a pattern of boom and bust. The present chapter shows how those economic forces, which so much altered the United States internally, also reshaped its international position. So, too, did many of the prejudices that shaped the Jim Crow system in the South and patterns of racial violence in the West.

OVERVIEW

In an effort to bring into more human focus the larger, often impersonal forces of American expansion abroad, we have opened the chapter with the stories of Minor Keith's United Fruit Company in Central America and the attempt by Singer to open the China market to the sewing machine trade. The two examples provide only a partial explanation, however, of why the United States after a century as a continental nation suddenly moved to expand its reach into overseas territories.

Visions of Empire

Europeans had practiced imperialism long before Americans took it up. And since Americans had long criticized European expansion and dominion over subject peoples, they had a hard time justifying it for themselves. But justify it they did. The chapter looks first at the human side of the equation, the people within American society who supported American expansionism: missionaries, naval officers, business interests, farmers, and a social/intellectual elite. These groups collectively generated a series of cultural, racist, and economic rationales to support imperialism.

Several ideas had broad appeal. Most peoples view themselves as in some way exceptional or superior. Americans of the late nineteenth century shared that sense. Part of that sense of superiority came from Social Darwinism, often translated into the idea that it was the "White Man's Burden" to civilize less developed peoples. Most important, much of the business community believed that expansion would provide new markets for surplus products.

Stirrings of Empire

After the Civil War some Americans still toyed with the idea of annexing either Canada or Mexico--or both. William Henry Seward envisioned growing American links to the Far East strengthened by a canal to be built across Central America, by a transcontinental railroad, and by island possessions acquired to support an expanded American navy. Seward realized few goals beyond the purchase of Alaska and the completion of the railroad. In the cases of Canada and Mexico most imperialists concluded that trade was better than annexation.

Seward's successors as Secretary of State included Americans like James Blaine, who saw Latin America as the proper outlet for American overseas ambitions. A failed attempt to acquire Hawaii in 1893 and conflict with Britain over Venezuela in 1895 suggested that the United States was on the verge of imperialism in some form. The rise of imperial rivalry from Japan, Germany, and Russia led the British to improve relations with the United States.

The Imperial Moment

The form imperialism would take soon became clearer. Unrest in Cuba, played out against the background of severe depression in the United States from 1893-1897, led to war with Spain. A series of incidents, peaking with the sinking of the battleship *Maine*, stirred a war fever President McKinley could not resist. The war had two arenas: the naval war in the Philippines and a combined naval-military struggle in Cuba. The war opened with Admiral Dewey's smashing victory over the Spanish fleet in Manila Bay. After more than three months of fighting the United States vanquished Spain, liberated Cuba, and took possession of the Philippines.

Sharp congressional debate preceded the United States decision to make the Philippines a colony. In many ways imperialists and anti-imperialists made similar arguments. Both, for example, saw the Philippines as unprepared for self-rule. Both saw a colony as a strategic burden. Each side, however, drew quite opposite conclusions. At the same time, Filipinos did not accept the change from Spanish to American rulers. That led in turn to a cruel and protracted guerrilla war lasting until 1902.

The acquisition of the Philippines was largely related to American desires for markets in China. To keep European powers from closing China to American trade, Secretary of

State John Hay sent two "Open Door" notes that not only asserted American interest in keeping China's markets open, but also of preserving China's sovereignty.

The Roots of Russian-American Conflict

The merging of British and American interests in both China and Latin America contributed unexpectedly to a worsening of relations with Russia. So too did Russia's treatment of its Jewish citizens. Having traditionally emphasized mutual interests rather than conflicting values between the United States and Russia, American leaders now allowed ideological conflict to influence their policy. Protest to the czar's government of its treatment of Jews did nothing to solve the problem, but it did pay political dividends for Theodore Roosevelt. Tensions over China and the evidence of Russian ambitions there also aggravated relations. Therein lay the roots of future Soviet-American tensions in the twentieth century. As the nineteenth century ended, the United States took its place among the great powers of the world.

KEY EVENTS

1850   *Clayton-Bulwer Treaty*: requires Anglo-American role in building an Isthmus canal

1867   *Alaska acquired*: Seward's Folly proves valuable in the long run

British North America Act: creates Canadian confederation

Fall of Maximilian III: French threat ends in Mexico

1871   *Minor Keith*: American imperialist arrives in Costa Rica

1878   *Samoan Treaty*: avoids Anglo-German-American Pacific crisis

1881   *Anti-Jewish pogroms*: persecutions begin in Russia

1883   *Naval building program*: Congress supports plan to build steel ships

1889   *First Pan-American Congress*: Blaine seeks stronger Latin American ties

1890	*The Influence of Sea Power Upon History, 1660-1783*: published by Admiral Alfred Thayer Mahan
	Naval Appropriations Bill: expands modern navy
1893	*Hawaiian revolution*: raises controversy over annexation of Hawaii
1893-1896	*Depression*: encourages expansionist policies
1895	*Venezuelan boundary dispute*: provokes Anglo-American tensions
	José Martí: patriot revives Cuban revolution
1898	*U.S.S. Maine*: sinking creates war crisis
	War with Spain
	Teller amendment: denies imperial goals in Cuba;
	Admiral Dewey captures the Philippines
	Tampa riots: race tensions explode
	Treaty of Paris: gives U.S. control of Philippines and Puerto Rico, grants Cuba independence
	Hawaii formally annexed
1898-1902	*Philippine insurrection*: Filipino nationalists resist U.S. rule
1899	*First Open Door notes*: assert U.S. concern over China
1900	*Boxer Rebellion*: uprising of Chinese nationalists
	Second Open Door notes: Secretary of State Hay asks foreign powers to respect China's sovereignty
1901	*Hay-Pauncefote Treaty*: gives U.S. control over isthmus canal

LEARNING OBJECTIVES

When you have finished studying this chapter, you should be able to:

1. Explain the similarities and differences between European and American imperialism

2. Name some important imperialists and explain their ideas

3. Define the political, economic, and cultural factors that determined the course of American overseas expansion

4. Explain the foreign policy of the United States toward key areas of the world such as the Western Hemisphere, the Pacific Basin, the Far East, Europe, and Russia

5. Explain why the United States went to war with Spain as part of its emergence as an imperial power

6. Explain the connection between Jewish immigration and rising Russian-American friction

Review Questions

MULTIPLE CHOICE

1. The chapter introduction tells the stories of Minor Keith and the Singer sewing machine to make the point that, in the late 1800s,
   a. in order to protect national security, American foreign policy, backed by the U.S. navy, induced American businessmen to invest abroad.
   b. in order to stabilize the domestic economy, American foreign policy, backed by Wall Street, induced American farmers and manufacturers to expand exports.
   c. with little government involvement, American influence overseas increased as U.S. businesses invested in foreign lands and opened foreign markets.
   d. with little government involvement, American technology emerged as the best and most sought after in the world.

   (pp. 802-804, 809-810)

2. Many Americans, despite their anti-European, anti-imperialist heritage, were able to justify joining the race for empire. Their rationale included all of the following assumptions EXCEPT:
  a. They believed themselves responsible for extending the benefits of free enterprise.
  b. They believed themselves responsible to spread Christianity.
  c. They believed themselves responsible to defend other peoples against European imperialists.
  d. They believed themselves responsible to promote democracy abroad.
  (p. 806)

3. Most businessmen were uninterested in foreign adventures, but there were some groups that were indeed "shapers of foreign policy"; these included all EXCEPT:
  a. adventuresome, profit-seeking investors in foreign economies.
  b. shipbuilders
  c. timber interests
  d. manufacturers plagued by overproduction
  (pp. 808-810)

4. Assess the significance of William Henry Seward to America's "new empire."
  a. Preparing the way for American acquisition, he led successful naval assaults on Honolulu and Manila.
  b. Believing that empire moves ever westward, he arranged U.S. acquisition of Hawaii and Samoa.
  c. Though all he actually accomplished was the purchase of Alaska, he envisioned U.S. commercial dominance of the Pacific.
  d. Though a "desk general," he persuaded Congress to reform America's defenses and build a modern army and navy.
  (pp. 812-814)

5. What was the goal of James Blaine's Latin America policy?
  a. reduce political unrest in the region in order to increase American trade .
  b. build an American controlled canal.
  c. assist nationalist groups in peacefully throwing of Spanish rule.
  d. acquiring naval bases and coaling stations.
  (p. 815)

6. What was the significance of the Venezuelan crisis of 1895 and America's "jingoistic" behavior?
   a. It provided Americans with control of the gold of the Orinoco basin.
   b. It revived the Monroe Doctrine and strengthened U.S. power in Latin America.
   c. It proved the cooperative partnership of the new Pan-American Union could work.
   d. It showed that the U.S. should not try to build a canal across Venezuela.

   (pp. 817-818)

7. Who pushed for a more assertive American response to the Cuban revolution?
   a. Social Darwinists like William Graham Sumner.
   b. anti-imperialist critics like Mark Twain.
   c. Republican expansionists like Theodore Roosevelt.
   d. politically sensitive leaders like Presidents Grover Cleveland and William McKinley.

   (p. 819)

8. Which was NOT an influence in leading the U.S. to declare war on Spain in 1898?
   a. American disgust with the brutality of Spanish efforts to suppress the Cuban revolution
   b. American enthusiasm for intervening in support of popular independence movements
   c. the revelation of an insulting letter written by a Spanish diplomat
   d. the sinking of a U.S. warship in Havana harbor

   (pp. 819-821)

9. John Hay issued the Open Door notes to
   a. encourage more Chinese exports to the United States.
   b. permit more Chinese laborers into the United States.
   c. keep Europeans from establishing exclusive closed Chinese markets.
   d. demonstrate America's new military power.

   (pp. 827-828)

10. As global power alignments shifted, the United States in the late 1800s became more friendly with
    a. Russia
    b. Japan
    c. Great Britain
    d. Spain

    (pp. 818, 828)

IDENTIFICATION QUESTIONS

You should be able to describe the following key terms, concepts, individuals and places, and explain their significance:

Terms and Concepts

reconcentration policy
continentalism
Social Darwinism
Anti-imperialists
sovereignty
non-intervention
Clayton-Bulwer Treaty
British North American Act

Manifest Destiny
White Man's Burden
Open Door
sphere of influence
anti-Semitism
Monroe Doctrine
dreadnought
Teller Amendment

Individuals and Places

Minor Keith
Henry and Brooks Adams
Isthmus of Panama
James Blaine
Admiral George Dewey
Somoa

Alfred Thayer Mahan
John Hay
Emperor Maximilian
Venezuelan Crisis
Emilio Aguinaldo
Boxers

MAP IDENTIFICATIONS

On the map on the next page, label or shade in the following places. In a sentence, note their significance to the chapter. (For reference, consult the map in *Nation of Nations* on page 822.)

1. Cuba
2. Haiti
3. Dominican Republic
4. Puerto Rico
5. Tampa
6. Havana
7. Santiago de Cuba
8. route of U.S. invasion forces to Cuba

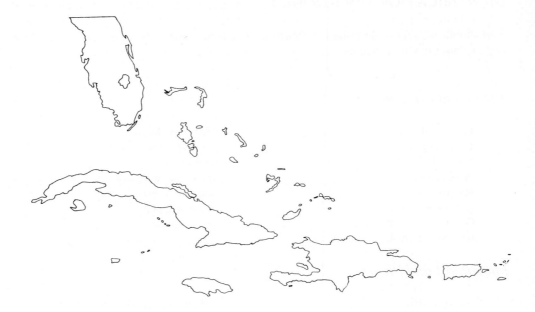

ESSAY QUESTIONS

1. Identify five major groups of Americans who supported overseas expansion.

2. Discuss three major events leading to America's war with Spain.

3. Explain several reasons why anti-imperialists opposed the acquisition of the Philippines.

4. What factors in the late nineteenth century led to the growth of tensions between Russia and the United States?

5. Discuss the role of popular opinion in America's emergence as a great power.

6. If you had been President McKinley's secretary of state, which of the following areas would you have argued should have been the primary focus of American foreign policy by the late nineteenth century: Canada and Mexico, Latin America, Europe, Russia, the Pacific Basin, the Far East, Africa, the Middle East. Why

should the area (or areas) you have suggested receive more attention from the United States?

7. Discuss the strengths and weaknesses of John Hay's policy towards China.

Critical Thinking

EVALUATING EVIDENCE (MAPS)

1. Looking at the map illustrating imperialist expansion (page 805), describe those geographic features that would explain why Russia and Japan might become rivals over China.

2. What does the map of the Spanish-American War (page 822) suggest about the ease with which the United States defeated the Spanish in Cuba?

3. Looking at the same map and the map of imperialism (page 804), explain what geographic factors led Germany to become a rival of Great Britain and the United States.

EVALUATING EVIDENCE (ILLUSTRATIONS AND CHARTS)

1. Look at the picture of the train presented by Commodore Perry to the Japanese (page 813). Is the artist Japanese or American? How can you tell? In fact, the size of the train is exaggerated in the painting. (It was so small that a person had to sit on top in order to drive it, on a circular track only 350 feet long.) Why would the Americans take space in their ship to carry a train that was essentially useless? Judging from the representation in the Japanese illustration, did the train have the effect the Americans intended?

2. Look at the two pictures (page 826) of opposing forces in the guerrilla war in the Philippines. How might the following factors affect the fighting attitudes and morale of the soldiers in each: race, culture, geographic location?

3. Examining the naval ships pictured on page 809, in what ways do the ships appear to contain remnants of the technology of the old Navy? What elements of the ship are more modern in technological design?

4. Looking at the graph of foreign trade (page 806), what significant change occurred in American foreign trade between 1876 and 1910? In what way might that help explain the rise of navalism and American interest in overseas possessions during the same period?

CRITICAL ANALYSIS

Read carefully the following excerpt from the text and then answer the questions that follow:

Yet as we have also seen, the success of western European expansion into colonial North America also benefited from ecological factors. European diseases, animals, and plants often devastated and disrupted the new worlds they entered. The coming of smallpox and measles; of pigs, cattle, and horses; and of sugar and wheat played equally important roles in opening the Western Hemisphere and the Pacific basin to European domination. In areas like the Middle East, Asia, and Africa, where populations already possessed hardy domesticated animals and plants (as well as their own devastating disease pools) European penetration was far less complete. Still, journalist Finley Peter Dunne's Irish characters Mr. Hennessy and Mr. Dooley best expressed the confidence with which Americans and Europeans viewed their self-proclaimed superiority. "`We're a gr-reat people,' said Mr. Hennessy earnestly. `We ar-re,' said Mr. Dooley, `We ar-re that. An' the best iv it is, we know we ar-re.'"

With a confidence so sublime, scholars, academics and scientists soon developed racial theories to justify European and American expansion. Charles Darwin's *Origin of the Species* (1859) had popularized the notion that among animal species, the fittest survived through a process of natural selection. Social Darwinists like Herbert Spencer in England and William Graham Sumner in the United States argued that the same laws of survival governed the social order. By natural as well as divine law, the fittest people--those descended from Anglo-Saxon and Teutonic stock--would assert their dominion over the lesser people of the world. When applied aggressively, the theory of white supremacy could rationalize the wholesale slaughter and enslavement of native populations who resisted. When combined with the somewhat more humane notions of the "White Man's Burden," conquest included not only the "burden" or obligation to impose order, but also to uplift the "lower" races by

teaching them western ideas, converting them to Christianity, and intro-
ducing law and government. Patricians like Theodore Roosevelt and
Henry Cabot Lodge eagerly accepted such notions.

Questions

1. In what ways do the authors suggest that ecological factors assisted the spread of
   Europeans across the globe? How would smallpox and measles help? cattle, pigs,
   and horses? What is a "disease pool"? How would it help "defend" against European invaders?

2. The first paragraph contains two points of view that in some ways contradict each
   other. What are they? In what ways does the first contradict, or at least cast doubt,
   on the second?

3. From the way the text describes Social Darwinist ideas, explain how the authors
   show they disagree with them.

4. Explain which theory about the success of European expansion seems most con-
   vincing to you.

5. Can you describe any ways that ideas like Social Darwinism still have an influence
   on foreign or public policy?

PRIMARY SOURCE: An English View of Imperialism[*]

*The English poet Rudyard Kipling had experienced much of his country's empire at first
hand. In 1899, while the United States was debating what to do with the Philippines, he
published this cautionary poem in* McClure's Magazine. *It was the title more than the content that struck his American audience. They saw the poem not as a warning, but as a noble
sentiment for empire.*

The White Man's Burden

Take up the white man's burden--
Send forth the best ye breed--
Go, bind your sons to exile

---

[*] From *McClure's Magazine, February*, 1899.

To serve your captives' need;
To wait in heavy harness,
On fluttered folk and wild--
Your new-caught sullen peoples,
Half devil and half child.

Take up the white man's burden--
In patience to abide,
To veil the threat of terror
And check the show of pride;
By open speech and simple,
A hundred times made plain,
To seek another's profit
And work another's gain.

Take up the white man's burden--
The savage wars of peace--
Fill full the mouth of famine,
And bid the sickness cease;
And when your goal is nearest
(The end for others sought)
Watch sloth and heathen folly
Bring all our hope to nought.

Take up the white man's burden--
No iron rule of kings,
But toil of serf and sweeper--
The tale of common things.
The ports ye shall not enter,
The roads ye shall not tread,
Go, make them with your living
And mark them with your dead.

Take up the white man's burden"
And reap his old reward--
The blame of those ye better
The hate of those ye guard--
The cry of hosts ye humor
(Ah, slowly!) toward the light:
"Why brought ye us from bondage,
Our loved Egyptian night?"

Take up the white man's burden--
Ye dare not stoop to less--
Nor call too loud on Freedom
To cloak your weariness.
By all ye will or whisper,
By all ye leave or do,
The silent sullen peoples
Shall weigh your God and you.

Take up the white man's burden--
Have done with childish days--
The lightly proffered laurel,
The easy ungrudged praise:
Comes now, to search your manhood
Through all the thankless years,
Cold, edged with dear-bought wisdom,
The judgment of your peers.

Questions

1. Express in your own words what you think Kipling means by the "white man's burden."

2. What view does Kipling express of colonial peoples? Indicate the words and phrases that convey that viewpoint.

3. What attitude does Kipling believe colonial people have towards their colonial rulers?

4. What words or phrases suggest that Kipling sees whites as biologically or racially superior?

5. What benefits does Kipling suggest that whites gain from their efforts to build colonies? Given your reading of Chapter 22, what benefits does Kipling not mention?

6. What in the tone of this poem strikes you as ironic? What point of view might the occupied of a colonial nation express upon reading the poem?

7. This chapter ends with an ironic comment made about the United States by a French diplomat. Compare that comment to the last stanza of this poem.

23

THE PROGRESSIVE ERA

THE CHAPTER IN PERSPECTIVE

In many ways, this chapter serves as a key pivot-point in the story. Previous chapters have charted the changes brought about by industrialization and urbanization--changes that transformed the United States into an industrial power of the first rank. Yet those changes came with high social costs that severely strained the political order, as we saw in Chapter 21. Indeed, it was the wrenching depression of 1893 that galvanized Progressivism, the first national reform movement. Progressivism began in the industrial cities, where the nation's problems were most evident. It was first promoted by middle class reformers who sought to apply expertise, professionalism, and the force of law to the many problems of the new industrial society. Unlike earlier reformers, they did not distrust government. In a pattern typical of liberal reform, Progressives used government as an instrument of change and an agent of the public interest. The modern liberal state--active and interventionist--emerged, and much of the rest of this text will chart the rise of that state.

OVERVIEW

Progressivism sprang from many impulses: desires to curb the advancing power of corporations and end widespread corruption; efforts to bring order and efficiency to economic and political life; attempts by new interest groups to make business and government more responsive to their needs; moralistic urges to rid society of such perceived evils as drink and prostitution. These problems reached a boiling point in the industrial city. The chapter therefore opens with an urban, industrial tragedy, the Triangle Shirtwaist fire. It is a case study of progressivism in action.

The Roots of Progressive Reform

The depression of 1893 underscored the national scope of these problems. Progressive reformers aimed to solve them without overturning the American system. They became moderate modernizers, at once nostalgic and innovative. They aimed at redeeming such traditional American values as democracy, Christian ethics, individual opportunity, and the spirit of voluntary public service. They operated on the pragmatic principles of philosophers William James and John Dewey, as they applied to contemporary problems the modern techniques of research, analysis, diagnosis, and prescription. Progressivism, with its emphasis on efficiency and the shaping effects of environment, found an appealing organizational model in the corporation. Like corporate executives, progressives relied on careful management and planning, coordinated systems, and specialized bureaucracies of experts to carry out their reforms.

A new breed of investigative journalists called "muckrakers" furnished an agenda of reform and the public indignation necessary to implement it. Factual and hard-boiled, they were also sentimental moralizers who rarely had solutions to the problems they discovered. When volunteerism and public anger failed to curb abuses, progressives turned to politics and government. At all levels, new agencies and commissions staffed by impartial experts began to investigate and regulate society.

The Search for the Good Society

If progressivism ended in politics, it began with social reform, mostly of cities, where poverty and blight were so evident. Mixing middle-class professionalism and lower-class uplift, progressive reformers redefined poverty as the social consequence of deprivation, not the individual consequence of personal failure or immorality. Settlement houses helped to produce a new profession, social work, which applied more scientific approaches to helping the poor and troubled.

Women, often single, well educated, and denied access to other professions, moved into the forefront of social reform. In the process they became "social housekeepers," extending the traditional woman's sphere of nurturance into society-at-large. Birth control, housing reform, factory safety, workers' compensation, child labor, consumers' issues: all were promoted by women and other reformers as matters of social welfare and social justice. For many progressives woman suffrage would also help to clean up society and, just as important, politics as well. In 1920, after much agitation, the Nineteenth Amendment finally granted women the right to vote.

Controlling the Masses

The drive for social justice reflected the optimistic, tolerant impulses of progressivism; the pursuit of social "welfare" for the masses, its paternalistic instincts. But for many progressives, urban society needed to be controlled, lest it be destroyed by immigrants and low-lifes. Occasionally allying themselves with more traditional Protestant evangelicals worried over losing America to foreigners, some progressives pressed for immigration restriction, prohibition of alcohol, and an end to urban crime, particularly prostitution. Whenever possible reformers tried to take the profit out of human misery.

The Politics of Municipal and State Reform

Increasingly politics seemed the only way to clean up the rest of society, but first politics itself had to be cleaned up. Through commission and city-manager plans, progressives tried to make municipal government less corrupt and political and more efficient. Colorful reform mayors such as Hazen Pingree of Detroit, Tom Johnson of Cleveland, and Samuel "Golden Rule" Jones fought boss-dominated machines and monopolistic transit and utility companies.

Building on municipal success, progressives turned to state government. In Wisconsin and elsewhere, governors like Robert La Follette injected democratic reforms but also more experts into state government, shifting power from interest-dominated legislatures to executives and administrative agencies. Boss politics, whether at the municipal or state level, nonetheless survived because machines promoted social welfare reforms that aided their working-class constituents. Working-class "urban liberalism" thus became a powerful instrument of reform.

Progressivism Goes to Washington

In the presidency of Theodore Roosevelt, progressivism moved to Washington and an era of federal reform began. A conservative reformer, Roosevelt accepted growth--whether of business, labor, or capital--as a natural development that promoted stability and order. He sought only to curb abuses with big government mediating among the various factions. The result, he said in 1904, would be a "Square Deal" for all Americans. Despite the compromises he usually made, Roosevelt established a dominant executive, enhanced the regulatory functions of the federal government (including regulation of the natural environment), and laid the groundwork for a widening federal bureaucracy. When he handed over the reins of government to his successor, William Howard Taft, conservatives in Congress had already begun to lash back. Taft's single term in office, in spite of its achievements, ended in frustration, divided the Republican Party, and allowed Democrat Woodrow Wilson to win the presidency in 1912.

Under Wilson national progressivism peaked. Rejecting Roosevelt's "New Nationalism" of private consolidation and public planning ("regulated monopoly"), Wilson promised a "New Freedom" of "regulated competition" and strict limits on size, whether in business or government. The achievements of his first term were considerable: downward revision of the tariff, centralization of the banking system, a federal trade commission, and a new anti-trust law. Together they raised progressive reform to new heights, even as they moved Wilson closer to the big government espoused by Roosevelt. In the end the weaknesses of progressivism--the narrowness of its social vision; the fuzziness of its definition of the "public interest"; the ease with which its regulatory agencies were captured by industry--were counterbalanced by its accomplishments in establishing the modern, activist state.

KEY EVENTS

1890   *General Federation of Women's Clubs:* women's clubs across the nation organize and soon become instruments of reform, especially for women and children

1892   *Sierra Club:* founded by John Muir to preserve the environment in its natural state

1893   *8-hour workday law for women:* Illinois legislature enacts first 8-hour workday law for women

                 Anti-Saloon League: created to prohibit the sale of alcoholic beverages by outlawing the saloon

1895   *United States v. E. C. Knight:* drawing a fine line between manufacturing and commerce, Supreme Court rules that the Sherman Anti-Trust Act applies only to monopolies involved in interstate commerce, thereby permitting the E. C. Knight company to continue owning 98 percent of the sugar refining business in America

1900   *Commission government:* following a devastating hurricane, the city of Galveston, Texas, creates first commission form of government to organize relief and recovery

1901   *McKinley assassinated:* Theodore Roosevelt becomes president;

                 La Follette's Wisconsin idea: Governor La Follette of Wisconsin begins a program of reform

                 Socialist Party of America founded

1902   *Northern Securities Case:* government brings successful antitrust suit to dissolve the giant Northern Securities Company

                 Anthracite coal miners' strike: in Pennsylvania, a successful strike supported by President Roosevelt

                 Workers' compensation law: Maryland adopts first law to compensate workers injured on the job

1903   *Department of Labor and Commerce created:* a step toward stricter regulation of business

Elkins Act: Congress outlaws rebates

Direct primary established in Wisconsin: part of La Follette's reform package

Wright brothers fly first airplane

1904   *The Shame of the Cities:* Lincoln Steffens publishes muckraking exposé of urban political corruption

Roosevelt elected president: promises a "Square Deal"

1906   *Hepburn Act:* strengthens Interstate Commerce Commission

The Jungle: Upton Sinclair's muckraking novel leads to passage of the Meat Inspection Act, which is followed by the Pure Food and Drug Act

1908   *Model T:* Henry Ford introduces the a new automobile that becomes the industry standard

Muller v. Oregon: accepting Louis Brandeis' sociological evidence, Supreme Court upholds 10-hour workday law for women

Taft elected president: William Howard Taft, Roosevelt's hand-picked successor, wins presidency

1909   *Ballinger-Pinchot controversy:* Secretary of Interior Richard Ballinger accused by Chief Forester Gifford Pinchot of accepting bribes to open public land

1911   *Triangle Shirtwaist fire:* factory fire kills 146 workers, mainly young women

1912   *Progressive ("Bull Moose") Party:* nominates Theodore Roosevelt for presidency

Wilson elected president: in a four-way race, Democrat Woodrow Wilson defeats Republican William Howard Taft, Progressive Theodore Roosevelt, and Socialist Eugene V. Debs

1913   *Sixteenth Amendment adopted:* federal income tax legalized

Seventeenth Amendment adopted: direct election of senators

Underwood-Simmons Tariff: tariff revised downward for first time in decades

Federal Reserve Act: creates federally-controlled banking system

1914   *Clayton Anti-Trust Act:* tightens antitrust laws

Federal Trade Commission: created to regulate competition

1916   *Birth Control League:* organized by Margaret Sanger

Keating-Owen Child Labor Act: bans child labor

1917   *Literacy test:* Congress enacts restriction for new immigrants

1920   *Nineteenth Amendment adopted:* grants women right to vote

LEARNING OBJECTIVES

When you have finished studying this chapter, you should be able to:

1. Describe the origins of progressive reform, including the system of beliefs upon which it rested and the methods it employed.

2. Explain how progressives sought to create the "good society" and the social reforms they pursued to achieve it.

3. Describe the origins and effects of progressive municipal and state reforms.

4. Explain why and how progressivism flowered on the national level.

5. Describe the contributions of the Roosevelt and Wilson administrations to progressive reform.

6. Evaluate the strengths and weaknesses of progressivism.

Review Questions

MULTIPLE CHOICE

1. The chapter introduction tells the story of the Triangle Shirtwaist fire to make the point that
   a. the time known as the Progressive era was when modern city services such as police and fire departments spread across America.
   b. reformers of the day sought to use government to curb abusive corporations and establish a good society.
   c. industrial society increasingly had to face the negative consequences of decades of wrenching economic change.
   d. economic depression was not the only harsh reality faced by anxious Americans at the turn of the century.

   (pp. 832-835)

2. Which one of the following ideas should NOT be associated with progressivism?
   a. a belief in efficiency and planning
   b. moral overtones that could be expressed as a desire to restore moral purity
   c. a commitment to using government to curb the influence of "special interests"
   d. a skeptical view of human nature and American potential

   (pp. 834-835)

3. The ideology of progressivism, insofar as it had one, generally
   a. mixed a liberal concern for the poor with a conservative wish to control social disorder.
   b. called for redistribution of incomes from wealthy to poor and a socialist approach to government.
   c. was rooted in firm and fixed standards of morality and truth.
   d. stressed trying to meet the special needs of each identifiable private interest.

   (p. 834)

4. *McClure's Magazine* pioneered a new style of journalism featuring writers like Ida Tarbell and Lincoln Steffens who
   a. scientifically analyzed social problems and proposed solutions.
   b. provided voter information to reveal where candidates stood and whose money they accepted.
   c. employed a gritty realism that portrayed life in the slums.
   d. presented carefully researched exposes of corporate and government abuses.
   (pp. 837-838)

5. Which statement about political progressivism at the local and state levels is true?
   a. Urban reforms strengthened middle class control and improved efficiency.
   b. Big city mayors, controlled by corrupt political machines, were the main obstacles to Progressive reform of municipal government.
   c. Municipal reformers sought to replace traditional forms of city government like the commission or city manager.
   d. In their quest for efficiency and expert rule, Progressives tried to invent alternatives to direct democracy.
   (pp. 849-852)

6. The Nineteenth Amendment granting women the right to vote was embraced by many Progressives because
   a. a large majority of American voters now favored it.
   b. it could offset growing jingoism and militarism, especially once World War I began.
   c. the women agitating for it moderated the radicalism of their campaign.
   d. the higher moral character of women would help clean up politics.
   (pp. 842-844)

7. How did the new amusement parks differ from earlier public entertainments?
   a. Earlier parks and fairs provided no opportunities for shows or rides.
   b. Amusement parks were located in urban rather than rural settings.
   c. No longer was there an obligation to instruct as well as amuse.
   d. No longer was commercial success enough; now progressive reform values had to be advanced.
   (pp. 846-847)

8. Which statement does NOT accurately compare Theodore Roosevelt and Woodrow Wilson?
   a. Both ran for president in 1912.
   b. Both used presidential power to promote pragmatic change.
   c. Both took significant symbolic steps to break down barriers of racial segregation.
   d. As his re-election campaign neared, Wilson began advocating programs that fit Roosevelt's "New Nationalism" ideas.

   (pp. 853, 861-866)

9. Many historians consider it the most important reform of the early 20th century, because it established the means for expanded federal action. It was:
   a. the Sixteenth Amendment permitting graduated income taxes.
   b. the Seventeenth Amendment providing for direct popular election of Senators.
   c. the Eighteenth Amendment authorizing prohibition.
   d. the Nineteenth Amendment granting women's suffrage.

   (p. 860)

10. What is an accurate comparison of the two competing brands of political progressivism in the 1912 presidential campaign (Theodore Roosevelt's "New Nationalism" and Woodrow Wilson's "New Freedom")?
   a. The New Nationalism accepted concentrations of capital, labor, and government; but the New Freedom stressed competitiveness among small business and reduced government power.
   b. The New Nationalism supported business and ignored social justice concerns while the New Freedom held to the reverse emphasis.
   c. Both welcomed assertive federal power and encouraged business growth.
   d. Neither was truly progressive.

   (pp. 861-862)

IDENTIFICATION QUESTIONS

You should be able to describe the following key terms, concepts, individuals and places, and explain their significance:

Terms and Concepts

Progressivism
Muller v. Oregon
McClure's Magazine
the "Ashcan" school
eugenics
Wisconsin Idea
The "Square Deal"
The New Nationalism
The Jungle
Federal Reserve Board

Theory of the Leisure Class
sociological jurisprudence
muckrakers
National Woman's party
General Federation of Women's Clubs
referendum
United Mine Workers
Sixteenth Amendment
the Underwood-Simmons tariff
Pure Food and Drug Act of 1906

Individuals and Places

William James
Louis D. Brandeis
Lincoln Steffens
Charlotte Perkins Gilman
Carrie Chapman Catt
Robert La Follette

John Dewey
Oliver Wendell Holmes, Jr
Jacob Riis
Margaret Sanger
Julia Lathrop
John Muir

MAP IDENTIFICATIONS

On the map on the next page, label or shade in the following places. In a sentence, note their significance to the chapter. (For reference, consult the map in *Nation of Nations* on page 844.)

1. States granting women suffrage before 1871
2. States granting women suffrage between 1871 and 1910
3. States granting women suffrage between 1910 and 1918
4. States without women suffrage in 1919

ESSAY QUESTIONS

1. Define the "progressive method."

2. Describe the three main beliefs on which progressivism rested, discuss where they came from, and explain how the "Brandeis brief" reflected them?

3. What was the "Wisconsin Idea," and how did it work? Discuss two ways in which it was progressive.

4. In what ways did Woodrow Wilson bring progressivism to high tide?

5. "Progressivism was at once both nostalgic, looking back to traditions of the past, and modern, seeking to apply the advances of science." Explain.

6. How did progressives redefine poverty? Why was that important? Where and why did progressive solutions for the problems of poverty fall short?

7. In what ways were immigration restriction, prohibition, and attacks on vice "progressive" reforms?

8. Compare and contrast progressives and Populists. Why were progressives more successful reformers than Populists?

Critical Thinking

EVALUATING EVIDENCE (MAPS)

1. Does the map illustrating woman suffrage (on page 844) support the notion posited by historian Frederick Jackson Turner that democracy spread from west to east? Is there any geographic pattern to the spread of woman suffrage? If so, how do you explain it?

2. Compare the 1912 election map (on page 863) with the 1896 election map (on page 795). What states might have voted Republican in 1912 had Theodore Roosevelt been the Republican candidate? Would that have altered the outcome of the election?

EVALUATING EVIDENCE (ILLUSTRATIONS AND CHARTS)

1. According to the chart on page 862, how has voter turnout changed from the late nineteenth to the early twentieth centuries? Why do you suppose the percentage of voter turnout declined as the number of eligible voters has increased?

2. What image of Theodore Roosevelt does the opening cartoon on page 833 project? How is Roosevelt depicted, and what does that illustrate about Roosevelt's impact on the presidency?

3. What does the photograph of the Triangle Shirtwaist fire on page 834 depict? How might photography have become an important instrument of reform?

4. How does the cartoon on page 838 depict the trust? What does it tell us about American attitudes toward big business at the turn of the century?

CRITICAL ANALYSIS

Read carefully the following excerpt from the text and then answer the questions that follow:

> The reform of character, the cure for poverty, the movement to liberate women and care for slum children, the need to take the profit out of human misery--all these problems seemed soluble with reform in government. Jane Addams learned as much outside the doors of her beloved Hull-House. For months during the early 1890s, garbage piled up all along Halstead Street. The filth and stench finally drove Addams and her fellow workers to city hall in protest--700 times in one summer--but to no avail. In Chicago as elsewhere, a corrupt band of city fathers ruled. For them, garbage collection was a plum to be awarded to the company that paid the most for it. Garbage inspectors won their posts by serving the machine, and garbage collection remained erratic, especially in poor neighborhoods, where boxes overflowed with stinking refuse.
>
> In desperation Addams submitted her own bid for garbage removal in the ward. It was thrown out on a technicality. Undaunted, she got herself appointed as a garbage inspector. For almost a year she dogged collection carts, but boss politics kept things dirty. So Addams ran candidates against local ward boss Johnny Powers in 1896 and 1898. Tossing cigars to the men and nickels to the children, Powers won both times. Addams continued her campaigns for honest government and social reform, not only at city hall but in the Illinois legislature and in Washington as well. Politics turned out to be the only way to clean things up.

Questions

1. Underline the passages in the excerpt that express the opinions or judgments of the authors rather than a narrative of facts.

2. What drove Jane Addams to city hall? Why did she go there rather than to the garbage collectors? Why were her petitions fruitless?

3. In what ways were the city fathers of Chicago "a corrupt band"? How was garbage collection a "plum"? How were contracts awarded? Why were garbage inspectors so ineffective?

4. What was Addams' solution? Why "having normally avoided politics" did she feel compelled to take political action?

5. In what ways does the story of Addams and garbage collection illustrate how progressivism started with social reform and ended in politics? How might a neighborhood association today handle a similar problem today?

PRIMARY SOURCE: A Progressive Proposes an Alternative to the Saloon*

Saloons were the target of many progressive reformers. Despite its role as a social center, reformers worried that the saloon was a rats' nest, where workers squandered their salaries and fell victim to drink, drugs, prostitution, and corrupt political bosses. This reformer described a new type of "rest room" being established in Wisconsin as a wholesome alternative.

The [rest room] at Chippewa Falls consists of one room located in the business portion of the city. The room is heated with steam, has city water, and is lighted with gas; the water and gas are donated. It is furnished with tables, easy chairs, couches, pictures, etc. On the tables are found some of the best magazines, the local and daily papers. The room is kept by a matron who receives $12 a month. The rent is $15 a month. This is the total expense, as the furniture, reading matter, and other incidentals are donated by the public. These expenses are borne by the merchants who have made monthly subscriptions, and the money is collected at the end of each month. The room is under the management and control of the Woman's Club. The average number of people daily accommodated is about twenty-five....

[Rooms like this] serve all classes of people, the farmer, the trader and stranger from the neighboring town, and the business man. They furnish a comfortable place for the farmer's wife to rest while waiting for him to finish his business. They are especially serviceable to mothers with small children who formerly were compelled to wait in the stores where they felt, and often rightly so, that they incommoded others. The wives and mothers are relieved from much care and worry by the comfort of these rooms. Through amusements, refreshments, and various kinds of reading matter, they may be made to serve the waiting or loafing farmer

---

* From A. D. Davis, "Rest Rooms in Cities," *The Municipality* (February 1901).

who now often goes to the saloon and spends money which the merchant should get....

It is generally believed by social reformers that the saloon is a social necessity until a satisfactory substitute is found. It is possible that, in providing dining, waiting, amusement, and toilet places, rest rooms may at least partially supplant the saloon as a social institution. Much can be done by placing toilet rooms in the Y.M.C.A. and public buildings. By keeping the rest rooms open at night when farmers do not need them, they may be made to serve the laboring men who are the best customers of saloons. They should, however, be made as attractive as the saloon. They should have smoking apartments, on the tables should be placed the best reading matter, cards, and all kinds of games, and refreshments should be served. In brief, rest rooms, to serve the laborer, should have all the attractions of the saloons without the evils of intoxicating liquors. The proper charges could be made for refreshments and games so that the laborer would not feel that this was a service of charity.

Questions

1. What is a "rest room," as this author describes it? How would rest rooms compete with saloons?

2. Why do you suppose that social reformers believe "the saloon is a social necessity"? What social functions did the saloon perform for laborers?

3. Are services of rest rooms limited just to working class patrons? Why should the "proper charges" be made for the services provided?

4. The text describes a number of qualities of temperament and approaches to reform shared by many progressives. In what way does the proposal to establish rest rooms reflect the progressive temperament and approach?

5. Why does the author not advocate closing down saloons entirely? What does his solution suggest about how progressives looked at laborers? At society in general?

6. How effective do you think rest rooms would be in "partially supplanting" saloons and the evils of drink? Should government, which was expected to sponsor rest rooms, be in the business of controlling social habits?

24

THE UNITED STATES AND THE OLD WORLD ORDER

THE CHAPTER IN PERSPECTIVE

he trends we have seen in previous chapters--towards industrialization, urbanization, and expansion to gain control of lands and resources--were characteristic of Europe as well as the United States. Chapter 20 has already taken note of the imperial designs of European nations, and how these designs brought them into conflict with one another and with the United States in Asia and Latin America. The present chapter traces the emergence of the United States as a world power by examining progressive diplomacy in the opening decades of the twentieth century. As the old order of alliances and empires proved unable to mediate the conflicts arising out of imperialism and international rivalry, the United States was drawn into the First World War. In its aftermath, Woodrow Wilson tried to establish a new world order based on international cooperation. Narrow nationalism, at home and abroad, prevailed instead. Not for an other 20 years would this new internationalism receive another chance.

OVERVIEW

The construction of the Panama Canal, opening the chapter, is emblematic of the rise of American power--power which has become increasingly nationalistic and interventionist, now spanning two oceans and looking toward Europe and Asia. By the early twentieth century expansionist diplomats in the United States and Europe had convinced themselves that they could maintain global order by dividing the world into spheres of influence and joining themselves in a series of political alliances. The system of alliances and spheres of influence, however, did not suffice, and the Old World order collapsed in a terrible war.

Progressive Diplomacy

Progressive diplomacy, like progressive politics, stressed moralism and order and stretched executive power to its limits. It was driven by a sense of global destiny, a commitment to civilizing the "lesser breeds," and an aggressive economic expansionism. In the Caribbean, Theodore Roosevelt attempted to encourage stable governments that would be fiscally responsible and open to American investment. His self-imposed "Roosevelt Corollary" (1905) to the Monroe Doctrine proclaimed the right of the United States to intervene in the internal affairs of Latin American countries to keep financial order and forestall European intervention.

Under its auspices, Roosevelt regularly wielded his "big stick," intervening in the affairs of Latin American countries and transforming the Caribbean into an American-dominated lake. In distant Asia he exercised tact rather than force, seeking to counterbalance Russian and Japanese ambitions in the Far East while recognizing their dominant positions in the region. His actions reflected two of his central beliefs: American interests were global; and armed conflict between great powers must be avoided.

Recognizing the reality of American economic expansion, President Taft and his secretary of state, Philander Knox, attempted to substitute "dollars for bullets," by undertaking "dollar diplomacy." In the end, however, Taft relied on both investment and intervention. Unsuccessful in China, the Taft-Knox policies did help American capital to penetrate Latin America more deeply. However, dollar diplomacy became so closely associated with unpopular regimes, corporations, and banks that Woodrow Wilson felt bound to disassociate himself with it as soon as he took office.

Woodrow Wilson and Moral Diplomacy

To the diplomacy of order, force, and finances, Woodrow Wilson brought a sincere commitment to justice, democracy, Christian values, and international harmony. He believed in a missionary diplomacy that preached the value of exporting democracy and capitalism (and American goods) to promote stability and progress (and American markets) in the world. His secretary of state, William Jennings Bryan, negotiated arbitration agreements with some 30 nations to keep peace. His administration opposed Japan's "Twenty-One Demands" to control China and gave the Philippines limited independence.

Yet like Roosevelt and Taft, Wilson failed to appreciate the near impossibility of trying to graft American-style democracy and capitalism onto foreign countries with their own traditions. Soon Wilson, like his predecessors, was intervening in Central America, and--with disastrous consequences--in Mexico. Wilson's missionary diplomacy, like Roosevelt's big stick diplomacy and Taft's dollar diplomacy before it, received a hostile reception.

The Road to War

The outbreak of war in Europe took Wilson and the American people by surprise. Wilson condemned both sides and proclaimed a policy of neutrality. By standing above the fray, he believed the United States could lead the world to a higher peace of international cooperation and collective security to replace the discredited old order of balanced powers and spheres of influence. But his natural sympathies, like the sympathies of most Americans, lay with the British. Their command of the high seas soon made a mockery of American neutrality, which in practice favored Britain and the rest of the Allied Powers. In desperation, Germany (leader of the opposing Central Powers) launched a vicious submarine assault on Allied and neutral shipping that brought the United States into the war in 1917.

War and Society

American society organized for war in peculiarly progressive ways. Fielding an army by democratic conscription, mobilizing the economy with centralized, executive agencies, propagandizing the war by using modern techniques of advertising--in all these ways progressive faith in planning, efficiency, patriotism, and publicity guided the war effort on the home front. The result was a deepening partnership between government and business in which regulation would increasingly give way to a business-dominated economy. Meanwhile, demographic changes, including a massive migrations of Latinos and African-Americans, reshaped the nation's cities and deepened tensions.

The darker side of progressivism also flourished. Its impulses toward social control turned into new drives for prohibition. Its penchant for assimilation became a frenzy for loyalty and conformity, leading to wholesale violations of civil liberties.

Overseas, the arrival of the American Expeditionary Force helped to break the European stalemate. Allied victory, negotiated on the basis of Wilson's 14-point peace plan, gave him the opportunity to put his progressive ideals into practice.

The Lost Peace

At the Paris peace conference Wilson fought for a new world order based on harmony, cooperation, democracy, self-determination, and rational dialogue. Softening some Allied demands for retribution, he achieved his greatest success in winning acceptance of the League of Nations, a new international organization. He believed it was the heart of the treaty because it could correct the mistakes made at the conference and ensure peace for the future.

Returning home, he found his hopes and his treaty dashed in the Senate, where his own refusal to compromise combined with Republican hostility to ensure defeat. Meanwhile, riots, strikes, and a "Red Scare" left the country reeling, sick of idealistic crusades and interested in returning to "normalcy."

KEY EVENTS

1901   *Hay-Pauncefote Treaty:* authorizes U.S. to build canal across the Central American isthmus

1902   *Platt Amendment:* U.S. reserves right to intervene in Cuban affairs

1904   *Roosevelt Corollary:* U.S. assumes right to police Caribbean affairs

1905   *Treaty of Portsmouth:* ends Russo-Japanese War

1907   *"Gentleman's Agreement:"* U.S. agrees to mutual restriction of immigration with Japan

          "Great White Fleet:" New U.S. battle fleet embarks on world tour

1911   *Mexican Revolution:* the overthrow of dictator Porfirio Díaz ignites a revolution in Mexico

1914   *Invasion of Vera Cruz:* U.S. Navy invades Mexican port city

          World War I: set off by assassination of Archduke Franz Ferdinand of Austria-Hungary

1915   *Lusitania torpedoed:* 114 Americans die when German submarines sink British liner

          Arabic Pledge: Germany pledges to restrict submarine warfare

1916   *U.S. invades Mexico:* General John Pershing crosses Mexican border in pursuit of Pancho Villa

1917   *"Peace without victory":* Wilson calls for negotiated peace

          Submarine warfare: Germany resumes unrestricted use of submarines

          Zimmerman telegram: German ambassador to Mexico promises American territory in return for Mexican declaration of war against U.S.

          Russian Revolution: Bolsheviks topple Czar Nicolas II

U.S. enters World War I: President Wilson receives declaration of war against Central Powers

Selective Service Act: Congress enacts draft

1918 *Fourteen Points:* President Wilson announces his peace plan

Influenza epidemic: global influenza pandemic kills more Americans than die in combat

Germany sues for peace: armistice declared

1919 *Paris Peace Conference:* Allied victors convene peace conference at Versailles

Schenk v. United States: Supreme Court affirms Espionage Act

Red Summer: nation erupts in race riots

Treaty of Versailles: Senate rejects Paris Peace Treaty

1920 *Palmer raids:* Attorney General orders arrest and deportation of radicals, igniting nationwide Red Scare

LEARNING OBJECTIVES

When you have finished studying this chapter, you should be able to:

1. Describe the underpinnings and aims of progressive diplomacy.

2. Discuss "big stick," "dollar," and "missionary" diplomacy in Latin America and Asia.

3. Explain how the United States moved from neutrality to war between 1914 and 1917.

4. Describe Woodrow Wilson's war aims, and explain how they constituted a new world order.

5. Describe how the federal government mobilized the economy and public opinion on the home front during World War I.

6. Explain how the peace was lost.

7. Explain the post-war "Red Scare."

Review Questions

MULTIPLE CHOICE

1. The chapter introduction tells the story of the Panama Canal to make the point that
   a. progressives were increasingly willing to flex American muscle to shape world order.
   b. the United States followed a pattern of arbitrary intervention in Latin America.
   c. the United States deliberately differed from European powers in the way they exercised influence abroad.
   d. Roosevelt took the canal.

   (pp. 870-873)

2. The text throughout the chapter links progressivism and American diplomacy. Which statement would best summarize this analysis?
   a. All three presidents between 1901 and 1920 were progressives.
   b. The Progressive administration of Woodrow Wilson led the United States into World War I.
   c. The humanitarian vision of Progressivism was violated by U.S. entry into World War I.
   d. Progressive moralism and desire for order were applied both to the international situation and to the wartime home front.

   (pp. 873, 887, 890, 897)

3. Under the "Roosevelt Corollary" the U.S.
   a. agreed to abstain from interfering in the internal affairs of the Caribbean nations.
   b. declared the canal zone open to all nations.
   c. established a system of mutual financial and commercial obligations with Panama.
   d. justified intervention in the internal affairs of Caribbean countries.

   (pp. 865, 874)

4. Roosevelt's objectives in Asian policy--which explain his actions in response to the Russo -Japanese War--included all EXCEPT:
   a. holding the U.S. navy in waters close to the U.S. for coastal defense.
   b. keeping the commercial door open in China.
   c. protecting U.S. Pacific holdings, especially the Philippines.
   d. maintaining the balance of power in the Pacific.

   (pp. 874-875)

5. Taft's "Dollar Diplomacy" was intended to accomplish all of the following EXCEPT:
   a. encourage private corporations to invest abroad.
   b. foster prosperity in nations abroad.
   c. tie debt-ridden nations to the U.S. instead of Europe.
   d. promote American corporate interests overseas through regular use of armed force.

   (p. 876)

6. Wilson's commitment to neutrality in the World War stemmed from his profound conviction that
   a. aggressive, threatening nationalisms would arise from the chaos of war.
   b. a neutral America could lead the warring nations to a "peace without victory".
   c. it was his Christian duty to impose America's will on the world.
   d. the U.S. had no security interests outside the Western Hemisphere.

   (pp. 881-883)

7. What circumstance led to an American posture in which true neutrality was dead?
    a. the British blockade, which cut off U.S. trade with Germany while supplies still flowed to the Allies.
    b. the British blockade, which infuriated Wilson to the point of embargoing U.S. trade.
    c. German war propaganda, which recruited thousands of influential German-Americans to lobby on behalf of the German cause.
    d. German war propaganda, which so alienated German-Americans that they shifted their support to the British.

(pp. 883-885)

8. The inflammatory Zimmerman Telegram proposed that in the event of war between the U.S. and Germany
    a. Mexico would attack the U.S.
    b. Germany would unleash unrestricted submarine warfare on U.S. merchant vessels.
    c. the U.S., once the Central Powers were defeated, would take over the German colonies.
    d. German nationals within the U.S. would be held in internment camps.

(pp. 886-887)

9. Characterize the "Fourteen Points."
    a. a pragmatic list of specifics undergirding Wilson's desire to mediate an end to the war
    b. an idealistic vision for a postwar world order freed of militarism and selfish nationalism
    c. a blueprint for a punitive peace that would prevent any resurgence of German aggression
    d. a code of moralistic guidelines for future diplomatic practice

(pp. 896-897)

10. The Treaty of Versailles never received Senate ratification because
    a. the vast majority of Americans came to oppose it.
    b. Wilson himself came to oppose it.
    c. Wilson could not compromise and appeal to the "mild reservationist" Republicans.
    d. it would have destroyed U.S. national security.

(pp. 902-903)

IDENTIFICATION QUESTIONS

You should be able to describe the following key terms, concepts, individuals and places, and explain their significance:

Terms and Concepts

Platt Amendment
Treaty of Portsmouth
Dollar Diplomacy
Central Powers
U-boats
Sussex Pledge
Selective Service Act
bond drives
National War Labor Board
Sedition Act
Fourteen Points
League of Nations
Palmer raids

Roosevelt Corollary
The Great White Fleet
August 4, 1914
Allies
Lusitania
Zimmerman telegram
War Industries Board
Committee on Public Information
"four-minute men"
Schenck v. United States
The Big Four
Treaty of Versailles

Individuals and Places

Dr. William Gorgas
Philander Knox
Francisco "Pancho" Villa
Charles Evans Hughes
George Creel

Elihu Root
Edward M. House
General John Pershing
Bernard Baruch

MAP IDENTIFICATIONS

On the map on the next page, label or shade in the following places. In a sentence, note their significance to the chapter. (For reference, consult the maps in *Nation of Nations* on pages 882 and 897.)

1. Great Britain, France, and Italy
2. Germany and Austria-Hungary
3. Belgium
4. Line of farthest German advance

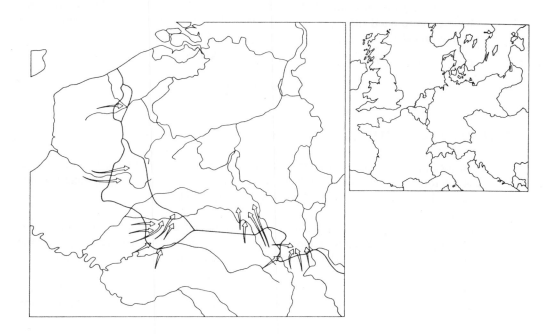

ESSAY QUESTIONS

1. Foreign policy decisions range anywhere from low-key negotiations (speaking softly) through the use of force (carrying a big stick). Explain where the following events fall on this spectrum of alternatives: the Platt Amendment, Treaty of Portsmouth, cooling off agreements, Pershing's "punitive expedition."

2. What ethnic divisions and tensions in American society helped to undermine neutrality? How important were they in bringing the United States into World War I?

3. How were women affected by the war? African-Americans? ethnic minorities?

4. Describe the differences between Roosevelt's policies toward Latin America and Asia. Why were they different? How were they similar?

5. Was American neutrality a realistic policy? What did Wilson hope to achieve with it? Why did it fail?

6. What ignited the anti-radical "Red Scare" of 1919-1920? What could the president have done to quell the rising tide of hysteria? Why did the Red Scare come to an end so quickly?

Critical Thinking

EVALUATING EVIDENCE (MAPS)

1. According to the map on page 872, by how many miles did the Panama Canal shorten the journey from New York to San Francisco? What topographical features made the isthmus an attractive spot for digging a canal?

2. According to the map on page 882, what advantages did Great Britain and the Allies enjoy for conducting a naval war and a blockade against Germany and the other Central Powers? What advantages did the Central Powers enjoy on land?

3. According to the map on page 897, how far had the Germans advanced by the time the American Expeditionary Force arrived? Where was American participation critical in the final Allied assault?

EVALUATING EVIDENCE (ILLUSTRATIONS AND CHARTS)

1. In the photograph of working women on page 893, what visual clues indicate that the women are relatively new to this job?

2. What does the poster of page 892 exhort Americans to do? How does it mock the Kaiser?

3. Compare the ideal and real trenches in the pictures on page 888. How does the ideal differ from the real?

4. In the picture of the signing of the Paris Peace Treaty on page 899, how are the victors depicted? What does the setting suggest about the nature of the peace that is being imposed on the defeated Germans?

CRITICAL ANALYSIS

Read carefully the following excerpt from the text and then answer the questions that follow:

> As the S. S. *George Washington* approached the coast of France in mid-December 1918 the mist suddenly lifted. On board were the president of the United States, a group of advisers called the "inquiry," and an entourage that included Committee on Public Information chief George Creel, there to make a movie of the historic mission. Woodrow Wilson was going to represent the United States at the peace conference to be held at Versailles, outside Paris. A world of problems awaited settlement. Large portions of Europe had been shelled into ruin and scarred with trenches barbed wire, and the debris of war. Fifty million people lay dead or maimed from the fighting. Starvation and typhus spread across the continent, eventually killing another 6 million people in the first year of the peace. In eastern Europe and the old Turkish empire, social chaos and revolution set Poles against Czechs, Slavs against Italians, Turks against Greeks, Bolshevik "Reds" against czarist "Whites," Jews against Arabs.
>
> With the old world order so evidently in shambles, it seemed clear to Wilson that vigorous, immediate action was imperative. Thus the president hand-picked the Peace Commission that accompanied him, including only loyal supporters like Secretary of State Lansing and Colonel House but not a single member of the Republican-controlled Senate. What promised to make negotiations easier at Versailles, however, created a crippling liability back in Washington, where Republicans cast a hostile eye on the impending Democratic peace treaty.

Questions

1. Underline the passages in the excerpt that express the opinions or judgments of the authors rather than a narrative of facts.

2. What happened when the *S. S. George Washington* approached the coast of France? What do the authors make of it?

3. Who accompanies President Wilson to the peace conference? Why? Why do you suppose the authors have chosen to tell us that a movie will be made of "the historic mission"?

4. What problems awaited Wilson and his entourage? Why did the authors *not* include among those problems the fact that European leaders wanted a vengeful peace? Whose point of view are the authors depicting?

5. Why does the absence of Republicans make negotiating the peace treaty "easier"? Why do the authors conclude that the absence of Republicans in the entourage was going to be a liability "back in Washington"? Would including them have changed the fate of the Treaty of Versailles?

PRIMARY SOURCE: A "Seditious" Pamphlet Opposing American Intervention in the Russian Revolution*

The Sedition Act of 1918 made it a felony "to utter, print, or publish disloyal, profane, scurrilous, or abusive language about the form of government, the Constitution [or] the flag...or by word or act oppose the cause of the United States." Jacob Abrams and others published pamphlets attacking President Wilson for intervening in the Bolshevik revolution by sending troops to Russia. He advocated resistance to the policy and was later convicted under the Sedition Act. Supreme Court Justice Oliver Wendell Holmes dissented, claiming that "a silly leaflet by an unknown man" constituted no clear and present danger to the safety of the United States. An excerpt from one of the pamphlets follows.

Yes, we, the Workers of America, have been duped--duped by the wonderful speeches of President Wilson. Although most of us did know the corruption of all the capitalists and rulers, be they Kaisers, Czars, Kings or Presidents, yet we have revered the attitude that "our" President had taken toward our COUNTRY, the country which is now the only country of the proletariat. We really thought that he would not consent to intervention, or in other words, that her, that he would keep his hands clean of this dirty business of destroying the Russian Revolution, the real proletarian revolution.

And here lies the hypocrisy of it. The President of the United States had not the courage to come forward straight and openly and say "We, as well as all other capitalist nations of the world, cannot have this revolution in Russia prolonged. We also are dead afraid of this proletarian government, which, when once in full power, will destroy capitalism forever and will spread its dangerous doctrines all over the world." No, he kept his policy secret, but instead fed us on pretty, empty phrases, and

---

* From *Abrams v. United States*, 250 U.S. 616 (1919). Briefs and Exhibits.

in the meanwhile American troops were already landing in Russia and were allying themselves with the other nations in the destruction of the Russian freedom, the real freedom of the working class, and not the so-called democratic "freedom."

Questions

1. According to the pamphlet, how have the "Workers of America" been "duped"?

2. Who are the "proletariat"? In the view of this pamphleteer, how are their interests threatened by American intervention in the Russian Revolution?

3. Why does the author equate the actions of President Wilson in sending troops to Russia with the actions of "Kaisers, Czars, [and] Kings"? What is the "hypocrisy" of such actions?

4. This pamphlet had nothing to do with the war against Germany but rather condemned American intervention in the Russian Revolution. How might the Sedition Act, designed to control wartime dissent, have been applied here?

5. As inflammatory as the pamphlet was, Mr. Justice Holmes nonetheless dissented from the majority opinion of the Supreme Court on the grounds that because relatively few pamphlets (about 5,000) had been distributed haphazardly by an "unknown man," there was no "present danger of immediate evil." Does this mean the status of the writer and the number of pamphlets printed are as important as the language itself? What *does* constitute a "present danger"?

25

THE NEW ERA

THE CHAPTER IN PERSPECTIVE

T he "New Era" of the 1920s, as contemporaries called it, was far more important than old stereotypes of a frivolous and self-absorbed "Jazz Age" imply. The decade witnessed the birth of modern America, as the transforming forces of modern life-- technology, bureaucratization, suburbanization, and consumerism--vastly accelerated. Yet modernism did not mix easily with more traditional values. The decade, therefore, looked simultaneously back toward a cherished past of neighborliness, small communities, and comfortable sameness and forward toward a glorious future of machines, consolidated organization, and middle-class urban living.

OVERVIEW

The chapter begins with a panoramic view of the 1920s that features evangelist Aimee Semple McPherson, Frederick Lewis Allen's fictional Smiths, and some real-life examples of changing times. Together they stress old and new, confidence and insecurity, modernism and traditionalism, all existing side by uncomfortable side.

The Roaring Economy

If anything roared in the "Roaring Twenties," it was industry and commerce. The economy experienced the greatest peacetime growth rate ever. Several factors accounted for it: technological advances; booming construction and automobile industries; corporate consolidation; new techniques of business and personnel management (called "welfare capitalism"); and the spread of advertising and the consumer culture. A modern ethic of high spending and high consumption worked its way into American society.

A Mass Society

New systems of mass distribution and mass marketing led not simply to a higher standard of living but increasingly to a mass culture and a mass society. Traditional institutions that had bound Americans together weakened. Local communities and churches, which had often been the arbiters of morality and propriety, found their authority undercut by new tastemakers in Hollywood and New York. Automobiles gave people new mobility and independence and so undermined the family and the community. Public education also undermined family control by creating competing centers of authority for children, including a new peer culture of students. Modern life emerged, complete with more independent women, the new mass media of radio and film, a standardized culture, impersonal cities, spectator sports, jazz music, alienated intellectuals, and a rising tide of black nationalism.

Defenders of the Faith

Mass society sharpened awareness of the differences between modern and traditional America. As modernism transformed the country, traditional culture hardened, looking on change with suspicion and diversity with dismay. The unspent antiradicalism of World War I combined with growing fear of foreigners to produce the most restrictive immigration laws in history. The National Origins Acts specifically reduced the flow of eastern and southern European immigrants, deemed most different (and therefore most threatening) to native Protestant America.

Prohibition, best understood as class and cultural legislation, rested on a similar antiurban and antiforeign bias and drew its strongest support from embattled Protestant evangelical churches. A resuscitated Ku Klux Klan fought to revive a lost America, free from "aliens," blacks, and uppity women, while a fundamentalist crusade succeeded in enacting legislation to prevent the teaching of modern theories of evolution. By the middle of the decade the defenders of an older faith had begun to falter, the victims of their own corruption and their own successes.

Republicans Ascendant

In government, the administration of Warren G. Harding ushered in a return to "normalcy," which was anything but normal. For the first time since Reconstruction a single party--the Republicans--ruled Washington. Dedicated to cautious, business-led policies, Harding and his successor, Calvin Coolidge, reversed the reformist trends of the previous two decades.

Government became the handmaiden of private enterprise. Lower taxes, higher tariffs, fewer antitrust suits, and more support for private collaboration and consolidation characterized public policy in the 1920s. Promoted by Secretary of Commerce Herbert Hoover, "associationism" encouraged trade associations and other business organizations to order and stabilize the economy, spreading a gospel of efficiency and cooperation among businesses. Oligopolies dominated nearly every basic industry, and by limiting competition, they helped to coordinate industrial policy and increase productivity. Meanwhile the interests of laborers and farmers received scant attention from Washington as prosperity soared.

In the election of 1928 a divided Democratic party swung from its rural to its urban wing and nominated former New York governor Al Smith. The majority Republicans ran Herbert Hoover, a Quaker, a "dry," and an enormously popular cabinet member. Hurt by his urban roots, his Catholicism, and his advocacy of Prohibition repeal, Smith won only 8 states. Buried in the returns were the stirrings of a major political realignment. The 12 largest cities, solidly Republican in 1924, went to Smith, moved to the Democratic column by their growing immigrant populations. Together with western farmers, urban immigrants would form the tangible nucleus of a powerful coalition that would transform the Democrats into the normal majority party in 1932.

KEY EVENTS

1903   *The Great Train Robbery:* First feature-length film released

1909   *Sigmund Freud:* psychoanalyst makes first trip to U.S.

1914   *Moving assembly line:* Henry Ford introduces new mass-manufacturing technique in automobile industry

1915   *Ku Klux Klan:* Modern Klan founded in Georgia

1916   *Marcus Garvey:* Jamaican black nationalist brings Universal Negro Improvement Association to America

1920   *Eighteenth Amendment adopted:* constitutional ban on alcohol

                 First commercial radio broadcast: from KDKA, Pittsburgh

                 Nineteenth Amendment adopted: grants women right to vote

                 Warren Harding elected president

                 Sacco and Vanzetti arrested: Italian immigrants charged with robbery and murder

1921   *National Origins Act:* sets quotas on European immigration

                 Budget and Accounting Act: new legislation puts federal government on budget

Sheppard-Towner Federal Maternity and Infancy Act: legislation to fight high rates of infant and maternal mortality

American Birth Control League founded: Margaret Sanger's National Birth Control League joins with Voluntary Parenthood League

1922   *Capper-Volstead Act:* federal law exempts farm cooperatives from anti-trust laws

Fordney-McCumber Tariff: raises rates

Babbitt: Sinclair Lewis' stinging attack on small-town business published

The Wasteland: T.S. Eliot's poem published

1923   *Time Magazine:* first weekly news magazine founded

Harding dies: Calvin Coolidge becomes president

Harding scandals: scandals involving members of Harding's inner circle begin to surface

1924   *Calvin Coolidge elected president*

1925   *The Man Nobody Knows:* Advertising man Bruce Barton's salute to Jesus published

Scopes trial: biology teacher John T. Scopes convicted of teaching evolution in Tennessee

The New Negro: Alain Locke publishes collection of works of young black artists and writers

1927   *Charles Lindbergh's flight:* young American crosses Atlantic alone by plane

McNary-Haugen farm bill: support for farmers but Coolidge vetoes

Sacco and Vanzetti executed: after years of appeals and protests, two Italian immigrants executed

The Jazz Singer: first talking film released

1928   *Herbert Hoover elected president:* defeats Democrat Al Smith, former
                    governor of New York

1929   *Middletown:* Robert and Helen Lynd's study of Muncie, Indiana, pub-
                    lished

LEARNING OBJECTIVES

When you have finished studying this chapter, you should be able to:

1. Describe the sources of economic growth and prosperity in the 1920s.

2. Explain the changes in business and advertising that occurred during the decade.

3. Explain the emergence of mass society and mass culture as well as the reactions
   against them.

4. Explain the tensions between modernism and traditionalism and how they mani-
   fested themselves.

5. Describe politics and public policies during the 1920s.

Review Questions

MULTIPLE CHOICE

1. The chapter introduction tells the story of Sister Aimee and the imaginary Smiths
   to make the point that
   a. Catholics, like other marginal groups, were becoming more culturally
      influential in the urbanized mass culture of the 1920s.
   b. transformations of the New Era mixed ambivalently with traditional beliefs
      and practices.
   c. in the Jazz Age, truth was often stranger than fiction.
   d. modern methods and values had taken over the minds of Americans by the
      1920s.

(pp. 913-915)

2. What might be called a "Second-or Post-Industrial Revolution," the "Roaring Economy" of the 1920s, involved all EXCEPT:
   a. a productivity revolution based on technology.
   b. a consumer-goods revolution that gave the U.S. the highest living standards on earth.
   c. a revolution in thinking, in which advertising persuaded consumers to buy now rather than save.
   d. a revolution in labor relations, marked by new growth in the size and influence of labor unions.

   (pp. 916-923)

3. Henry Ford's great contribution to modern industrial culture was
   a. the invention of the gasoline engine.
   b. his sensitivity to the needs of the modern worker.
   c. his commitment to standardization and assembly-line mass production.
   d. his canny use of product diversification to appeal to a wide range of individual tastes.

   (pp. 917-918)

4. For labor unions, the 1920s was a decade of
   a. unprecedented membership growth.
   b. holding on, retaining but not increasing membership or influence.
   c. retooling to become eager partners with business in a cooperative welfare capitalism.
   d. serious decline in membership.

   (p. 921)

5. What piece of federal legislation in the 1920s was a significant shift from a historic American practice?
   a. tariff reduction.
   b. immigration restriction.
   c. Prohibition repeal.
   d. antitrust enforcement.

   (pp. 933-934)

6. The National Origins Act fixed immigration patterns for four decades; it
   a. greatly increased immigration from eastern Europe.
   b. allowed for increased immigration from Asia, particularly well-educated Japanese.
   c. put strict quotas on the number of immigrants to be allowed into the U.S. every year.
   d. authorized discrimination against American citizens who had a particular national origin.

   (p. 934)

7. As Secretary of Commerce, Herbert Hoover practiced "associationalism." That is, he gave government encouragement and assistance to private business in all of the following ways EXCEPT:
   a. he encouraged the creation of trade associations.
   b. he fought for standardization to eliminate waste and inefficiency in industry.
   c. he advocated laissez faire policies to avoid government control.
   d. he urged businesses to treat workers decently and fairly ("welfare capitalism").

   (pp. 940-941)

8. In their tariff and taxation policies, the Republican administrations of the 1920s wanted
   a. tariff and tax reductions.
   b. tariffs raised and taxes reduced.
   c. tariffs and taxes raised.
   d. tariffs lowered and taxes raised.

   (p. 940)

9. What was an element of U.S. economic diplomacy in the 1920s?
   a. reduce the tariff to allow other nations to sell their goods in the U.S.
   b. reduce German reparations payments to the victorious Allies in return for helping stabilize the German economy
   c. cancel World War I debts owed by European nations to the U.S. in order to make it feasible to reduce German reparations
   d. promote arms sales abroad to bankrupt rival powers

   (pp. 940-943)

10. The beginnings of political realignment were already in evidence in the returns of the election of 1928, after which the Republicans
    a. lost the Southern vote.
    b. lost power in the cities.
    c. gained strength in the industrial northeast.
    d. gained support among union members.

(p. 944)

IDENTIFICATION QUESTIONS

You should be able to describe the following key terms, concepts, individuals and places, and explain their significance:

Terms and Concepts

The Man Nobody Knows	flappers
technological unemployment	mass production
American Plan	*Middletown*
League of Women Voters	*National Origins Act*
Kellogg-Briand Pact	*The Fundamentals*
Prohibition	associationalism
Fordney-McCumber Tariff	the Spirit of St. Louis
Scopes trial	Washington Naval Conference
the Dawes Plan	
Universal Negro Improvement Association	
Sheppard-Towner Federal Maternity and Infancy Act	

Individuals and Places

Al Smith	Charles Lindbergh
Andrew Mellon	Clarence Darrow
Albert Fall	Aimee Semple McPherson
Frederick Lewis Allen	Henry Ford
Albert Lasker	Miriam "Ma" Ferguson
Amos 'n' Andy	George Gershwin
Marcus Garvey	Claude McKay
Sacco and Vanzetti	William Simmons

MAP IDENTIFICATIONS

On the map below, label or shade in the following places. In a sentence, note their signifi-cance to the chapter (For reference, consult the map in *Nation of Nations* on page 915.)

1. Chicago
2. Detroit
3. New York
4. Paths of African-American migration northward

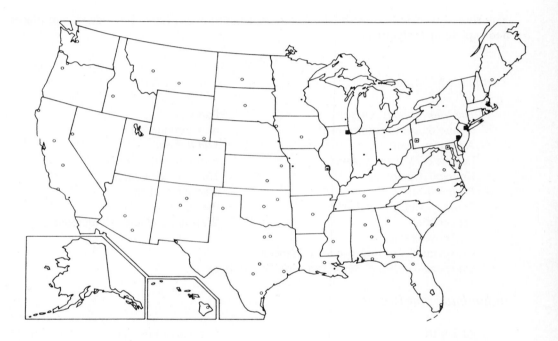

ESSAY QUESTIONS

1. In what ways did the automobile serve simultaneously as an economic catalyst, transportation revolution, and cultural symbol in the 1920s? What role did Henry Ford play in these developments?

2. What was welfare capitalism? How did it work? Why did employers use it? What was its most important effect on wage earners during the 1920s? On unionization?

3. Discuss three features of American society in the 1920s that alienated some artists and writers.

4. What was "normalcy," and how normal was it?

5. How did motion pictures, radio, and mass-circulation newspapers and magazines shape American life in the 1920s? Which of these media was most important?

6. Describe and evaluate the policies of the Harding and Coolidge administrations. Who was helped and who hurt or ignored? Why?

7. "The era of the 1920s witnessed a continual pull between the traditional and the modern." Explain how the following events reflected either the pull of the traditional or the modern--or both: Aimee Semple McPherson, the New Woman, Prohibition, the KKK, fundamentalism, advertising.

8. What economic problems plagued Europe after World War I? How and why did the United States attempt to help? What steps did the United States take to avoid another war? Why were they weak?

Critical Thinking

EVALUATING EVIDENCE (MAPS)

1. According to the map illustrating population changes between 1920 and 1930 (on page 915), what areas of the country are experiencing growth and what areas loss of population? Can you identify any geographic pattern? What influence might the automobile have had? What influence might cities have had?

2. Why are the twelve largest cities included in the 1928 election map (on page 943)? What is their significance in the election?

EVALUATING EVIDENCE (ILLUSTRATIONS AND CHARTS)

1. In what ways does the picture at the opening of the chapter (on page 913) conjure up an appropriate image of the 1920s? In what ways is the image misleading?

2. Compare the two contrasting images of the "New Woman" offered in the photographs of birth-control advocate Margaret Sanger (on page 926) and the first Miss America, Margaret Gorman (on page 925).

3. What effect might a theater like the Roxy (on page 928) have on those entering it? Why would theater-owners build such palaces?

CRITICAL ANALYSIS

Read carefully the following excerpt from the text and then answer the questions that follow:

> To the blare of trumpets on New Year's Day in 1923 she [Aimee Semple McPherson] unveiled a $1.5 million Angelus Temple graced by a 75-foot, rotating electronic cross. It was visible at night from 50 miles away. Inside was a 5000-seat auditorium, radio station KFSG (Kall Four Square Gospel), a wardrobe room that rivaled those of the movie studios, a "Cradle Roll Chapel" for babies, and a "Miracle Room" filled with the crutches, trusses, wheelchairs, and other aids Sister Aimee's cured faithful had discarded. Services were not simply a matter of hymn, sermon, and prayer. Aimee staged pageants, Holy Land slide shows, dramatized sermons, circuses, and healing sessions to ease the pain and boredom of the folks who flocked to see her.

> Sister Aimee succeeded because she was able to blend the old with the new. Her lively sermons had a simple message, easy to remember. They carried the spirit of what people were calling the "New Era." Casting aside hellfire evangelism, wrote one observer, she "substituted the cheerfulness of the playroom for the gloom of the morgue." Where country preachers menaced their congregations with visions of eternal damnation, she offered "flowers, music, golden trumpets, red robes, angels, incense, nonsense, and sex appeal." To that she added the sophistication of the booming media industries of the 1920s. She had a nose for publicity, a great capacity for self-dramatization, and a gift for improvising new

activities to entertain her followers. Here was one brand of evangelism eminently suited to a new consumer age.

Questions

1. Underline the passages in the excerpt that express the opinions or judgments of the authors rather than a narrative of facts.

2. What details do the authors include in describing the Angelus Temple? What message do they convey with their description?

3. How was Sister Aimee able to "blend old and new"? Why do the authors conclude that she succeeded by doing this?

4. How did her sermons carry "the spirit of what people were calling the `New Era'"? Why do the authors conclude that her evangelism was "eminently suited to a new consumer age"?

5. In what ways does Sister Aimee foreshadow the "televangelists" of a later day? Is there anything paradoxical about her methods of spreading the gospel of Jesus?

PRIMARY SOURCE: A Mexican Laborer Sings of Life in America*

As Mexican immigrants crossed the border into the United States, they brought many traditions with them, including music. The corrido is a ballad, common in the folk music of Mexico, that chronicles "current happenings." The following corrido tells the story of an anonymous Mexican contract laborer or enganchado *and his struggle with modern American life in the 1920s. Like many Americans caught between traditionalism and modernism, he longs for a simpler past and worries about his newly-liberated wife and children.*

> I came under contract from Morelia
> To earn dollars was my dream,
> I bought shoes and I bought a hat
> And even put on trousers.
>
> For they told me that here the dollars
> Were scattered about in heaps;

---

* From Paul S. Taylor, *Mexican Labor in the United States*, Vol. II (1932).

That there were girls and theaters
And that here everything was good fun.

And now I'm overwhelmed--
I am a shoe maker by trade
But here they say I'm a camel
And good only for pick and shovel.

What good is it to know my trade
If there are manufacturers by the score,
And while I make two little shoes
They turn out more than a million.

Many Mexicans don't care to speak
The language their mothers taught them
And go about saying they are Spanish
And denying their country's flag.

Some are darker than *chapote* [black tar]
But they pretend to be Saxon;
They go about powdered to the back of the neck
And wear skirts for trousers.

The girls go about almost naked
And call *la tienda* [store] "estor"
They go around with dirt-streaked legs
But with those stockings of chiffon.

Even my old woman has changed on me--
She wears a bob-tailed dress of silk,
Goes about painted like a pinata [brightly colored container filled
with candies]
And goes at night to the dancing hall.

My kids speak perfect English
And have no use for our Spanish
They call me "fader" and don't work
And are crazy about the Charleston.

I am tired of all this nonsense
I'm going back to Michoacan;

As a parting memory I leave the old woman
To see if someone else wants to burden himself.

Questions

1. Why did this immigrant come to the United States? Is he typical of immigrants coming to the United States in the early years of the twentieth century? What was his job in Mexico? What does he do in the United States? What does he think of his new job?

2. Why is he upset with Mexicans who "don't care to speak the language their mother taught them"? Why would they say they are "Spanish," deny "their country's flag," and "pretend to be Saxon"? What is wrong with Mexicanized English words like "estor"?

3. What upsets the immigrant about young Mexican men and women in the United States? About his wife? His children? Would any of his complaints about women be shared by native-born American men? Would his complaints about children be shared by native-born American parents?

4. How do his complaints about his new life in the United States reflect the conflict between traditionalism and modernism in the 1920s? What is his solution?

5. Of what use are such ballads to historians? What can folklore tell us about the past?

26

CRASH AND DEPRESSION

THE CHAPTER IN PERSPECTIVE

By the 1920s, the corporate industrial economy had grown for more than half a century. Along with its strengths, serious weaknesses developed. Few Americans noticed them because of the hot pursuit of material wealth. The consumer culture of the 1920s and a business-oriented government promoted not only the pursuit of money but of debt as well. When mass purchasing power could no longer sustain prosperity, the economy collapsed. The greatest depression in history dawned: bringing massive unemployment, withering prices, and a stagnated economy. Unlike his predecessors, Herbert Hoover took action. No president before him had dared to stimulate the economy, for fear of throwing it hopelessly out of balance. But Hoover's policies, for all his good intentions, were too wedded to the old order to make any difference.

OVERVIEW

Get-rich-quick schemes obsessed the nation in the 1920s. Thus this chapter begins with a montage of easy-money schemes. Speculative ventures, including the Florida real estate boom and the soaring stock market, dominated the news and diverted national attention from the economy's problems. The stock market crash of 1929, one of the worst in the nation's history, signaled the onset of a precipitous decline that shrunk the economy by almost half. The Great Depression caught the nation by surprise. Despite the best efforts of its leaders, recovery remained elusive.

The Great Bull Market

For most of the decade a great "bull market" had been building on Wall Street. By 1928 speculative fever, a new breed of aggressive investors and inexperienced young brokers, a host of shady financial devices, and skyrocketing corporate profits fueled rising stock prices and transformed the market into a glittering gambling casino.

Warning signs went unnoticed but reflected real economic weaknesses. Corporate profits rose at twice the rate of productivity and, in some industries, nearly eight times the rate of real wages. Mass purchasing power therefore declined relative to production. The consumer debt rose, and the gap between the wealthy and the middle and working classes widened. The resulting pattern of income distribution could not sustain prosperity. The percentage of national income going to farmers dropped by almost half between 1916 and 1929. Rural banks began to fail, and with little centralized control of the banking business, others soon followed suit. "Sick" industries--coal, textiles, lumbering, and railroads--were characterized by over expansion, declining demand, heavy competition, and weak management.

In October 1929 the speculative bubble on Wall Street burst and the market crashed in a heap of near-worthless stock. The Great Crash did not bring about the Great Depression that followed; it only accelerated the slide. Over expansion of major industries, uneven distribution of wealth and income, the relative decline of mass purchasing power, a weak banking and corporate structure, and plain economic ignorance were the underlying causes.

The American People in the Great Depression

The Great Depression was also the great leveler. It reduced differences of class, ethnicity, geography, and race through deprivation. Most people did not plummet to rock bottom; they simply lived leaner lives. Some tightened family budgets; others moved to cheaper quarters. A few starved to death, and more than a few foraged for food. For the first time more people left rather than entered the country. With hard times came shame, self-doubt, and a loss of confidence. Birth and marriage rates dropped, and troubled unions broke apart. In strong and weak families alike, the role of homemaker took on added importance. More and more women worked outside the home to supplement meager family incomes, and the home itself became an inexpensive center of recreation and companionship. A depression culture emerged, but whether on film, radio, or in print, it tended to reinforce the basic social and economic tenets of American culture: middle class morality and family life, capitalism, and democracy.

An ecological disaster transformed 1500 square miles from the Oklahoma panhandle to western Kansas into a gigantic "Dust Bowl." Made partly by man, partly by nature, the Dust Bowl emptied of large numbers of its people, as 3.5 million farmers left the Great Plains, the only states of the country to suffer a net loss of population. "Agribusiness," the corporatization of farming, pushed as many farmers from their land as nature did. A growing migration of rural refugees wandered the country in search of work, more of them than ever before and more of them white and native-born.

Meanwhile outsiders, especially Mexican- and African-Americans, suffered more than their share of hardship. Beginning in 1931, after more than a decade of local encouragement, the federal government launched a series of deportations or "repatriations" of Mexican migrants (and with them their Mexican-American children). The Latino population of the country declined by 500,000, even as Hispanic "barrios" in Los Angeles and other cities continued to grow. The nation's largest minority, African-Americans, reported unemployment rates as high as 50 percent. The Great Depression, moreover, aggravated racial prejudice as the number of recorded lynchings tripled between 1932 and 1933. African-Americans refused to be victimized by the depression. Some urban blacks, like George Baker ("Father Divine"), stressed economic cooperation and opened shelters, while a few rural blacks joined with whites in the newly founded Southern Tenant Farmers Unions.

The Tragedy of Herbert Hoover

The depth of the crisis soon exhausted private and municipal resources. By 1931 only New York had a statewide relief agency. The federal government became the court of last resort. It alone possessed sufficient resources to meet the manifest need. Unfortunately President Herbert Hoover proved ineffective. He used the techniques of the New Era--self-help, voluntarism, publicity, and public calls for private cooperation. Though he did more than any of his predecessors to combat a downturn, he could not bring himself to do enough, for fear that too much government activity would unbalance the budget, impede the return of business confidence and recovery, and create an unwieldy and intrusive bureaucracy.

Resentment grew and peaked in the disastrous march of the Bonus Army on Washington in 1932. In the election that fall, Hoover suffered a thundering rebuke as Democrat Franklin D. Roosevelt won nearly 58 percent of the popular vote and laid the foundation of a powerful coalition that would dominate politics for decades to come.

KEY EVENTS

1926   *Miami real estate bust:* hurricane devastates southern Florida and land prices plummet

1928   *Great Bull Market:* stock market begins to peak

            Herbert Hoover elected president: defeats Democrat Al Smith of New York

1929   *Stock market crash:* after a record climb, stock market plunges

            Agricultural Marketing Act: Congress authorizes federal help for farmers

1930   *Hawley-Smoot Tariff:* rates raised to protect U. S. from growing global depression

President's Emergency Committee on Employment: Hoover appoints panel to study unemployment

1931   *Mexican repatriation:* federal government orders return of Mexican laborers to Mexico

Scottsboro boys: arrest of 9 young African-Americans leads to their unjust conviction for rape

Temporary Emergency Relief Administration: New York establishes first state relief agency

President's Organization on Unemployment Relief: second of Hoover's panels on unemployment created

1932   *Glass-Steagall Banking Act:* to guard against another Great Crash, Congress separates investment from commercial banking

Reconstruction Finance Corporation: Congress establishes federal agency to aid ailing banks

Farm Holiday Association: Milo Reno forms organization farm recovery

Bonus Army: World War I veterans march on Washington for payment of war bonuses

Franklin Roosevelt elected president: defeats Republican incumbent Herbert Hoover

1933   *"black blizzards":* giant dust storms begin to create Dust Bowl

1934   *Southern Tenant Farmers Union:* tenant farmers organize

1935   *Communist Party:* announces "popular front" to join with capitalist democracies to fight fascism

1936   *Gone With the Wind:* Margaret Mitchell's epic novel of the Civil War
                     published

1939   *The Grapes of Wrath*: John Steinbeck's chronicle of dispossessed Ameri-
                     can migrants published

LEARNING OBJECTIVES

When you have finished studying this chapter, you should be able to:

1. Describe the operation of the Great Bull Market and explain why it crashed.

2. Explain the weaknesses in the economy of the 1920s that led to the Great Depression of the 1930s.

3. Describe the impact of the Great Depression on individuals, families, minorities,
   and popular culture.

4. Describe the Hoover depression program, assess its successes and failures, and
   evaluate the leadership of Herbert Hoover.

5. Explain the rise of Franklin Roosevelt and evaluate the significance of the election
   of 1932.

Review Questions

MULTIPLE CHOICE

1. The chapter introduction tells the story of the Florida land boom to make the point
   that
   a. despite the speculative fever, significant weaknesses plagued the U.S.
      economy in the 1920s.
   b. the national economy enjoyed good times in the 1920s, making the crash that
      much more traumatic.
   c. several crashes, not just the Great Crash of 1929, caused the Depression.
   d. the Depression created the first wave of migration to the Sunbelt.

   (pp. 952-954)

Questions

1. Underline the passages in the excerpt that express the opinions or judgments of the authors rather than a narrative of facts.

2. What do the authors imply was Dwight Eisenhower's reaction when George S. Patton, Jr., charged a crowd of Bonus marchers?

3. Why might there have been fears that the Bonus march carried the potential for insurrection?

4. How does the language of the passages indicate the authors' opinion of the attack on the Bonus marchers?

5. How is Herbert Hoover depicted in the passage? What message are the authors communicating when they liken him to "the hero of a classical tragedy"?

6. Is it justifiable to control protests in the nation's capital during a crisis such as the Great Depression? When does such control violate the rights of protesters in a democratic society that guarantees freedom of speech and peaceable petitions of government to redress grievances?

PRIMARY SOURCE: An Editor Loses His Job in the Great Depression*

Ward James was born in Wisconsin and educated there. When the Great Depression struck, he was working at a small publishing house in New York. In 1935 he lost his job and went on relief. Forty years later he recalled his experiences.

> I was out of work for six months. I was losing my contacts as well as my energy. I kept going from one publishing house to another. I never got past the telephone operator. It was just wasted time. One of the worst things was occupying your time, sensibly. You'd go to the library. You took a magazine to the room and sat and read. I didn't have a radio. I tried to do some writing and found I couldn't concentrate. The day was long. There was nothing to do evenings. I was going around in circles, it was terrifying. So I just vegetated.

---

*From Studs Terkel, *Hard Times: An Oral History of the Great Depression* (1978) Copyright 1970 by Studs Terkel. Reprinted by permission of Pantheon Books, a division of Random House, Inc.

With some people I knew, there was a coldness, shunning: I'd rather not see you just now. Maybe *I'll* lose my job next week. On the other hand, I made some very close friends, who were merely acquaintances before. If I needed $15 for room rent or something, it was available....

I finally went on relief. It's an experience I don't want anybody to go through. It comes as close to crucifixion as.... You sit in an auditorium and are given a number. The interview was utterly ridiculous and mortifying. In the middle of mine, a more dramatic guy than I dived from the second floor stairway, head first, to demonstrate he was gonna get on relief even if he had to go to the hospital to do it.

There were questions like: Who are your friends? Where have you been living? Where's your family? I had sent my wife and child to her folks in Ohio, where they could live more simply. Why should anybody give you money? Why should anybody give you a place to sleep? What sort of friends? This went on for half an hour. I got angry and said, "Do you happen to know what a friend is?" He changed his attitude very shortly. I did get certified some time later. I think they paid $9 a month.

I came away feeling I didn't have any business living any more. I was imposing on somebody, a great society or something like that....

I feel anything can happen. There's a little fear in me that it might happen again. It does distort your outlook and your feeling. Lost time and lost faith....

Questions

1. What effect did unemployment have on Ward James? How did he spend his time?

2. How did people treat him after he lost his job? Why?

3. How did he feel about going "on relief"? What questions were asked during his interview, and what purpose do you suppose they served? Why do you suppose he reacted so strongly to them?

4. Why was the experience of going on relief so difficult for James?

5. In the textbook the authors write about an "invisible scar" left by the Great Depression on its victims. What overall effect does the Great Depression seem to have had on Ward James? What did he mean by "lost time and lost faith"? Did he carry an invisible scar?

6. What use can historians make of such interviews (which in this case was conducted over 40 years after the events described took place)? What are the dangers of such oral histories?

27

THE NEW DEAL

THE CHAPTER IN PERSPECTIVE

The New Deal was no revolution in public policy. In many ways it was quite conservative. It sought ultimately to reform capitalism by modifying some of the excesses that led to the Great Depression. If there were a revolutionary aspect, however, it lay in the New Deal's willingness to commit government to compensating for swings in the economy and to supporting those in need. The New Deal marshaled the government activism and executive leadership of Progressivism but with none of the moralizing that often accompanied progressive reform. With the New Deal the modern liberal state was born.

OVERVIEW

This chapter opens with federal investigator Lorena Hickok traveling across America in search of the New Deal's impact on the lives of ordinary people. The deprivation, anguish, and courage she finds upsets the common stereotype of lazy loafers in search of government hand-outs. She also discovers that the New Deal is restoring hope and confidence, and because of it, Americans are looking to Washington as never before for help.

The Democratic Roosevelts

Part of the reason was the warmth, dynamism, and willingness to experiment of the new president, Franklin Roosevelt, and the insistent fights for the underdog waged by his wife Eleanor. Even more to the point, a spirit of activism emanated from Washington. Roosevelt's first "hundred days" in office were marked by an unprecedented flood of legislation: banking and securities acts to restore the credit structure and safeguard investment markets; relief measures to aid the dispossessed; the Tennessee Valley Authority to provide flood control and to siphon federal building funds into one of the poorest regions of the country.

Reform and relief were less important themes in the early New Deal than recovery. Here Roosevelt proceeded cautiously but vigorously, combining new federal planning with associational techniques pioneered during the 1920s to revive the economy. The National Recovery Administration promoted industrial cooperation and self-regulation through codes of fair practices, while the Agricultural Adjustment Administration similarly relied on private cooperation to raise farm prices by reducing acreage under cultivation. Although more successful than the NRA, the AAA (like the NRA before it) was voided by the Supreme Court in 1936.

A Second New Deal (1935-1936)

The limited economic progress of the New Deal bred political success in the 1934 off-year elections, when Democrats actually increased their majorities in Congress. New Deal critics, too, experienced success, as progress failed to keep pace with rising public expectations. Among the most popular voices of protest were Louisiana governor and senator Huey Long, Detroit radio priest Charles Coughlin, and Dr. Francis Townsend, an advocate of aid to the elderly. They helped, along with Congress and the public-at-large, to push Roosevelt and the New Deal farther to the left in 1935.

A second "hundred days" of legislation signaled a break from the earlier partnership with business and stressed longer term relief and more sweeping reform. The Works Progress Administration substituted federal work relief for earlier give-away programs and made aid to the needy a centerpiece of administration policy. The Social Security Act institutionalized a semi-welfare state with a relatively conservative social insurance program. The National Labor Relations Act created a federal board to oversee unionization and labor relations with management, thereby giving a powerful boost to organized labor. Legislation regulating banking, holding companies, and new taxes strengthened federal control over the private sector and further alienated many business leaders.

In 1936 Roosevelt won reelection by the largest majorities to date in American history. Victory was built on a powerful coalition of the traditionally Democratic South, big city ethnics, and labor. It reflected the wide impact of the New Deal on the American people, particularly those at the middle and bottom of the economic ladder.

The New Deal and the American People

In the most stunning electoral reversal of the century, African-Americans turned their allegiances from the Republican party to the Democrats. Though local administration often meant that racial discrimination persisted in New Deal programs, black citizens still received more attention than they had since Reconstruction.

So, too, did Mexican-Americans and women. None of these groups prospered but all benefited to greater or lesser degree. Organized labor probably benefited most of all, but splits between the American Federation of Labor and the Committee for Industrial Organization weakened solidarity. A wave of sit-down and other strikes alienated Democrats and Republicans alike.

The End of the New Deal (1937-1940)

Some of the troubles of Roosevelt's second term were brought on by the president himself. In 1935 and 1936 a conservative Supreme Court had begun to invalidate several New Deal measures on the very grounds used by the administration to expand executive authority. Roosevelt fought back by trying to "pack" the courts with new judges. Later, because of deaths and retirements, Roosevelt was able to appoint five justices to the Supreme Court, but his court-packing plan, badly formulated and ineptly handled, succeeded only in angering the public and bolstering a conservative coalition of Republicans and rural Democrats. A presidential effort to balance the budget in 1937 led to a deep recession in 1938, and a vindictive attempt to unseat anti-New Deal Democrats ended in failure.

By 1938, with passage of a public housing act and a wages-and-hours law, the New Deal had come largely to an end. Though Roosevelt and the New Deal never succeeded in achieving recovery, their legacy was a lasting one: the creation of economic stabilizers to compensate for future swings in the economy, the modernization of the presidency, the establishment of a limited welfare state, and the revitalization of the Democratic party.

KEY EVENTS

1933   *Franklin Roosevelt inaugurated*

Bank "holiday": Roosevelt closes banks for eight days

"Hundred days": in first three months of Roosevelt's term, Congress enacts record fifteen pieces of major legislation, including the National Industrial Recovery Act and the Agricultural Adjustment Act

Eighteenth Amendment (Prohibition): repealed

Townsend movement: Dr. Francis Townsend organizes the aged

1934   *Securities and Exchange Commission:* new federal agency begins to oversee stock exchanges and issuance of securities

American Liberty League: ultra-conservative organization created to fight Roosevelt and New Deal

Indian Reorganization Act: returns control of Indian lands to tribes

1935   *Emergency Relief Appropriation Act:* continued aid for the unemployed, most of which goes to the new work-relief program of Works Progress Administration

Rural Electrification Administration: federal program to bring electricity to rural America

Schecter Poultry Corp. v. United States: invalidates National Recovery Administration

Share Our Wealth Society: Louisiana's Huey Long creates organization to redistribute wealth

"Second hundred days": a second burst of New Deal legislation, including Social Security Act and National Labor Relations Act

National Union for Social Justice: Father Charles Coughlin, Detroit's "radio priest," organizes political vehicles for his ideas

Huey Long: assassinated on steps of Louisiana state capitol

1936   *Butler v. U.S:* invalidates Agricultural Adjustment Administration

Congress of Industrial Organizations: labor leader John L. Lewis forms confederation of unskilled workers

Roosevelt reelected

Sit-down strikes: United Auto Workers sponsor first strike in which workers take over factory

The General Theory of Employment, Interest, and Money: economist John Maynard Keynes publishes his new economic theory of counter-cyclical spending

1937   *Court "packing" plan:* Roosevelt announces his plan to add justices to Supreme Court and federal courts

Roosevelt recession: economy plunges when Roosevelt cuts federal expenditures

1938   *Fair Labor Standards Act:* sets minimum wages/maximum hours

                 Temporary National Economic Committee: in a display of business
                 hostility, Congress creates committee to investigate monopolies

1939   *Marian Anderson concert:* denied the use of Constitution Hall by
                 Daughters of the American Revolution, African-American soprano
                 sings on steps of Lincoln Memorial

LEARNING OBJECTIVES

When you have finished studying this chapter, you should be able to:

1. Explain the presidential effectiveness of Franklin Roosevelt and describe the role played by the first lady, Eleanor Roosevelt.

2. Describe the approaches of the early New Deal to recovery, relief, and reform.

3. Explain why the New Deal failed to achieve recovery.

4. Describe the "Second New Deal" and explain why it was pursued.

5. Describe the impact of the New Deal on ordinary Americans, including African- and Hispanic-Americans, women, and Indians.

6. Explain the demise of the New Deal.

7. Describe and evaluate the legacy of the New Deal.

ESSAY QUESTIONS

1. What assumptions did Roosevelt hold about the effects of relief on people, and what measures did he recommend for relief during the early New Deal? How did he resolve the contradictions between his assumptions and actions?

2. What were three aims of the Tennessee Valley Authority, and what were its two most important effects?

3. Describe the policies of the "Second New Deal." In what way did they represent a shift to the left?

4. How did African- and Mexican-Americans fare under the New Deal? What impact did the New Deal have on women?

5. How did the policies of the "Second New Deal" differ from those of the "First New Deal"? Which were more successful?

6. What strides did unions make in the 1930s, and why? What role did Roosevelt play?

7. Compare and contrast Herbert Hoover's approach to the depression with Franklin Roosevelt's, in terms of both style and substance.

Critical Thinking

EVALUATING EVIDENCE (MAPS)

1. How does the map of the Tennessee Valley Authority on page 995 illustrate the many purposes of the TVA? How might the influence of the TVA spread beyond the Tennessee River watershed?

EVALUATING EVIDENCE (ILLUSTRATIONS AND CHARTS)

1. What feelings are conveyed in the painting opening the chapter (page 987)? In what ways does the style of painting harken back to an earlier America? Why might such a style be appealing to Americans during the Great Depression?

2. What is unusual about the photograph of FDR at Warm Springs, Georgia, on page 990? Why might photographs like this one be rare?

3. What does the painting of the Communist riot (on page 999) illustrate about the nature of conflict during the Great Depression? Why weren't there more such violent clashes in the 1930s?

4. What are the cartoonists on pages 993 and 1015 trying to say about Roosevelt's New Deal and Supreme Court "packing" plan? Are they critical of them? If so, why?

5. In what ways does the post office painting on page 1013 (depicting a post-Civil War scene) reflect local and regional influences on art? What messages might it communicate to those entering the post office?

CRITICAL ANALYSIS

Read carefully the following excerpt from the text and then answer the questions that follow:

> The lights did not go on in the Hill Country of Texas until 1939. Before then, farmers read books after dusk and milked cows before dawn by the light of 25-watt kerosene lamps. Hill Country wives washed eight loads of laundry a week, all by hand. They hauled 200 gallons of water a day from wells and heated seven-pound "sadirons" on wood-burning stoves to press clothing. Farms had no milking machines, no washers, no automatic pumps or water heaters, no refrigerators. After sundown people could barely see each other. While other Americans enjoyed evenings listening to Jack Benny and the Lone Ranger on radio, Hill Country farmers sat in silence broken only by their own voices. "Living--just living--was a problem," recalled one woman.
>
> The reason for this limited life was simple: the Hill Country had no electricity. Utility companies resisted electrifying rural America because more money could be made in cities. Thus no agency of the Roosevelt administration changed the way people lived more dramatically than the Rural Electrification Administration (REA), created in 1935. At the time less than 10 percent of American farms had electricity. Six years later 40 percent had electricity, and by 1950, 90 percent did.

In the Smoky Mountains, along the Upper Peninsula of Michigan, on the slopes of the Continental Divide, and in the Hill Country of central Texas, communities saw their churches, stores, schools, and homes set aglow with a dazzling new light. Electric machines eased the drudgery of rural people. Radios cut the isolation of rural folk. Light bulbs reduced the strain on their eyes and even improved the school grades of their children, who could now study at night. The New Deal did not always have such a marked impact. And overall its record was mixed. But time and again it changed people's lives as government never had before.

Questions

1. Underline the passages in the excerpt that express the opinions or judgments of the authors rather than a narrative of facts.

2. What do the authors mean when they write that "the lights did not go on in the Hill Country of Texas until 1939"?

3. In 1935, how many rural Americans lived without electricity? Why?

4. What impact did the absence of electricity have on the lives of rural Americans? How might the Great Depression have accentuated the plight of rural Americans? How did electrification change their lives? How might historians have discovered those changes?

5. The New Deal vastly expanded the responsibilities and authority of the federal government. Yet some critics contended that even in the 1930s that government had grown too large and intrusive. Should government be involved in promoting such ventures as electrification? At what point does government become so large and meddlesome as to threaten private enterprise and private initiative?

PRIMARY SOURCE: A Worker, Protected by the NRA, Loses His Job[*]

The National Industrial Recovery Act promoted industrial self-regulation by encouraging businesses to draw up codes of fair competition to spread work and avoid "cutthroat competition." Section 7a guaranteed workers the right "to organize and bargain collectively."

---

[*] From Russel Bowker, letter to Franklin D. Roosevelt, November 8, 1933

Russel Bowker, a hosiery worker from New Jersey, found that not all employers were willing to abide by it.

According to the N.R.A. the workers have a right to join unions and organize. According to the papers recently General [Hugh] Johnson [head of the N.R.A.] said we don't have to strike to get our rights, that the Government would protect us in these rights....

I am hosiery knitter and was working for the Swan Hosiery Co., Pleasantville, N.J. until two weeks ago. About three weeks ago one of the organizers of the Amer. Federation of Hosiery Workers, of which I was a former member, called at my home and told me that there was going to be a meeting of the workers in our shop for the purpose of organizing into a union. This meeting was to be held on Saturday, October 14th. On the Friday before the meeting Mr. John Miller, our superintendent, came around to each worker and asked them if they were going to the meeting and told them they had better not go because if they did go there were going to be "changes" around the shop. When he talked to me he said he would be outside the meeting place with a pencil and paper to take the names of all who attended so he would know what changes to make on Monday morning.

After the meeting there were rumors that all those who went to the meeting would be fired. On the following Friday when I received my pay I called Mr. Miller's attention [to the fact] that I hadn't been paid for a day I put in repairing my machine. He said that was because I had [earned?] more during the rest of the week. I showed him in the Hosiery Code where I must be paid the minimum wage for each and every hour I worked. He as much as said I knew too much and went back to his office. A few minutes later he called me to his office and showed me twelve (12) stockings which he claimed were bad work and said "you are fired."

This is the first time in 16 years as knitter that I was fired for any reason.... When I was fired Mr. Miller told one of his workers that he would get the rest who attended the meeting before he was through.

I have made a complaint to the local N.R.A. board and the Union has filed one with the Code Authority for the Hosiery Industry but I am still out of work and wish you would see if something couldn't be done about it.

Questions

1. What prompted Russel Bowker to go to a union meeting in the first place? In what ways did the federal government encourage Bowker to join a union?

2. How did Bowker's superintendent respond?

3. What price does Bowker say he paid for attending the meeting? What evidence does he present? Why did Bowker's superintendent say he was fired?

4. If the N.R.A. guaranteed labor the right to organize and bargain collectively, how could Bowker's employer threaten him for attending a union meeting in the first place? What does this suggest about the power of the federal government and the power of organized labor in the early 1930s?

5. Bowker addressed his letter to the President of the United States. What does this tell us about how ordinary people regarded President Roosevelt? How useful are such letters to historians?

28

AMERICA'S RISE TO GLOBALISM

THE CHAPTER IN PERSPECTIVE

World War II was in some ways like no other event in American history. It involved more people and resources from more places around the world than the United States had ever been called upon to organize before. Still, those who managed and fought the war could draw on the experience of World War I (Chapter 24). In that war Americans raised an army, produced war materials in huge quantities, and transported them to Europe. On the battlefields they confronted such modern weapons as tanks, submarines, and airplanes. During the 1920s, as Chapter 25 explains, American industry improved products like the automobile and also techniques for manufacturing them. Despite the Great Depression, Americans had the most productive industrial plant in the world at the time Japan attacked Pearl Harbor. And the New Deal had created a variety of agencies that helped prepare the government to face the huge task of organizing the war's truly global crusade. The combination of fighting a depression and a war made the government much more a part of every level of American life, as the following chapters will show.

OVERVIEW

World War II did not begin with the bombing of Pearl Harbor. That attack culminated a long period of tension caused by Japanese, Italian, and German aggression. Despite that tension, and despite the fact that much of the world had been at war since 1939, when the Japanese attacked, they found Americans both militarily and psychologically unprepared. Pearl Harbor shocked Americans into a war they had been reluctant to fight.

The United States in a Troubled World

The causes of World War II extended back to the peace talks at Versailles that ended World War I. Issues that divided victors and vanquished then, like German reparations and the naval arms race, continued to trouble international relations for another twenty-five years. Despite its economic power, the United States played only an indirect role in the postwar world. The most direct threat to the peace during the 1920s arose from Japan's aspirations in Manchuria. The United States could propose little besides the Stimson Doctrine of nonrecognition to restrain Japanese aggression. In Latin America the United States under

Hoover and Roosevelt took some constructive steps to become a "Good Neighbor," although that did not lessen in any way American dominance of the region's economies.

Franklin Roosevelt was one of the most internationally minded American Presidents. Yet domestic pressures against foreign political entanglement left him largely powerless to play a role in containing the spread of German and Italian fascism or Japanese militarism. Neutrality legislation limited FDR's power to support victims of aggression like Ethiopia and China. That impotence made him sympathetic to the efforts of French and English leaders, who at Munich in 1938 sought to negotiate an end to Hitler's aggression in Europe. Munich proved a sellout of Czechoslovakia, not a diplomatic triumph. With the German invasion of Poland in 1939 Europe was once again plunged into war. Determined to play a decisive role in Europe, Roosevelt tried to avoid a showdown in the Pacific with Japan. Diplomatic talks produced no compromises, while the Japanese extended their empire and then began secretly planning an attack on the American naval base at Pearl Harbor.

A Global War

When the United States entered the war, it suffered a string of demoralizing defeats. But the key to victory was the productive capacity of American factories and the ability of the Americans and their Russian and British allies to coordinate a strategy, first to defeat Germany and only then to concentrate on defeating Japan. In Roosevelt, Churchill, and Stalin the Allies had exceptional leadership.

Despite agreement to defeat Germany first, the Allies' first successes came in naval engagements in the Pacific, highlighted by a smashing victory at Midway. After the Anglo-American invasion of North Africa, victories at El Alamein and Stalingrad in late 1942 marked the turning point of the war with Germany. By then American factories were at full production and the armed forces prepared to battle the enemy on all fronts.

Those Who Fought

The war mobilized not just soldiers, but also women and minorities. All of them made unprecedented contributions. Many young men and women found themselves far from home for the first time. For African-Americans service offered an unusual opportunity for education and decent living conditions. They volunteered in great numbers. Unfortunately the prejudices of civilian life often led to interracial tensions in the military. Gay men and women had a similar experience. They too had new opportunities and encountered widespread prejudices. Women were a third group who showed their patriotism by joining the services. While they achieved equal status in some ways, they were often restricted socially and allowed only a limited role.

War Production

Before the United States entered the war President Roosevelt spoke of the nation as "the arsenal of democracy." But it became that only after the government eliminated the initial bottlenecks that disrupted war industries. A pattern emerged. Shortages led to the search for explanations and solutions. Industries developed new techniques or new products that ended the shortages. Henry Kaiser was one example of an entrepreneur who helped create a "miracle of production." In the long run organization for war increased the consolidation of key industries into fewer, but larger corporations. Scientists too made critical contributions like radar and the proximity fuse that may have proved decisive and introduced new peacetime technologies. The fear of German advances in fission research prompted Roosevelt to authorize the Manhattan Project. American scientists raced the Germans to chain the power of the atom to a weapon of war.

War production brought back prosperity, but also created headaches, as Americans adjusted to shortages and dislocations. In all facets of the war economy the Roosevelt administration tried to achieve its results through voluntary means such as the sale of war bonds. It resorted to compulsion only when necessary, as for example when it increased taxes to finance the war. Issues such as what taxes ought to be levied divided liberals and conservatives.

Labor unions generally cooperated in keeping industry functioning smoothly, but a few militant leaders like John L. Lewis insisted on winning major concessions even if it hurt war production. Labor shortages increased the demand for women workers. These were not only the traditional young and single women, but also married women with children. The need for income, new opportunities, and a sense of patriotism all attracted women to jobs. There they found that many of the old barriers to advancement remained.

A Question of Rights

World War I had resulted in severe infringements of civil rights. The United States had a better record during World War II. German and Italian aliens faced restriction for less than a year. Japanese-Americans suffered a harsher fate as the government, in response to hysteria and bigotry, herded them into concentration camps. Even the Supreme Court gave its blessing to this injustice.

At the same time, traditional forms of prejudice limited the opportunities of African-Americans and Hispanics. Black leader A. Philip Randolph pressured Roosevelt into creating the Fair Employment Practices Commission, which in some cases was able to end job discrimination. The movement of minorities into industrial centers outside the South often created frictions, which in Detroit, New York, and Los Angeles erupted into violence. De-

Destroyers-for-bases deal: fifty destroyers aid England

Roosevelt wins third term

1941   *Lend-Lease Act:* aid to America's potential allies

German invasion of the Soviet Union

Atlantic Charter: Roosevelt and Churchill agree on grand strategy

A. Philip Randolph threatens a March on Washington: forces Roosevelt to create Fair Employment Practices Commission

Pearl Harbor attacked: Hitler and Mussolini join Japan in declaring war on the United States

1942   *Philippines surrender*: Bataan and Corrigedor fall

War Production Board and War Labor Board: created to boost war production

Midway, El Alamein, and Stalingrad: key victories for Allies

Civil Rights issues: Roosevelt lifts restrictions on enemy aliens, but Japanese-Americans interned

Operation Torch: American and British troops invade North Africa

Manhattan Project begun: scientists seek to harness the atom

1943   *Invasion of Italy*: Allied offensive forces Italian surrender

Race riots disrupt Detroit, New York, and Los Angeles

Teheran Conference: Roosevelt, Churchill, Stalin meet for first time

1944   *D-Day*: invasion of France

Battle of the Bulge: Allies turn back German counterattack

Island-hopping campaign: U.S. forces reach Guam and Saipan, MacArthur returns to Philippines

Dumbarton Oaks and Bretton Woods meetings: Anglo-American plan for peace organizations

Roosevelt wins fourth term: defeats Thomas Dewey

G.I. Bill of Rights: benefits to reward war service

War Refugee Board: created to aid holocaust survivors

Allies invade Germany

1945   *Yalta Conference*: Roosevelt makes controversial concessions

Roosevelt dies: Truman becomes president

Holocaust: Allied troops liberate extermination camps

United Nations Organization: first meeting

Potsdam Conference: Allies fail to settle differences or adopt atomic policy

Atom bombs dropped on Japan

World War II ends

LEARNING OBJECTIVES

When you have finished studying this chapter, you should be able to:

1. Explain why the United States was unable to remain isolated from the German, Italian and Japanese aggression in the 1930s.

2. Understand the long-term lessons Americans brought away from the policy of isolation that led to appeasement at Munich and the attack on Pearl Harbor.

3. Explain how the Allies' grasp of global military, diplomatic, and economy strategy led to victory.

4. Discuss and evaluate the praise and criticism Franklin Roosevelt received for his leadership during World War II.

5. Explain how war work affected the lives of ordinary Americans, especially women.

6. Discuss the experiences and responses of minorities during the war.

7. Discuss key issues of domestic politics during the war, especially those involving labor, taxes, New Deal reforms, and Roosevelt's reelection to a fourth term.

8. Describe how the end of the war forced Americans to confront the Holocaust, the atomic bomb, and deteriorating Soviet-American relations.

Review Questions

MULTIPLE CHOICE

1. The chapter introduction tells the story of Hawaiian pipefitter John Garcia to make the point that
   a. the Japanese surprise attack on Pearl Harbor was used as justification for interning Japanese-Americans.
   b. Mèxican-Americans made significant gains in acceptance because of their contribution to the war effort.
   c. the attack on Hawaii and subsequent global war taught Americans that they could not be isolated from the perils of the rest of the world.
   d. tragically, it now appears that U.S. entry into World War II could have been avoided if Roosevelt had been less preoccupied with Europe.

   (pp. 1022-1024)

2. The "Good Neighbor Policy" intended that the U.S.
   a. assert the right to defend Latin America from the Nazis unilaterally.
   b. give up military, political, and economic intervention in Latin America.
   c. renounce military intervention in Latin America.
   d. exercise political influence rather than economic intervention in Latin America.

   (pp. 1025-1026)

3. Most fundamentally, over what did internationalists and isolationists disagree?
    a. whether war could be prevented by collective security
    b. whether an international consultation or a North Atlantic military alliance would best preserve peace.
    c. which political party could best protect American security
    d. whether international alliances or policies like the Stimson Doctrine were the more effective strategy against aggression

(p. 1027)

4. Concerning the background to the Pearl Harbor attack, which of the following statements is true?
    a. Right up until the Japanese attack on Pearl Harbor, President Roosevelt was one of the country's most outspoken isolationists.
    b. The text ultimately explains the coming of war with Japan by showing how each side came to understand the other's intentions.
    c. Clear evidence now exists that President Franklin Roosevelt knew and even encouraged the Japanese to attack Pearl Harbor in 1941.
    d. Before Pearl Harbor, the U.S. provided substantial military aid to the British and Russians.

(pp. 1029-1035)

5. The war aims of the Allies were articulated before U.S. entry into the war, in the so-called Atlantic Charter. This document included all of the following EXCEPT:
    a. a call for a new association of nations.
    b. a condemnation of Nazism.
    c. a commitment to the Four Freedoms.
    d. the combined approval of Churchill and Roosevelt.

(p. 1032)

6. The impact of World War II on American society included all of the following EXCEPT:
    a. It brought recovery from the stagnation and unemployment of the Great Depression.
    b. Military life served as a melting pot as well as taking Americans far from home.
    c. Women and minorities felt resentment at being barred from military service.
    d. Women found new economic opportunities despite little change in gender attitudes.

(pp. 1040-1043, 1047-1052, 1070-1071)

7. Which of the following statements about American economic activity during World War II is NOT true?
   a. Workers and farmers enjoyed sharply increased earnings which instead of saving they spent on new model cars and other available consumer goods.
   b. The huge increase in federal spending was paid for by both borrowing (war bonds) and higher taxes.
   c. New federal agencies were created to manage war production.
   d. Women, along with lower income wage earners, made significant economic gains.

   (pp. 1044-1050)

8. What happened to the New Deal during the war?
   a. Since wartime spending brought recovery, neither Roosevelt nor Congress thought the New Deal was needed any more.
   b. Since "Dr. New Deal" had become "Dr. Win-the-War," there was little political interest in domestic legislation.
   c. An anti-New Deal coalition moved to end many New Deal programs, and the president adapted to the new political environment.
   d. Although cloaked in wartime labels, several additional New-Deal style agencies were in fact created to provide relief, recovery, and reform.

   (pp. 1058-1059)

9. The text portrays the key agreements at the Roosevelt-Churchill-Stalin Yalta Conference of 1945 as:
   a. A one-sided diplomatic victory for the Americans--until the Soviets broke their pledges.
   b. A sellout and betrayal of American ideals and interests by a naive and ill President Roosevelt.
   c. A series of compromises and U.S. concessions, relying for fulfillment on Soviet cooperation.
   d. A diplomatic stalemate: there was no agreement because the U.S. sought maximum territorial control and the Soviets wanted a new collective security organization.

   (pp. 1065-1066)

10. At the Potsdam Conference,
    a. the United Nations was organized.
    b. Roosevelt, Churchill and Stalin agreed on the fate of Germany.
    c. Truman, Churchill and Stalin agreed on occupying Germany but had to compromise on reparations.
    d. representatives of smaller allied nations met with the Big Three to hammer out a comprehensive peace treaty ending the war.

(pp. 1068-1069)

IDENTIFICATION QUESTIONS

You should be able to describe the following key terms, concepts, individuals and places, and explain their significance:

Terms and Concepts

isolationism	non-recognition
Mexican oil expropriations	Neutrality Acts
Benito Mussolini (Il Duce)	Quarantine Speech
Panay incident	fascism
neutrality	quarantine
cash-and-carry	fission
total war	balance of power
war conversion	voluntarism
concentration camps	Issei
Nisei	bracero program
GI Bill of Rights	anti-Semitism
Stimson Doctrine	Lend-Lease Act

Individuals and Places

Winston Churchill	Joseph Stalin
Munich Conference	Midway
General Douglas MacArthur	WACs
D-Day	Yalta Conference
"Rosie the Riveter"	A. Philip Randolph
Zoot Suiters	John L. Lewis
George C. Marshall	Thomas Dewey
Henry Morgenthau	Harry Hopkins

Leslie Groves
El Alamein

Hiroshima
Admiral Chester Nimitz

MAP IDENTIFICATIONS

On the map below, label or shade in the following places. In a sentence, note their significance to the chapter. (For reference, consult the maps in *Nation of Nations* on pages 1030
and 1036-37.)

1. Midway
2. Potsdam
3. Teheran
4. El Alamein
5. Normandy
6. Stalingrad

ESSAY QUESTIONS

1. Identify three events that drew the United States into World War II.

2. Describe the major war aims of the Allied Powers.

3. Explain why the battles at Midway, El Alamein, and Stalingrad were turning points in the war.

4. Why do you suppose so many people remain suspicious of Roosevelt's role in the attack on Pearl Harbor? Discuss the merits of the case.

5. Why did women play such an important role in war industries?

6. Why did the United States fail to take steps to help Europe's Jews during the Holocaust?

7. Compare the treatment of Italian-Americans with that of Japanese-Americans during World War II. How do you account for the differences?

8. Some historians have charged the United States dropped the atom bomb not to end the war quickly, as Truman argued, but to make the Soviet Union more cooperative. Explain why you think this may or may not be true.

Critical Thinking

EVALUATING EVIDENCE (MAPS)

1. Looking at the map of World War II in Europe and North Africa (page 1030), why do you suppose the Americans favored an invasion at Normandy over Churchill's proposal to attack Europe's "soft-underbelly" along the Mediterranean Coast?

2. Looking at the map of World War II in Europe and North Africa (page 1030), why would it have been natural for Hitler to expect the Allies to invade France at Calais?

3. In what ways do the maps illustrating the Geography of Global War (pages 1036-37) highlight the supply problems the Allies faced during World War II?

4. Looking at the map illustrating the Pacific campaigns of the war (page 1037), why would Roosevelt have been eager to have Stalin declare war on Japan? Looking at a map of the world (in Volume 2, see Appendices; in hardcover edition, see the endpaper, back cover of the text), why would Stalin have been reluctant to declare war on Japan?

EVALUATING EVIDENCE (ILLUSTRATIONS)

1. The picture on page 1024 of sandbags in front of the telephone company in San Francisco, suggests one reason West Coast Americans feared a possible attack by Japan. What else in the picture suggests a reason for fear among some residents of San Francisco?

2. Hitler was a master in the manipulation of patriotic propaganda. What are some of the techniques revealed in the photograph on page 1029?

3. How does the "Zoot Suit" fashion (page 1058) compare with styles that are considered outrageous today?

4. Examine the chart on government spending on page 1049. How does the level of government spending rise during the Depression years? How does that rise compare with the level of government spending during World War II?

5. Critics of the New Deal charged that the budget deficits accumulated through government spending programs did not bring the United States out of the depression, but that World War II did. What does the graph on page 1049 suggest about that argument? What does it suggest about the relationship of government spending and deficits and economic recovery? In what ways might critics counter this argument?

CRITICAL ANALYSIS

Read carefully the following excerpt from the text and then answer the questions that follow:

> Had Roosevelt known the attack on Pearl Harbor was coming? For months American intelligence had been cracking some of Japan's secret codes. Much information indicated that Pearl Harbor was at risk. Yet Roosevelt left the fleet exposed, seeming almost to provoke an attack to bring the United States into the war. Was it mere coincidence that the

vital aircraft carriers were at sea? That only the obsolete battleships were left a Pearl Harbor? Some critics have charged that Roosevelt deliberately contrived to bring war about. But the argument is based on circumstantial, not documentary, evidence. Roosevelt wanted to fight Germany more than Japan. If he had wished to provoke an incident, one in the Atlantic would have served him far better. More important, the intelligence signals were confusing and analysts lost track of the Japanese fleet as it moved toward Hawaii.

In the end, cultural misperceptions explained the coming of the war better than any conspiracy theory. American leaders were surprised by the attack on Pearl Harbor because they could not believe the Japanese were daring or resourceful enough to attack an American stronghold 4000 miles from Japan. Japanese militarists counted on a surprise attack to give them time to build a line of defense strong enough to discourage weak-willed westerners from continuing the war. As it turned out, both calculations were wrong.

Questions

1. The passage makes a distinction between "circumstantial" and "documentary" evidence. Explain that distinction. Give an example of each kind of evidence.

2. Explain what the authors think is a "conspiracy theory" to explain the attack on Pearl Harbor.

3. Why do the authors suggest it is more important that "intelligence signals were confusing" than to know that Roosevelt wanted an incident with Germany to provoke war?

4. How do you know from the chapter that both Japanese and American cultural assumptions about each other proved wrong?

5. Can you think of "cultural misperceptions" that exist today between the Japanese and Americans?

PRIMARY SOURCE: Two Views on the Evacuation of Japanese-
                    Americans*

*When President Roosevelt issued Executive Order 9066 on February 19, 1942, he author-
ized the evacuation of Japanese-Americans from the West Coast. Soon after, a Congressional Committee heard testimony from both California public officials and representatives
of the Japanese community who both favored and opposed evacuation. The following ex-
cerpts are from California Attorney-General Earl Warren (later the Chief Justice of the Supreme Court) and from James Omura.*

EARL WARREN: Unfortunately, however, many of our people and
some of our authorities ...are of the opinion that because we have had no
sabotage and no fifth column activities in this State since the beginning
of the war, that means that none have been planned for us. But I take the
view that is the most ominous sign in our whole situation. It convinces
me more than perhaps any other factor that the sabotage we are to get
...[is] timed just like Pearl Harbor....

We believe that when we are dealing with the Caucasian race we have
methods that will test the loyalty of them, and we believe that we can, in
dealing with the German and Italians, arrive at some fairly sound conclusions because of our knowledge of the way they live in the community.... But when we deal with the Japanese we are in an entirely different field and we cannot inform any opinion we believe to be sound.
Their method of living, their language, make for this difficulty....

JAMES OMURA: It is doubtlessly difficult for Caucasian Americans to
properly comprehend and believe in what we say. Our citizenship has
even been attacked as an evil cloak under which we expect immunity for
the nefarious purpose of conspiring to destroy the American way of life.
To us--who have been born, raised, and educated in American institutions and in our system of public schools, knowing and owing no other
allegiance than to the United States--such a thought is manifestly unfair
and ambiguous.

I would like to ask the committee: Has the Gestapo come to America?
Have we not risen in righteous anger at Hitler's mistreatments of the
Jews? Then, is it not incongruous that citizen Americans of Japanese de-

* From *Hearings before the Select Committee Investigating National Defense Migration,
House of Representatives*, Washington, 1942

scent should be similarly mistreated and persecuted? ...We cannot understand why General DeWitt can make exceptions for families of German and Italian soldiers in the armed forces of the United States while ignoring the civil rights of Nisei Americans. Are we to be condemned merely on the basis of our racial origin? Is citizenship such a light and transient thing that which is our inalienable right in normal times can be torn from us in times of war?

Questions

1. On what points, if any, do Warren and Omura agree?

2. What is Warren's proof that sabotage is imminent?

3. If you were a Japanese-American, how could you answer that charge?

4. On what basis do you think Warren makes the claim that authorities can deal with Germans and Italians more confidently than with Japanese-Americans? Do you think he is right?

5. In what ways do you agree or disagree with Omura's analogy between Japanese-Americans and European Jews?

6. Based on your reading of the text's discussion of the Supreme Court decisions on the evacuation, how did the Court answer Omura's question about civil rights? How would you answer that question?

7. Suppose Iran launched a surprise attack against the United States in the near future, with terrorists planting bombs in urban areas across the country. Would you recommend detaining Iranian Americans? What if Iran declared war but had only bombed embassies abroad? Discuss the parallels and construct other hypothetical situations, in order to explore what factors contributed most to the internment of Japanese-Americans in World War II.

29

COLD WAR AMERICA

THE CHAPTER IN PERSPECTIVE

T he postwar era in two critical ways marked a departure from Americans' past. For one, isolationism ended. In an attempt to contain Communism and Soviet expansion, the United States entered into the sort of "entangling alliances" that George Washington had once warned against. On the domestic scene, the country entered a period of economic growth that lasted around twenty-five years. Although dampened by occasional recessions, this economic expansion was not punctured by the sort of boom-and-bust depressions that had characterized earlier business cycles. Despite these departures from the past, connections to earlier experiences remained critical. Chapter 28 discussed both the appeasement of Hitler at Munich and Japan's surprise attack on Pearl Harbor. Those events helped determine the postwar generation's attitude toward national security. And when President Truman sought to in his Fair Deal to extend the New Deal programs discussed in Chapter 27, a sharp national debate occurred over the legacy of the Roosevelt era.

OVERVIEW

In many ways the history of the immediate postwar years was as much about adjusting to the past as to the present or future. This chapter thus begins with three individual stories of people making their peace with their war experience and then getting on with their lives. Much, of course, would never be the same. In particular, the growing antagonism between the Soviet Union and the United States shaped the way the nation adjusted to the postwar world.

The Rise of the Cold War

The Cold War had its roots in the unresolved issues of World War II, especially the questions of German reparations and boundaries, Poland's government, the future of China, and the relationship of the Soviet Union to its bordering nations. As president, Truman lacked Roosevelt's easy confidence in foreign affairs. He felt compelled to take a much harder line with the Russians, lest Stalin underestimate his resolve to strike tough bargains. Early tensions arose over Greece and Turkey.

For Americans, old hostilities to the Bolsheviks and new fears raised by Stalin's aggressive posture toward Eastern Europe aroused profound suspicions about the Soviets' postwar territorial ambitions. Persuaded that those ambitions were global, the Truman Administration adopted a policy of containment, outlined in George Kennan's 1946 "long telegram" from Moscow. Events in Iran helped persuade government officials of the importance of Kennan's views. Containment had its first real test when Truman persuaded Congress to support aid for Greece and Turkey. Political and economic turmoil in both Eastern and Western Europe made the case for the Truman Doctrine's theory of bipolar conflict compelling. Congress in 1948 authorized massive aid to Europe under the Marshall Plan. Stalin's effort to consolidate the Soviet sphere in Eastern Europe encouraged reluctant members of Congress to support economic and military initiatives in Europe. After the fall of Hungary and Czechoslovakia and a crisis in Berlin, the United States formed NATO. All of this took place under the shadow of the atomic bomb. The United States rejected any UN oversight that might compromise the nuclear monopoly. Military planners viewed the expansion of that monopoly as a way to deter possible Soviet aggression.

Postwar Prosperity

The end of the war brought wrenching readjustments as the government, industry, and individual citizens converted from war to peace. Women and minorities often lost their jobs. Inflation, shortages, layoffs, strikes, and a host of inconveniences created political headaches for the Truman Administration. Voters took their revenge against Democratic candidates in the 1946 elections and the new Congress resisted any attempts to revive the New Deal. One exception was the "G.I. Bill of Rights" that gave generous benefits to former soldiers.

Prosperity did not automatically spell political success for Harry Truman, as a new conservative spirit threatened to splinter the once-dominant New Deal coalition. Yet the defection of northern liberals and southern segregationists from the Democratic Party actually helped Truman defeat Thomas Dewey in the 1948 election. After his shocking upset win, Truman tried to revive social reform with his Fair Deal program. Congress blocked the way, forcing Truman to use executive authority to make gains on civil rights, such as the desegregation of the armed forces.

The Cold War at Home

A combination of conservative and liberal anticommunists brought the atmosphere of the cold war home. Fear of domestic subversion led the government to launch a massive loyalty review program. The House Un-American Activities Committee investigated the Hollywood film industry; labor unions expelled radicals. Under the 1947 Taft-Hartley Bill labor leaders, though not management, were required to take loyalty oaths. The mood of conspiracy influenced the tone of many popular movies in the *film noir* genre. The espionage cases of

Alger Hiss, Klaus Fuchs, and the Rosenbergs all fed the growing hysteria. In 1950 Congress passed the McCarran Act to bar subversives.

It was Senator Joe McCarthy who captured the tide of anticommunism and lent his name to the postwar "Red Scare." The Wisconsin Senator made spectacular charges, though he never authenticated any of them. In part his reckless style made him effective at first, but McCarthyism owed some of its credibility to Truman's own anti-red crusade.

Frustrated at home, Truman looked to foreign policy to assert his leadership. The new NATO alliance promised to strengthen Europe's defenses. But then came the two shocks of 1949: the communist overthrow of Chiang Kai-Shek and the Soviet detonation of an atom bomb. With a hotter cold war in prospect, the National Security Council proposed to accelerate national defense spending under the doctrines of NSC-68. Congress resisted the huge costs until war erupted as North Korea invaded South Korea.

From Cold War to Hot War and Back

Truman did not hesitate to commit American forces to the United Nations effort. General Douglas MacArthur reversed the initial North Korean successes with a brilliant amphibious operation at Inchon. But the decision to move across the 38th parallel to reunite North and South Korea brought China into the war. Truman eventually fired MacArthur for insubordination, as the Korean stalemate undermined the President's political position at home. In the election of 1952, war hero Dwight D. Eisenhower and his anticommunist running mate, Richard Nixon, used the formula of "K1C2" (Korea, Communism, and Corruption) to defeat Adlai Stevenson.

Ike's popularity complicated Senator McCarthy's efforts to extend his crusade. The Senator's excesses embarrassed the President and finally the Republican Party. Eisenhower never openly attacked McCarthy, though he did criticize the "book burners" inspired by the excesses of his aides, Roy Cohn and David Schine. Some of Eisenhower's actions actually encouraged McCarthy, especially the execution of Julius and Ethel Rosenberg and the security case against nuclear physicist Robert Oppenheimer. McCarthy went too far, however, in attacking the United States Army. When the Senate finally condemned him in 1954, the Red Scare began to wane.

It was also clear by the early 1950s that no matter whether the Republicans or Democrats sat in the White House, the nation's economy and its defenses were tied more than ever to a global order.

KEY EVENTS

1945   *Iran crisis and civil war in Greece*: early Cold War issues promote containment

1946   *George Kennan's "Long Telegram"*: explains Soviet threat and defines containment

Stalin and Churchill: "cold war" speeches harden divisions

1946 elections: Republican congressional victories

McMahon Bill: creates Atomic Energy Commission

Baruch plan: international control of atomic energy fails

1947   *Truman Doctrine*: aids Greece and Turkey

Taft-Hartley Act: restricts labor unions

HUAC: House committee investigates Hollywood

National Security Act: creates Defense Department and CIA

1948   *Marshall Plan* adopted to aid Western Europe

Berlin blockade: airlift saves Berlin

Truman upsets Dewey in presidential election

Truman recognizes Israel

1949   *Soviet A-bomb test*: Truman orders H-bomb research

China: falls to the Communists

NATO established: new U.S. defense commitments

1950   *Senator Joseph McCarthy launches his anticommunist campaign*

Korean War: North attacks South

McCarran Act: antisubversive bill

NSC-68: defines new national security policy

Alger Hiss: former government official convicted

1951   *Truman fires MacArthur:* general dismissed for insubordination

1952   *Dwight D. Eisenhower elected president*

1953   *Korean War ends*

1954   *Army-McCarthy hearings:* McCarthy censured

LEARNING OBJECTIVES

When you have finished studying this chapter, you should be able to:

1. Discuss the origins of the cold war between the Soviet Union and the United States.

2. Explain what factors complicated the conversion from war to peace.

3. Explain the concept of containment.

4. Discuss the domestic consequences of the cold war and the rise and decline of McCarthyism.

5. Explain Truman's upset win over Dewey in 1948.

6. Explain the decline of Truman's political fortunes and the Republican success in capturing the White House in 1952.

Review Questions

MULTIPLE CHOICE

1. In the general introduction to "The U.S. in a Nuclear Age," the text highlights all of the following themes EXCEPT:
    a. The U.S. and U.S.S.R., Europe's peripheral powers, confronted each other in the realigned global power politics of the postwar era.
    b. The Soviet-American Cold War was a surprising development in world history, considering the historic pattern of relations and the cooperative wartime alliance between the two powers.
    c. Wars in Vietnam and Afghanistan showed the limits of superpower action.
    d. Environmental deterioration emerged as an obstacle for continuing the great postwar economic expansion.

    (pp. 1074-1076)

2. What was the "Munich analogy"?
    a. if the Russians could blockade Munich, they could blockade London
    b. national power is as enticing and intoxicating as beer at Oktoberfest
    c. an aggressor might launch a surprise attack at any place, at any time
    d. you dare not appease aggressors

    (p. 1082)

3. Several factors explain the rise of the Cold War, according to the text. Which is NOT a correct statement of one these factors?
    a. geopolitical: the Truman administration harbored suspicions about Soviet designs on its neighbors
    b. ideological: both Soviet communism and the "American dream" represented ends and means that the other side hated
    c. economic: both the U.S. and U.S.S.R. were economically devastated after World War II
    d. historic: the Soviets remembered earlier invasions; the Americans remembered the pre-war Nazi-Soviet pact

    (pp. 1082-1084)

4. America's basic cold war strategy emerged when the Truman administration adopted the recommendations of U.S. diplomat and Soviet specialist George Kennan. It is known as
    a. the containment doctrine.
    b. the counterinsurgency strategy.
    c. the anticommunist crusade.
    d. the appeasement policy.

(pp. 1084-1085)

5. What did the Secretary of State offer in his Marshall Plan?
    a. to provide financial aid to rebuild Europe's war-torn economies
    b. to station U.S. troops in Europe to defend democratic nations
    c. to train free-world armies in the art of Oriental hand-to-hand combat
    d. to place atomic energy research under United Nations control

(pp. 1086-1087)

6. In the absence of sufficient U.S. troops to confront the Soviet Army in Eastern Europe, what defense strategy was developed by the late 1940s?
    a. atomic detente
    b. nuclear deterrence
    c. a combined NATO army
    d. French and German rearmament

(pp. 1090-1091)

7. Which statement about the post-war world of work is most accurate?
    a. The percentage of women in the work force declined below 1930s figures.
    b. The cultural and economic status of women's work rose for those women who found jobs.
    c. Minority workers lost their jobs under "last hired, first fired" rules.
    d. A patriotic spirit coupled with pay hikes for unionized white workers prevented strikes.

(pp. 1092-1093)

8. The Taft-Hartley Act of 1947
    a. provided for loan and educational benefits for veterans.
    b. imposed legal penalties for avowed communists.
    c. restricted the power of labor unions.
    d. outlawed collective bargaining.

(p. 1094)

9. NSC-68, a proposal of Truman's National Security Council, called for
    a. a protective nuclear strike against the Soviet Union.
    b. massive U.S. defense expenditures to counter the worldwide Soviet threat.
    c. a U.S. invasion of North Korea.
    d. limited military assistance to Vietnam.

    (p. 1104)

10. How did the Korean War finally end?
    a. The U.S. withdrew its troops unilaterally when the fighting died down.
    b. China persuaded the North Koreans to retreat within their own borders.
    c. A military deadlock and protracted negotiations finally ended in an armistice that maintained a divided Korea.
    d. With the fighting stalemated, the United Nations interposed its own peacekeeping force.

    (pp. 1107-1110)

IDENTIFICATION QUESTIONS

You should be able to describe the following key terms, concepts, individuals and places, and explain their significance:

Terms and Concepts

cold war	reconversion
segregation by gender	Taft-Hartley
Truman Doctrine	Dixiecrats
Munich analogy	containment
"Long Telegram"	Marshall Plan
NATO	Federal Employee Loyalty Program
Atomic Energy Commission	HUAC
blacklist	McCarthyism
GI Bill of Rights	Fair Deal
NSC-68	police action
Checkers Speech	

Individuals and Places

Robert Taft	Winston Churchill
George Kennan	Berlin blockade

Leslie Groves
George Marshall
Syngman Rhee
Iran
Turkey

Bernard Baruch
Alger Hiss
Henry Wallace
Hungary

MAP IDENTIFICATIONS

On the map below, label or shade in the following places. In a sentence, note their significance to the chapter. (For reference, consult the map in *Nation of Nations* on page 1088.)

1. Berlin
2. Czechoslovakia
3. Hungary
4. Turkey
5. Iran

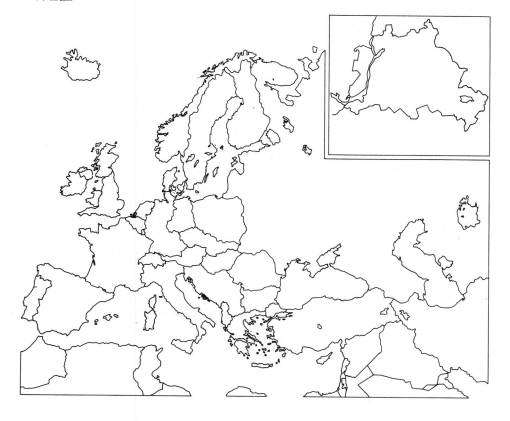

ESSAY QUESTIONS

1. Identify the countries in which early cold war crises occurred. What do these countries have in common?

2. What was the policy of containment?

3. How did the United States use nuclear weapons to deter aggression?

4. What were the major steps taken to prevent subversion in the United States?

5. Why did Truman relieve MacArthur of his command in Korea? Was he justified?

6. How did the cold war affect the film industry and popular culture? Explain by discussing both the content of films and the reactions of the larger political community.

7. How were the rights of African-Americans advanced or blocked during the Truman years?

Critical Thinking

EVALUATING EVIDENCE (MAPS)

1. Berlin is the capital of West Germany; locate it on the map of cold war Europe (page 1088). Where is it? Why is it not in West Germany?

2. Looking at the cold war map on page 1088, identify the countries that had fallen under Communist control since the outbreak of World War II. Based on the narrative in the text, identify those countries in which crises led to the cold war and the development of a policy of containment.

3. Looking at the Korean War map on page 1106, locate MacArthur's landing at Inchon; then his drive into Northern Korea. Why did the decision to cross the 38th parallel prove so fateful?

EVALUATING EVIDENCE (ILLUSTRATIONS AND CHARTS)

1. The image of the mushroom cloud in the photograph opening this chapter has been described by some observers as an "icon" of the era. What is an icon? What is meant by the comparison and what values or ideas do you associate with this particular "icon"?

2. What does the cartoon on page 1090 tell you about Europe's view of the atomic bomb?

3. "Politics are more image than substance." Apply that comment to the photograph of McCarthy, Cohn, and Schine (page 1111). Apply it to the authors' *selection* of that photo for inclusion in the text.

4. The picture of "My Son John" (page 1101) might also be called an icon, in its own way. What symbolic elements does the photograph contain that are particularly revealing about American cold war concerns and fears?

CRITICAL ANALYSIS

Read carefully the following excerpt from the text and then answer the questions that follow:

It was less clear, however, whether anticommunism could be contained. Eisenhower prided himself on being a "modern" Republican, distinguishing himself from what he called the more "hidebound" members of the GOP. Their continuing anticommunist campaigns were causing him increasing embarrassment. Senator McCarthy's reckless antics, at first directed at Democrats, began to hit Republican targets as well. In 1953 the Wisconsin senator tried to defeat the appointment of Soviet expert Charles Bohlen as ambassador to Moscow. Only the parliamentary skill of Senator Robert Taft saved the appointment and grave embarrassment to the administration.

By the summer of 1953 the Senator was on a rampage. He dispatched two young staff members, Roy Cohn and David Schine, to investigate the State Department's overseas information agency and the Voice of America radio stations. Behaving more like college pranksters, the two conducted a whirlwind 18-day witch hunt through Western Europe. To the chagrin of the administration, they insisted on purging government library shelves of "subversive" books, including those by John Dewey and Foster Rhea Dulles, a conservative historian and cousin of Eisenhower's Secretary of State. Some librarians, fearing for their careers, burned a number of books. That drove President Eisenhower to denounce "book burners," though soon after he reassured McCarthy's supporters that he did not advocate free speech for communists....

In such a climate--where Democrats remained silent for fear of being called elitists and Eisenhower refused to "get in the gutter with *that* guy"--McCarthy eventually lost all sense of proportion. When the army denied his staff aid David Schine a commission, McCarthy decided to investigate communism in the army. The new American Broadcasting Company network, eager to fill its afternoon program slots, televised the hearings. The public had an opportunity to see McCarthy badger witnesses and make a mockery of Senate procedures. When Joseph L. Welch, the outraged lawyer for the army, asked, "Have you no sense of decency, sir?" he laid bare the Senator's weak spot. The Senate gallery and the wide television audience had seen for themselves the senator's abusive behavior. As McCarthy's popularity dwindled and the 1954 elections safely passed, the Senate finally moved to censure him. He died three years later, destroyed by alcohol and the habit of throwing so many reckless punches.

Questions

1. Underline the passages in the excerpt that express the opinions or judgments of the authors rather than a narrative of facts.

2. In what way is McCarthy's attack on Charles Bohlen "less discriminating" than his earlier "reckless antics"?

3. In what ways does the language of the passage clearly indicate the authors' low opinion of McCarthy? What are their attitudes toward Roy Cohn and David Schine? How do they portray Eisenhower?

4. To what degree are the authors' opinions of McCarthy backed up by factual examples? In what areas would you need to do further research of your own to form an opinion on the accuracy of the authors' judgments?

5. McCarthy and his aides are characterized as "reckless" and as pursuing "witch hunts." Yet surely during the cold war, there was a legitimate need for the United States to guard against Soviet espionage. At what point does the threat to national security force legitimate limits on the freedoms of a democratic society? At what point do such limits threaten democratic society itself?

PRIMARY SOURCE: A Blueprint for National Security*

The National Security Council's position paper, NSC-68, served both as a summary of major American cold war assumptions and as a blueprint for its foreign policy over the next two decades. Although the document accurately reflected the views of Secretary of State Dean Acheson, it provoked a dissent from the State Department's two leading experts on the Soviet Union and containment, George Kennan and Charles Bohlen. Kennan questioned the assumptions about Soviet expansionist designs and the proposal to militarize containment.

> Two complex sets of factors have now basically altered [the older] distribution of power. First, the defeat of Germany and Japan and the decline of the British and French Empires have interacted with the development of the United States and the Soviet Union in such a way that power has increasingly gravitated to these two centers. Second, the Soviet Union, unlike previous aspirants to hegemony, is animated by a new fanatic faith, antithetical to our world. Conflict has, therefore, become endemic and is waged, on the part of the Soviet Union, by violent or non-violent methods in accordance with the dictates of expediency. With the development of increasingly terrifying weapons of mass destruction, every individual faces the ever-present possibility of annihilation, should the conflict enter the phase of total war.
>
> On the one hand, the people of the world yearn for relief from the anxiety arising from the risk of atomic war. On the other hand, any substantial further extension of the area under the domination of the Kremlin would raise the possibility that no coalition adequate to confront the Kremlin with greater strength could be assembled. It is in this context that this Republic and its citizens in the ascendancy of their strength stand in their deepest peril.

---

*From *NSC-68: A Report to the National Security Council from the Executive Secretary on United States Objectives and Programs for National Security, April 14, 1950.*

The issues that face us are momentous, involving the fulfillment or destruction not only of this Republic but of civilization itself. They are issues which will not await our deliberations. With conscience and resolution this Government and the people it represents must now take new and fateful decisions....

The fundamental design of those who control the Soviet Union and the international communist movement is to retain and solidify their absolute power, first in the Soviet Union and second in the areas now under their control. In the minds of the Soviet leaders, however, achievement of this design requires the dynamic extension of their authority and the ultimate elimination of any opposition to their authority.

The design, therefore, calls for the complete subversion or forcible destruction of the machinery of government and structure of society in the countries of the non-communist world and their replacement by an apparatus and structure subservient to and controlled from the Kremlin. To that end Soviet efforts are now directed towards the domination of the Eurasian land mass. The United States, as the principal center of power in the non-Soviet world and the bulwark of opposition to Soviet expansion, is the principal enemy whose integrity and vitality must be subverted or destroyed by one means or another if the Kremlin is to achieve its fundamental design.

Questions

1. This passage contains some difficult vocabulary. What are the meanings of the words *aspirants, hegemony, antithetical, endemic, expediency, and subservient?* Reread the sentences in which they appear to ensure that you understand the thrust of the argument.

2. Why, in the opinion of the authors of NSC-68, has conflict become "endemic" to the cold war world? Why is the Soviet Union seen as being qualitatively different from previous empires, such as the French or British? What strategy will the Soviets use, according to NSC-68, to dominate "the Eurasian land mass"?

3. Although much of the vocabulary in the passage is scholarly and complex, the authors also use language that contains strong value judgments designed to persuade. Underline those words and phrases that are judgmental and emotion-laden.

COLD WAR AMERICA   193

4. What assumption does NSC-68 make about the relationship between communist parties around the world and the Kremlin?

5. George Kennan believed Stalin had no grand design for world conquest, but was concerned primarily with affairs in the Soviet bloc. Kennan argued that the Russian dictator, as a conservative, feared overextending Soviet power. In what ways do Kennan's arguments challenge the major assumptions of NSC-68? Based on what you have read in this chapter, how would you weigh the two contrasting positions?

30

THE SUBURBAN ERA

THE CHAPTER IN PERSPECTIVE

Historians often remark on the similarities between the 1950s and the 1920s. Both were prosperous decades, both had economies led by the automobile and construction industries, both had pro-business administrations in Washington, and both seemed marked by a retreat from social reform. Beyond those superficial similarities, the differences are perhaps more informative. By the 1950s the nation was rapidly becoming more suburban and less rural and urban. Twelve years of depression and five years of war had made the government, industry, and bureaucratic organizations far bigger and more impersonal. Further, the United States had become an activist member of the world community, as Chapters 28 and 29 have made clear. In the 1950s prosperity at home became not only an end, but an instrument to fight the Cold War.

OVERVIEW

As the introduction makes clear, the automobile and the culture of the highway were in many ways the ties that bound Americans to one another in the 1950s. Automobiles reflected the increasing abundance of the era, with newly designed models being presented yearly, graced in this decade by ever more upswept tail fins. The fears of many Americans during the depression era--that differences of class might lead to social conflict--now gave way to concern that the rise of a consensus among Americans, in support of anticommunism and middle-of-the-road suburban values--might be breeding a suffocating conformity.

The Rise of the Suburbs

Two factors shaped suburban growth in the postwar era: the baby boom and prosperity. More children created a need for more housing, as well as for other goods and services. Rapid economic growth and government policies like the G.I. Bill made home ownership practical for far more people. Developers like William Levitt used mass production techniques to build housing rapidly at affordable prices.

Levittown, begun in 1947, typified the new auto-dependent suburbs. The interstate highway system begun during the period symbolized a continuation of moderate New Deal-style involvement in the economy, in the guise of Eisenhower's "modern Republicanism." And the new highways encouraged suburban growth as the most popular form of housing. As highways paved the exodus to suburbs, cities began to decline. They were unable to provide recent African-American migrants from the South and Hispanics in the Southwest the opportunities that earlier immigrants had found.

The Culture of Suburbia

The new suburbs blurred class distinctions and celebrated the single-family dwelling, where family rooms and live-in kitchens afforded more space for baby-boom families. The notion of "civil religion"--that civic-minded Americans ought to hold some core of religious belief, regardless of the particular creed--gained in popularity. Public leaders proclaimed religion a weapon in the cold-war struggle against Communism.

At the center of this idealized world stood the mother and father of the family. Father, the organization man, worked increasingly in more bureaucratic settings, often for large conglomerate firms. Although more women than ever worked outside the home, the public image of the ideal mother promoted the notion that housework and family provided sufficient outlet for female talent. Though women more often worked and received more education, the social patterns of the decade segregated them more than in earlier eras.

Emphasis on exclusive gender roles reflected a larger concern with sexuality. The research of Alfred Kinsey challenged a number of conceptions and taboos about normal sexual behavior. New sexual attitudes were also a consequence of increased leisure time. For most Americans, more free time meant more opportunity to gather in front of the television as the new medium became the center of family entertainment.

The Politics of Calm

Former General Eisenhower brought a gift for organization and political maneuvering to the White House. Reflecting the politics of the era, he resisted the demands of conservative Republicans to dismantle New Deal programs. He preferred his own brand of modern Republicanism. While initiating a number of modest social welfare programs, he rejected more far-reaching proposals of liberal Democrats to provide large-scale federal housing aid or a universal health care system.

In face of Democratic demands for government activism, Eisenhower maintained a pragmatic approach that led him to support programs like the Interstate Highway Act and the construction of the St. Lawrence Seaway, neither of which took any funds from general revenues. Still, partisan politics flourished. Issues about corrupt officials and the President's health dogged the administration. Recessions hurt the Republicans in Congressional elections of 1954 and 1958. Eisenhower's personal popularity remained so high, however, that he easily defeated Adlai Stevenson in the 1956 election.

The recessions marked temporary downturns in a generally expanding economy. Large multinational and conglomerate firms managed much of the private sector of the economy. Fears of excess concentration of corporate power were balanced by the stabilizing effects of diversity. New technologies such as computers made it easier to manage complex corporate empires.

Nationalism in the Age of Superpowers

The prosperity of the 1950s at home depended on maintaining a stable international system of markets and resources. Eisenhower shared responsibility for foreign policy with his experienced but somewhat belligerent secretary of state, John Foster Dulles. Under Dulles, U.S. anti-Soviet rhetoric became more confrontational, with an expressed willingness to push to the "brink" of nuclear war in order to counteract Soviet influence. As many nations worldwide clamored for independence and an end to the old colonial remnants of imperialism, both superpowers competed for the allegiance of former colonies and nonaligned nations. Although the Korean War ended in 1953, regional conflicts in Vietnam, Quemoy and Matsu, Hungary, Guatemala, Iran, and the Middle East all demonstrated how the cold war struggle inflamed international tensions. Often Eisenhower and Dulles supported covert action, as in Iran and Guatemala, when they wanted to topple popular governments that seemed to have a pro-Communist tilt.

The death of Stalin eased some cold war tensions. While Eisenhower made moves toward conciliation (the Geneva Summit and his "Open Skies" proposal), they were offset by renewed rivalry (the U-2 incident, the race into space, Castro's Cuban revolution). Nationalism, especially in the Middle East, Eastern Europe, and Latin America, posed special problems. A brief war between Egypt and Israel, France, and Britain closed the Suez Canal. A simultaneous uprising in Hungary found the U.S. unprepared to act. To discourage Soviet gains in the Middle East, the administration won approval for the Eisenhower doctrine and briefly sent troops to Lebanon. The launching of the Soviet space satellite *Sputnik* in 1957 made Americans fear they had lost their edge in defense technology. In his farewell address, Eisenhower warned not to allow such unrealistic fears to lead to over-spending on the military-industrial complex.

Civil Rights and the New South

At home, the material prosperity of the 1950s did not spread evenly. At a time when many whites were moving to suburbs that were effectively segregated either by custom or law, African-Americans were moving out of the rural South and into urban cities in large numbers. As black reformers began concentrating on ways to end legal segregation, the National

Association for the Advancement of Colored People succeeded in challenging the Supreme Court to overturn, in *Brown v. Board of Education*, the prevailing doctrine of allowing separate but equal facilities. That victory inspired civil rights leaders to adopt more assertive approaches. In Montgomery, Alabama, Martin Luther King, Jr. led a campaign to desegregate the city's bus system, while public school desegregation sparked conflict at Little Rock, Arkansas. President Eisenhower was forced to send in federal troops to assure respect for government.

Cracks in the Consensus

Thus, for all the rhetoric about "consensus" in the 1950s, the budding civil rights movement showed that the United States had not eliminated striking differences between racial or ethnic groups or economic classes and regions. Culturally, American society often seemed split. "Highbrow" intellectuals celebrated the achievements of abstract expressionists like Jackson Pollock or Mark Rothko. At the same time they condemned television sitcoms, westerns, and other forms of "middlebrow" entertainment. They feared mass media would produce mass conformity reminiscent of the 1930s in fascist Europe. Large organizations added to a loss of individualism and a sometimes powerful pressure to conform.

Another group of social critics arose among the nation's adolescents. As baby boomers became teens, they adopted their own culture, exemplified by rock and roll idols like Bill Haley and Elvis Presley. Many conventional adults were alarmed by what they saw as "juvenile delinquency." But the revolution in rock and roll produced a new cultural idiom that paved the way for cultural and political ferment in the 1960s. So, too, did the "beatniks," an urban group that rejected mainstream values in search for "IT." Thus, as the 1950s ended, the seemingly calm United States stood on the brink of a profound upheaval.

KEY EVENTS

1950   *The Lonely Crowd:* David Riesman's critique of corporate conformism published

1951   *abstract expressionism:* first major exhibit at the Museum of Modern Art

1953   *Mossadeq overthown:* Iranian nationalist toppled with the help of CIA

1954   *Brown v. Board of Education*: Supreme Court strikes down "separate but equal" doctrine

St. Lawrence Seaway Act: major public works project

Arbenz overthrown: Guatemalan leader toppled with CIA assistance

1955   Montgomery bus boycott: protest begun that eventually ends bus segregation in that city

Elvis Presley: ignites rock and roll

Geneva summit: thaw in Cold War

1956   Interstate Highway Act: huge project to expand nation's highways

Suez Crisis: U.S. intervenes to stop war on Egypt

1957   Sputnik: Soviet satellite launched

Little Rock crisis: Faubus defies federal order

Eisenhower Doctrine: Eisenhower seeks free hand to resist Communism

1958   National Defense Education Act: Congress responds to Sputnik fears

1959   Fidel Castro seizes power in Cuba

Nikita Khrushchev visits United States

1960   U-2 incident: Soviet Union captures CIA pilot; Paris summit canceled

1961   Eisenhower farewell address: warns of military-industrial complex

LEARNING OBJECTIVES

When you have finished studying this chapter, you should be able to:

1. Explain how mass automobility affected American lifestyles in the 1950s.

2. Discuss the impact of organizations and the pressures for conformity on suburban living, both for men and women.

3. Distinguish Eisenhower's "modern Republicanism" from both New Deal Reformism and Taft conservatism.

4. Compare the Eisenhower-Dulles "New Look" approach to the Cold War with the concept of containment pursued by Truman and Acheson.

5. Explain how demographic and economic patterns in the 1950s contributed to greater civil rights activism.

6. Explain how the emergence of a teen culture contributed to the debate over the values of American culture.

Review Questions

MULTIPLE CHOICE

1. The chapter introduction uses the automobile as a symbol for the 1950s, in order to make the point that
   a. a culture of mobility developed, featuring abundance and a high degree of movement, especially to the suburbs.
   b. all the variations and yearly changes in automobile design reflected the immense diversity and divisions in American life.
   c. government programs no longer focused on people, as in the New Deal, but on things, as with the Interstate Highway system.
   d. car-buying adults, rather than children and their simpler toys, were more influential in shaping American culture.

   (pp. 1114-1116)

2. All help explain the rise of suburbia EXCEPT:
   a. "white flight," which lured rural residents to the glamour and high living standards of metropolitan areas.
   b. the "baby boom," which provided a large number of young families seeking their own houses.
   c. availability of cheap single-family houses on their own lots.
   d. availability of a transportation system that allowed commuting to a job elsewhere.

   (pp. 1116-1119)

3. As Henry Ford had been to mass production of automobiles, so William Levitt was to the mass production of
   a. ships.
   b. houses.
   c. baby products.
   d. religion.

   (pp. 1117-1118)

4. Church membership in the 1950s
   a. for the first time in the 20th century declined to less than half the population.
   b. for the first time in the 20th century grew to more than half the population.
   c. grew steadily in the suburbs but declined sharply in cities and rural areas.
   d. became irrelevant to the consumer-oriented culture of the suburbs.

   (p. 1122)

5. Which stereotype of women was most common in the 1950s?
   a. independent and career-oriented
   b. an equal partner in American democracy
   c. domestic and motherly
   d. genteel and cultured

   (p. 1123)

6. What phrase did President Eisenhower coin to describe the vulnerable neighbors of a country like Vietnam threatened with a communist takeover?
   a. "sitting ducks"
   b. "at the brink of war"
   c. "our firm friends"
   d. "a row of dominoes"

   (p. 1133)

7. At the height of the Cold War in the 1950s all of the following were true EXCEPT:
   a. The United States tended to rely on nuclear weapons in order to save money.
   b. The hostility between the U.S. and U.S.S.R. grew more and more intense and uncompromising.
   c. The two superpowers competed for the allegiance of the newly independent nations of the Third World.
   d. Unrest, nationalism, and even revolution plagued the countries of the "Third World."

   (pp. 1123-1136)

8. In the final stages of the French-Vietnamese war, the United States:
   a. adopted a policy of strict neutrality.
   b. was subsidizing the costs of the French war effort.
   c. deployed nuclear weapons in support of the French.
   d. contributed ground combat troops in support of the French.

   (p. 1133)

9. The case of *Brown v. Board of Education of Topeka* concerned:
   a. prayers in public schools.
   b. federal aid to education.
   c. racial segregation in public schools.
   d. equal access to school busing.

   (pp. 1141-1142)

10. Martin Luther King, Jr., rose to leadership in the civil rights movement during the 1950s. His strategies, different from the recent past, would become the primary techniques of the Civil Rights movement into the 1960s. What is the most accurate summary of this transition in the movement?
    a. Direct and often violent confrontation replaced nonviolent passive resistance.
    b. King's rhetorical skills on TV rather than organized action caught the nation's attention.
    c. King appealed directly to President Eisenhower to lend his support to efforts to speed up desegregation.
    d. King proposed non-violent confrontation rather than the NAACP's strategy of legal challenges to segregation in the courts.

    (pp. 1140-1143)

IDENTIFICATION QUESTIONS

You should be able to describe the following key terms, concepts, individuals and places, and explain their significance:

Terms and Concepts

Interstate Highway Act	civil religion
organization man	conglomerate
modern Republicanism	mass automobility
New Look	brinksmanship
covert operations	Open Skies

Eisenhower Doctrine

Sputnik

"all deliberate speed"

beatniks

U-2

Sunbelt phenomenon

abstract expressionism

Individuals and Places

St. Lawrence Seaway

William Whyte

Jacobo Arbenz Guzman

Beirut, Lebanon

Earl Warren

Little Rock

Billy Graham

John Foster Dulles

Nikita Khrushchev

Gary Powers

Rosa Parks

MAP IDENTIFICATIONS

On the map on the next page, label or shade in the following places. In a sentence, note their significance to the chapter. (For reference, consult the map in *Nation of Nations* on page 1133.)

1. Quemoy
2. Dien Bien Phu
3. South Vietnam
4. Taiwan
5. Hanoi

ESSAY QUESTIONS

1. Identify three factors that explain suburban growth after World War II.

2. Explain how each of the following affected (or were affected by) the growth of the suburbs: the federal highway system, the film industry, housewives, African-Americans.

3. Describe the key features of conglomerates and diversified corporations.

4. What important ideas influenced Martin Luther King's approach to civil rights protest? How did he put those ideas into practice?

no other way for a woman to be a heroine. Here is a typical specimen from a story called "The Sandwich Maker" (*Ladies Home Journal*, April, 1959). She took home economics in college, learned how to cook, never held a job, and still plays the child bride, though she now has three children of her own. Her problem is money. "Oh nothing boring, like taxes or reciprocal trade agreements, or foreign aid programs. I leave all that economic jazz to my constitutionally elected representative in Washington, heaven help him."

Questions

1. From reading this passage, how would you define the feminine mystique?

2. How would you describe Friedan's tone in this passage? What words or phrases influence your reading of it?

3. What historical source material does Friedan use to document her case about changing women's attitudes?

4. What does Friedan's choice of sources tell you about her view of the role the media play in shaping popular values?

5. If you were a historian, what would you do to test Friedan's interpretation of the causes of the rise of the feminine mystique?

6. Based on Friedan's brief description of "The Sandwich Maker," sketch a hypothetical story you would write that would be consistent with what the women's magazines were publishing. How would the happy homemaker reconcile her need for more money with her obligations to family?

7. Check your version against either the original or Friedan's summary of the story in *The Feminine Mystique* (pages 39-40).

31

LIBERALISM AND BEYOND

THE CHAPTER IN PERSPECTIVE

In some ways the political and social upheavals of the 1960s stand in sharp contrast to the calmer mood of the 1950s. In fact the ground work for many of the era's reformist causes had been laid earlier. Much of the Kennedy-Johnson legislative agenda extended programs launched under the New Deal discussed in Chapter 27. The important initiatives taken by African-Americans during the 1940s and 1950s prepared the way for the major push of the 1960s. And as Chapter 30 emphasized, a whole series of demographic shifts -- the maturing of the baby boomers, the shift of population to the West Coast, the migration of African-Americans from South to North and West, and the increase in the middle class -- all contributed to the ferment of the 1960s.

OVERVIEW

In the last two chapters you have seen the groundwork laid for the momentous achievements of the civil rights movement. But great movements have smaller, often painfully human dimensions, as the introduction to this chapter shows. Six-year-old Ruby displayed one kind of courage; an Atlanta school teacher showed quite another. Both made essential contributions to a dream too long deferred.

A Liberal Agenda for Reform

The roots of social upheaval in the 1960s lay beneath the calm surface of the 1950s. John F. Kennedy opened the new era with his call to "get the nation moving again." As a Catholic and playboy son of the wealthy Joseph Kennedy, Jack Kennedy seemed an unlikely presidential candidate. Yet he showed superb organizational skills, laid to rest the religious issue, and bested Richard Nixon in televised debates. For all that, Kennedy won the election by an unprecedentedly narrow margin.

As president, Kennedy was not instinctively a liberal. Still, he brought to the White House a crew of pragmatic liberals convinced they could reach "New Frontiers." That meant practical reforms at home and a more dynamic policy to contain Communism abroad.

Kennedy shared with his advisers the belief that they could use power when and where it was needed to get optimal results.

New Frontiers

The new administration turned its attention abroad to the instabilities of the third world, hoping to counter them with programs like the Alliance for Progress, the Peace Corps, and "special forces" military advisers. Almost immediately the aborted invasion of Cuba at the Bay of Pigs raised doubts about Kennedy's judgment. So, too, did his confrontation with Khrushchev in Vienna and the Soviet decision to build a wall in Berlin. Kennedy countered by stepping up aid to South Vietnam. And when intelligence sources discovered in October 1962 that the Soviets had placed offensive missiles in Cuba, the President faced the worst crisis of the nuclear age. Using restraint, he rejected air strikes in favor of a blockade. Privately he offered Soviet Premier Khrushchev a face-saving way out of the crisis. The next year Kennedy negotiated a nuclear test ban treaty, which eased slightly the heated-up cold war.

At home Kennedy and his advisors applied the ideas of John Maynard Keynes to increase economic growth without inflation. Even as they succeeded, they could not overcome the mistrust of the business community. And when Kennedy found his liberal reform package stymied by congressional conservatives, the Supreme Court under Chief Justice Earl Warren took the lead with critical decisions on civil liberties, voting, and civil rights.

The Civil Rights Crusade

Civil rights proved to be the crucial test of liberalism. Kennedy only reluctantly took up the cause which threatened to split the Democratic Party. Leadership came instead from black political and religious organizations such as the Congress on Racial Equality, the Student Nonviolent Coordinating Committee, and Martin Luther King's Southern Christian Leadership Council. Sit-ins, Freedom Rides, and other forms of nonviolent protest became the weapons to fight segregation. The sometimes brutal reactions of southern police and white supremacists shocked national television audiences and especially Kennedy's brother, Attorney General Robert Kennedy. On several occasions the younger Kennedy ordered federal marshals to protect civil rights groups. The President introduced a major civil rights bill and on August 28, 1963, over 200,000 people gathered in Washington to hear Martin Luther King speak of his dreams for integration.

Kennedy committed himself to a civil rights bill, but was assassinated in Dallas. Lyndon Johnson, a Southerner, honored Kennedy's commitment by passing a broad Civil Rights Act in 1964 and a Voting Rights Act in 1965. But even those advances could not quiet the increasingly militant and radical demands of black nationalist groups like the Student Nonviolent Coordinating Committee (SNCC), the Black Muslims, and the Black Panthers.

In the North, civil rights leaders discovered de facto barriers to integration far more difficult to remove than the "Jim Crow" laws in the South. Beginning in the summer of 1964, a series of race riots tore through the nation's cities.

Lyndon Johnson and the Great Society

As President, Lyndon Johnson was determined to leave an enduring mark on the nation, much in the spirit of his hero, Franklin Roosevelt. Not only did he commit himself to civil rights, but to liberal tax cuts, aid to education, health benefits for the elderly and poor, job training, housing, urban renewal, the environment, and more. He called his program "The Great Society" and with it surpassed Roosevelt's legislative achievements. In beating conservative Barry Goldwater in the 1964 presidential race, Johnson also bested Roosevelt's landslide victory in 1936.

Johnson's vision proved heady indeed. In whirlwind fashion, he passed laws affecting almost every area of life from health to education to jobs to immigration to auto safety to equal rights to the environment. Many of the initiatives had a higher price tag than he or his supporters imagined. Inefficiency, corruption, soaring costs, and political infighting dogged many Great Society programs. But more than flawed legislation or political corruption, the Vietnam War shattered Johnson's hopes to create his Great Society.

The Counterculture

Among young Americans, there were many who had given up on the traditional methods of politics and society. One politically left group centered around Students for a Democratic Society (SDS). These young radicals distinguished their brand of politics from the Marxists of the 1930s by describing themselves as the New Left. A battle over free speech at the University of California at Berkeley, in 1964 brought their movement wide national exposure.

Other young people rejected politics altogether and sought non-materialistic lifestyles, experimenting with sex, drugs, and music in search of altered consciousness. In their outrageous clothes and personal style they flouted convention. Much of the style of the "counterculture" came from West Coast hippies and rock musicians. Drugs played a central role in defining hippie styles. So, too, did the folk music of Bob Dylan and rock music revitalized by the Beatles and other English groups. West Coast acid rock groups like the Grateful Dead and Jefferson Airplane adapted rock to the drug culture. By the late 1960s, the hope of building a better world, whether through a Great Society or through radical politics and cultural revolution, began to collapse. The era's soaring dreams were brought to earth under the weight of an invasive commercialism, the lack of coherence within the movements, growing violence, and, above all, the impact of the war in Vietnam.

KEY EVENTS

1958   *Kingston Trio*: popularizes folk music

1960   *Greensboro sit-ins*: college students push civil rights

                  Kennedy elected president: first Roman Catholic to win the office

1961   *Alliance for Progress*: Kennedy program for Latin America

                  Peace Corps: sets idealistic tone

                  Alan Shepard, Jr. becomes first American in space

                  Bay of Pigs invasion: American-aided Cuban rebels fail to overthrow Castro

                  Vietnam: Kennedy steps up U.S. role

                  Communists erect Berlin Wall

                  CORE organizes freedom rides

1962   *The Other Americans:* Michael Harrington's book about poverty published

                  Cuban missile crisis: to the brink of nuclear war

                  James Meredith desegregates University of Mississippi

                  Engel v. Vitale: school prayer case

                  Baker v. Carr: case for one person, one vote

                  Students for a Democratic Society issues Port Huron Statement

1963   *Ngo Dinh Diem*: South Vietnamese leader assassinated

                  American-Soviet nuclear test ban treaty signed

University of Alabama desegregation crisis: Gov. Wallace defies court order

March on Washington: crowds hear Martin Luther King support civil rights

Kennedy assassinated: Lyndon Johnson becomes president

1964   *Escobedo v. Illinois*: critical criminal rights case

Civil Rights Act: most important rights bill since Civil War era passed

SNCC Freedom Summer: campaign for voting rights meets with violence

First of the decade's urban race riots

Kennedy tax cuts: Johnson enacts key economic reform

Economic Opportunity Act: cornerstone of Great Society

Wilderness Preservation System Act: major environmental reform

Lyndon Johnson elected president

Berkeley Free Speech Movement: inspires student unrest

Beatles introduce British rock

1965   *Great Society*: Johnson legislative blitz

Selma protest: King leads voting rights march

Voting Rights Act: second major civil rights bill

Watts riots: Los Angeles in flames

Malcolm X: Black Muslim leader assassinated

Medicare and Medicaid Acts: major health care reforms

Elementary and Secondary Education Act: federal aid to education

Immigration Act: ends quota system

1966   *Stokely Carmichael calls for "Black Power"*

1967   *First "be-in"*: counterculture flourishes

1968   *Fair Housing Act*: last major Great Society bill

1969   *Woodstock Music Festival*: celebration of counterculture

LEARNING OBJECTIVES

When you have finished studying this chapter, you should be able to:

1. Discuss the Kennedy administration's application of pragmatic liberalism.

2. Explain how Kennedy's cold war foreign policy led to crises in Cuba and Vietnam before Soviet-American tensions eased.

3. Outline the Supreme Court's role in promoting reform.

4. Describe how the non-violent achievements of moderate civil rights activists gave way to black nationalism and violence.

5. Explain why Lyndon Johnson's extraordinary efforts to frame a Great Society resulted in disillusionment and social friction.

6. Explain how a youth culture gave birth to a radical New Left and an apolitical counterculture.

Review Questions

MULTIPLE CHOICE

1. The chapter introduction tells the story of a schoolgirl and a teacher to make the point that
   a. education was an important focus of the liberal agenda for reform.
   b. the civil rights movement's emphasis on integration actually proved a failure.
   c. adult white Southerners, steeped in racial stereotypes, could not adjust to school integration.
   d. the wrenching changes of the 1960s, which affected most Americans, grew out of the social trends and conditions of the 1950s.

   (pp. 1150-1153)

2. Kennedy's foreign policy stressed
   a. pragmatism and flexibility within a cold war liberal framework.
   b. high ideals and rejection of military action.
   c. rigidly ideological cold-war rhetoric and hostility toward Third World development.
   d. detente and human rights.

   (pp. 1156-1158)

3. What foreign policy crisis did NOT occur during Kennedy's thousand-day Presidency?
   a. assassination of the U.S.-backed Prime Minister of Vietnam
   b. the Berlin wall crisis
   c. the Soviet launch of Sputnik
   d. the Bay of Pigs invasion

   (pp. 1158-1161)

4. Why did the United States impose a blockade on Cuba in October 1962?
   a. Intelligence revealed the presence of Soviet offensive missiles.
   b. Intelligence revealed a large buildup of Soviet and Cuban troops.
   c. To carry out a CIA plan to overthrow Castro's government.
   d. To initiate preparations for a counter-insurgency invasion of Cuba.

   (pp. 1159-1161)

5. Which of the following was NOT a consequence of the missile crisis of 1962?
   a. installation of a "hot line" communication link between the Kremlin and the White House
   b. renewal of negotiations for a nuclear test ban treaty
   c. jump in Kennedy's prestige as a Cold Warrior
   d. jump in Khrushchev's power as a Soviet leader

   (p. 1162)

6. What finally pushed the Kennedy administration to commit to federal legislation to end segregation and protect voting rights?
   a. the rulings of the Warren Court.
   b. the riots in Northern cities.
   c. the bus boycott in Montgomery, Alabama.
   d. the violent repression of a non-violent demonstration in Montgomery, Alabama.

   (pp. 1168-1169)

7. The Civil Rights Act of 1964, according to your text, "marked one of the great moments in the history of American reform." It provided for all of the following EXCEPT:
   a. requirements that persons accused of crimes must be informed of their rights and allowed to consult a lawyer.
   b. banned discrimination in public facilities.
   c. banned discrimination in employment.
   d. protected the right to vote.

   (p. 1170)

8. All of the following were elements of Johnson's "Great Society" programs, EXCEPT:
   a. a health insurance program for the elderly.
   b. an anti-poverty program.
   c. an aid program for education.
   d. a funding program to return tax revenues to states.

   (pp. 1175-1177)

9. What geographic reorientation of popular culture had occurred by the later 1960s?
   a. The rise of the West Coast as trend-setter.
   b. A return to the southern roots of both black rhythm and blues and white rock and roll.
   c. The shift from rural to urban settings in television shows.
   d. The rise of the "Big Apple" (New York City) as the center of the recording and film industries.

(pp. 1184-1185)

10. One of the key concepts articulated in the "Port Huron Statement" of the Students for a Democratic Society was
    a. bureaucratic efficiency.
    b. participatory democracy.
    c. Marxist ideological purity.
    d. personal moral autonomy.

(p. 1179)

IDENTIFICATION QUESTIONS

You should be able to describe the following key terms, concepts, individuals and places, and explain their significance:

Terms and Concepts

hyphenated Americans	Camelot
liberalism	Alliance for Progress
special forces	Peace Corps
domino theory	missile gap
hotline	*Engel v. Vitale*
Freedom Riders	voter registration
black power	Medicare and Medicaid
Port Huron Statement	New Left
mod	soul sisters

Individuals and Places

McGeorge Bundy	Bay of Pigs
Berlin Wall	Earl Warren
Selma, Alabama	Watts

Eldridge Cleaver
Timothy Leary
Daniel Patrick Moynihan
James Meredith

Michael Harrington
Motown
George Wallace

MAP IDENTIFICATIONS

On the map below, label or shade in the following places. In a sentence, note their significance to the chapter. (For reference, consult the map in *Nation of Nations* on page 1166.)

1. Greensboro, North Carolina
2. Montgomery, Alabama
3. Oxford, Mississippi
4. Watts (Los Angeles)

ESSAY QUESTIONS

1. Describe three steps President Kennedy took to deal with Third World unrest.

2. What were three major achievements of the civil rights movement during the 1960s?

3. In what ways did the student protest movements and civil rights campaigns of the 1960s arise out of the generally placid decade of the 1950s?

4. Compare the achievements and shortcomings of President Lyndon Johnson's Great Society with Franklin Roosevelt's New Deal.

5. In what ways did the New Left and the counterculture have roots in traditional American practices and beliefs?

6. In what ways did the West coast play a prominent role in the youth rebellion of the 1960s?

Critical Thinking

EVALUATING EVIDENCE (MAPS)

1. Study "The World of the Superpowers" (pages 1160-61) for a moment in order to orient yourself to the map's somewhat unusual projection. (Note the location of the North Pole, and, to the south, the edges of Africa and South America.) Which nations were the sites of crises during the early years of the cold war, from 1946-1952? From 1952-1960? During the 1960s?

2. What does the location of forces along the Soviet Union's eastern borders in 1960 suggest about Sino-Soviet relations? About American cold war calculations of a monolithic communist alliance?

3. In what ways does the evidence in the superpower map (pages 1160-61) support American charges of Soviet expansion? In what ways does it support Soviet charges of hostile "capitalist encirclement?"

4. On the map, "Civil Rights: Patterns of Protest and Unrest" (page 1166), locate the route of the Freedom Ride of May 1961 and reread the description of it in the text. Where does the sharpest confrontation occur?

4. How does the map of civil rights activities suggest the idea that the movement had at least two major phases during the 1960s?

5. John F. Kennedy ran as a Democrat. What does the election map of 1960 (page 1155) suggest to you about the Catholic issue and previously strong areas of Democratic support? How does the map compare with the election results for 1928 (page 943)? Why would the two elections be compared?

EVALUATING EVIDENCE (ILLUSTRATIONS AND CHARTS)

1. What evidence do Ruby's drawings (page 1152) give to support the Supreme Court's position in the *Brown* decision?

2. In what way does the picture from the Birmingham demonstrations (page 1168) underscore the success of nonviolent tactics by the civil rights movement?

3. Compare and contrast the images of John Kennedy and Lyndon Johnson from the photographs on pages 1156 and 1173. How does the text use them to make points about both men's presidential images?

4. Discussions of the growth of government spending usually center on the debates or merits of federal spending. In the chart on page 31-29, how do federal and state government spending levels compare? How might that affect discussions on government spending?

CRITICAL ANALYSIS

Read carefully the following excerpt from the text and then answer the questions that follow:

> In the face of such violence, many Americans came to doubt that programs of gradual reform or nonviolence could hold the nation together. A few black radicals believed that the Kennedy assassination was a payback to a system that had tolerated its own racial violence--the "chickens coming home to roost," as separatist Malcolm X put it. Many younger

black leaders observed that civil rights received the greatest coverage when white, not black, demonstrators were killed. They wondered too how Lyndon Johnson, a consummate southern politician, would approach the civil rights programs.

The new president, however, saw the need for action. Just as the Catholic issue had tested Kennedy's ability to lead, Johnson knew that without strong leadership on civil rights, "I'd be dead before I could ever begin." On November 23, his first day in office, he promised one civil rights leader after another that he would pass Kennedy's bill. Despite a southern filibuster in the Senate, the Civil Rights Act of 1964 became law the following summer.

The bill marked one of the great moments in the history of American reform. Embodying the provisions of the Kennedy bill, it barred discrimination in public accommodations such as lunch counters, bus stations, and hotels; it authorized the attorney general to bring suit to desegregate schools, museums, and other public facilities; it outlawed discrimination in employment by race, color, religion, sex, or national origin; and it gave additional protection to voting rights. Within months, the Supreme Court upheld the controversial public accommodations section, in what Justice Arthur Goldberg described as a "vindication of human dignity."

Questions

1. Identify information in the passage that indicates the Civil Rights Act applied to more than the black minority.

2. Underline the two most sweeping generalizations the authors make.

3. What tensions does the passage reveal existed in both the black and white communities over the questions of civil rights?

4. What do the authors suggest is the relationship between violence and the promise of liberal reform? Why are the two related?

5. What areas of civil rights, if any, does the 1964 act fail to cover?

6. Do you agree with the authors' assertion that the act's passage was one of the great moments in the history of American reform? Why or why not? If the act was a watershed, does it have any relevance for the decade of the 1990s?

PRIMARY SOURCE: Dome-Building at Pacific High School*

In the spring of 1968, the counterculture movement was in full swing. Lloyd Kahn, who had been teaching at Pacific High School, an experimental school set in the Santa Cruz mountains, in California, recalled how the school evolved into a communal settlement housed in geodesic domes. His account, published in 1971, gives a fine sense of both the frustrations and exaltations of the counterculture.

Three years ago Pacific High School was probably one of the freest places around. We had forty acres of beautiful land, a lot of close friends, some money, a daily influx of students, and no idea of what education meant or was for. Almost everyone lived in the flatlands and came in busses every day; it was like coming to a little haven of comrades, getting stoned and playing at everything from submarine building to James Joyce. In the winter the rain kept us inside and drove us mad with lack of space and dirt. People started hating each other. It didn't seem worth driving for 45 min. to get to a lot of intense conflicts.

Everyone had plans to make the school better (Pacific's greatest trouble has always been its unlimited potential) and all the plans involved firing someone or changing the government or embarking on some sophisticated program of cognitive development. The students fired all the staff, totally reorganized, restructured the educational process, and went steaming off for a good three weeks of scheduled classes and work lists.

Things started to pick up when the weather cleared and we ran out of money. The staff (we had all been rehired) that didn't care stopped coming, the rest started camping out and sharing food expenses. There were less people around and less conflicts, nobody cared really.

People had toyed with the idea of making it a live-in school but we were so lame and could barely keep the buses running and everyone out of jail, much less feed and house 60 people. It was the best idea, because

* From "Pacific High School," in LLoyd Kahn, ed., *Domebook 2* (1971), pp. 32-33.

everything we were trying to do to give students a sense of independence and autonomy was contradicted by their life at home.

By the end of the spring there were about 15 people living on the property and were very high. There was no doubt that students and staff living in a community was the next step. We had a small kitchen running with a new cook every night. People lived in tents, parachutes, trucks, trailers and one beautiful house. The school was really on the edge of disaster; every time I went to the flatlands someone would ask if it was true that the school had folded....

[After seeing a geodesic dome at Big Sur] we decide to build some, we start driving back and forth to the school. Martin and kids make a conduit frame dome, put together on a hot day with funky ladder and beer. School meetings are held outside, under that dome framework. It's a symbol of what's in our heads. Sarah and I getting more and more attached to the people and the place, despite no place to live, no water, hot and dusty dry climate. We pitched a tent on the ridge, looking about 20 miles through rolling hills to the summer ocean fog. Martin lived about 50' away in a pup tent, reading late each night by kerosene lantern. Fresh ground coffee and schemes at Mark's house each morning, swimming in the lake on hot afternoons. Problems seemed insurmountable, but we had nothing to lose. No water, no money, no unifying principles.

Kids and lumber for the first domes arrived about the same time. Fantastic vitality. Energy, movement. We walked around, picked out dome sites. We held an impromptu dome class; everyone came.... Many people got in on the building, if they wanted to build a dome they'd come around and watch. We went into operation in an old tin building that had housed a horse, and was full of horseshit. We cleaned it out, ran in electricity, saws and drill press went into operation. As struts were being cut, kids would look in to see how. Everyone rushing to get their dome built. Things moving along of their own accord, no one directing. When I look back I see that what happened was a community forming itself, created with no real plan other than the need to live together. No grand design, no master plan. Joys, tension, both with the vitality implicit in beginnings.

We somehow governed ourselves enough to jointly survive. Community more economical way to live than single family. One sink, washing machine, kitchen for 50 people. An exercise in expanded awareness. Many problems. Your consciousness will change, or you'll leave the group. Your consciousness may change and *then* you'll leave the group, but if you can ride with it for a while, you'll learn a fantastic amount about yourself, and others. So different from anything you've done in the white middle class trip with all roads open to you from birth, color and poverty not wrecking your chances to do something.

Questions

1. During the time period described, how does Pacific High school evolve in its organization and structure? (Distinguish at least three stages in the life of the school.)

2. Kahn says, "Things started to pick up when the weather cleared and we ran out of money." Why does he believe things got better when the school ran out of money?

3. What does Kahn mean when he says that of making Pacific High a "live-in school" is the "best idea, because everything we were trying to do to give students a sense of independence and autonomy was contradicted by their life at home"?

4. Underline all the words and phrases in the passage whose language seems characteristic of the counterculture movement. What are the aspects of the counterculture that the underlined passages reflect?

5. How is the educational philosophy reflected at Pacific High a reaction against the educational systems of the 1950s and 1960s, as described in *Nation of Nations?*

6. In your opinion, what are the strengths and weaknesses of the educational philosophy described here? Do the strengths outweigh the weaknesses?

32

THE VIETNAM ERA

THE CHAPTER IN PERSPECTIVE

No event since the Civil War divided Americans as deeply as did the Vietnam War. The contrast between the patriotism evoked during World War II offers a strong contrast. The contrast becomes perhaps even stronger when it is remembered that World War II began at the end of the nation's most severe depression, while the Vietnam War came at the end of a long period of economic expansion. Yet the broader roots of social discontent put these contrasts into perspective. As we saw in Chapter 30, the crisis atmosphere of the Cold War had encouraged a majority consensus during the 1950s. During the 1960s a younger generation began to challenge that consensus--to campaign for "free speech, to revolt against conformity, to question the conditions that allowed segregation, poverty and racism to persist. It is not so surprising that, as draft calls and casualty lists rose for a war halfway across the globe, the questioning also spread to challenge the black-and-white battlelines of the cold war.

OVERVIEW

The consensus that had united the nation to fight the cold war cracked during the Vietnam conflict, as Americans fought in Vietnamese jungles and the streets of American cities. In a guerrilla war without battle lines and against an often unseen enemy it was easy to wonder who was the friend and who the enemy. At home Americans could ask the same question when both the supporters of the war and its opponents claimed to represent the best interests of the nation.

The Road to Vietnam

The struggle that wracked Vietnam for some thirty years was deeply rooted in history. Ho Chi Minh drew as much or more on the traditions of his people as he did on Marxist-Leninist ideas. Before Lyndon Johnson committed the United States fully to the war, presidents from Franklin Roosevelt to John Kennedy had made decisions interlocking the fate of the two nations.

An incident in the Gulf of Tonkin in August 1964 led President Johnson to launch retaliatory air strikes on North Vietnam. More important, Congress adopted the Gulf of Tonkin Resolution giving Johnson in effect a blank check to retaliate. The following year, Operation Rolling Thunder began the bombing of selected targets in the North, but Ho Chi Minh refused to negotiate unless the bombing stopped and all U.S. troops went home. With air bases to defend, the United States had to send troops, and when the troops became involved in combat, reinforcements were brought in, until American forces assumed the major fighting role in the South.

Social Consequences of the War

Due to a draft system that made it easier for students and the more affluent to receive exemptions, the soldiers that served in Vietnam tended to be younger, poorer, and less well educated. Still, morale at first remained high in the face of unrelenting combat, booby traps, and the physical rigors of the jungle. Yet American forces made little headway against the enemy. Even as the United States poured in supplies, men, and modern equipment, the Viet Cong maintained control of much of the countryside. The advanced technologies of war that were used (napalm, cluster bombs, and defoliants) too often destroyed the land, villages and people that American policymakers were intending to help.

By 1967 antiwar protest at home had spread outward from college campuses. Hundreds of thousands of people rallied to halt the bombing and end the war. In 1968 protesters ringed the Pentagon. The grim lack of progress led to defections even within Johnson's cabinet, most notably Secretary of Defense Robert McNamara. And as the cost of the war rose, so did inflation.

The Unraveling

The issues of the war came to a head in 1968, after the shock of the Vietcong's Tet offensive. Americans won a costly military victory, but the Vietcong came away with a political triumph. Within Johnson's Cabinet, Defense Secretary Clark Clifford led a movement to deescalate. When antiwar candidate Eugene McCarthy almost beat Johnson in the New Hampshire primary, the president announced he would not run for reelection, a victim of America's longest war.

Four days later an assassin gunned down Martin Luther King, sparking riots in the nation's major cities. Two months later Robert Kennedy was shot and killed while campaigning for the presidency. America had lost its most articulate liberal leaders. Frustrated protesters ran into hostile police at the Democrats' Chicago convention and rioting erupted in the streets. The presidential race of 1968 came down to a contest among Johnson's vice president, Hubert Humphrey; conservative Republican Richard Nixon; and the former segregationist Governor of Alabama, George Wallace. Despite Humphrey's last-minute surge, Nixon won a narrow victory.

The Nixon Era

Richard Nixon admitted in private that the Vietnam war needed to be ended, while publicly he escalated the bombing to force North Vietnamese concessions. In 1970, he briefly extended the war into Cambodia. As a result, domestic protest mounted and Congress repealed the Tonkin Gulf Resolution. Meanwhile, Nixon steadily withdrew American troops-- "Vietnamizing" the war. That reduced both American casualties and the morale of American troops.

Nixon saw Vietnam as part of a larger pattern of America's declining world power. In the Nixon Doctrine, he announced a shift of increased responsibility to allies like the South Vietnamese and Shah of Iran. He also made a dramatic trip to China and initiated a policy of détente with the Soviet Union that included a Strategic Arms Limitations Talks (SALT) agreement limiting some nuclear weapons.

At home, Johnson's insistence on pursuing both the war and his domestic welfare programs (both "guns *and* butter") without paying for them through tax increases led the economy into stagflation (low growth combined with inflation). Nixon sought to stem the economic slide and shift power from Washington to state and local government through his "New Federalism." Despite a reputation as a conservative, the president accepted a number of reforms, including the Clean Air an Clean Water Acts. He even resorted to Keynesian wage and price freezes to stem inflation. Nixon aimed to bring together a middle class coalition of voters he called "the silent majority" to win reelection in 1972.

"Silent" Majorities and Vocal Minorities

Nixon's appeal to the silent majority did not recognize the plight of significant minorities. Hispanics had grown increasingly vocal in insisting that they, like African Americans, had been held back by discrimination and poverty. They campaigned for a greater political voice and for economic power. Cesar Chavez organized Mexican-American migrant farmworkers, while more militant groups like *La Raza Unida* sought to gain power in communities where Chicanos were a majority. Indians, whose population had swelled during the twentieth century to about 800,000 by 1970, became similarly active. Through various forms of protest and legal challenge they sought to reclaim old tribal rights and more responsive government policy. And one of the most long silent groups, gays, gave voice to new demands for respect and equal rights.

Even with Nixon appointee Warren Burger replacing the liberal Earl Warren as chief justice, social activists still looked to the Supreme Court to redress their grievances. The

Court upheld school busing as one way to redress segregation. When President Nixon tried to make two controversial appointments to shift the Court's balance to the right, Congress rejected them. Nixon increasingly resorted to legal harassment by federal agencies to crush groups he saw as enemies. When the Democrats in 1972 nominated George McGovern, an antiwar liberal, to run for president, Nixon and his vice president, Spiro Agnew, won a smashing victory.

The End of an Era

In 1973, after untold material and personal loss, the United States ended its almost thirty-year involvement in Vietnam's internal conflicts. An intense bombing campaign in 1972 allowed negotiator Henry Kissinger to claim "peace with honor" rather than defeat--although in fact, the administration had accepted the terms offered by the North Vietnamese before the bombings. Even Richard Nixon, whose career had begun as an arch-cold warrior, came to recognize there were limits to what the United States could do to contain Communism.

KEY EVENTS

1945   *Ho Chi Minh unifies Vietnam:* his forces are soon fighting to expel French

1947   *Puerto Rico:* given commonwealth status

1954   *Battle of Dienbienphu:* defeat for French leads to withdrawal from Vietnam

                 Geneva accords: establish guidelines for peace and national elections in Vietnam

1963   *Ngo Dinh Diem assassinated:* instability plagues South Vietnam's government

1964   *Tonkin Gulf incident:* North Vietnamese engage American destroyers

                 Tonkin Gulf Resolution: Congress grants Johnson power to expand the war

1965   *Rolling Thunder:* U.S. begins bombing of North Vietnam

Antiwar "teach-ins": major protests begin on college campuses

César Chavez: leads national campaign on behalf of farm workers

1967   *March on the Pentagon*: antiwar protests spread

1968   *U.S. troop levels peak in Vietnam:* at 536,000

Tet offensive: Viet Cong attacks discredit notion that U.S. is steadily winning war

U.S. troops commit My Lai massacre

Paris peace talks open with North Vietnam

Eugene McCarthy: peace candidate challenges Johnson in New Hampshire primary

Johnson withdraws: decision stuns nation

Martin Luther King, Jr. assassinated: riots erupt

Robert Kennedy: enters presidential race and is assassinated

Democratic Convention in Chicago: riots spread discord and dim Humphrey's chances

George Wallace: launches third party candidacy

Presidential election: Nixon wins narrowly over Humphrey

1969   *Secret bombing of Cambodia*: Nixon escalates the war

Vietnamization: leads to reduction of American forces

Nixon Doctrine: spreads defense burdens to allies

1970   *U.S. troops invade Cambodia*: protests lead to killings at Kent State and Jackson State

March on Washington: renewed antiwar protest

Clean Air and Water acts: Nixon era reforms

Recession: creates stagflation

Congress repeals Tonkin Gulf resolution

1971 *Wage and price controls*: Nixon seeks to control inflation

Swann v. Charlotte-Mecklenburg Board of Education: Court upholds school busing

1972 *Nixon trip to China*: opens new Cold War era

SALT: arms control opens détente with Soviet Union

Presidential election: Nixon crushes McGovern

Renewed air war: mining of Haiphong Harbor and Christmas bombings of North Vietnam

1973 *Vietnam peace treaty*: America's longest war ends

Wounded Knee: AIM supporters occupy site of massacre

LEARNING OBJECTIVES

When you have finished studying this chapter, you should be able to:

1. Explain the steps taken that involved the United States more deeply in the Vietnam War.

2. Describe the way Americans fought the Vietnam War and how the conditions of fighting differed from previous conflicts.

3. Explain the rise of the antiwar movement at home and its role in shaping American policy for Vietnam.

4. Explain why 1968 was such a pivotal year for both the Vietnam War and for domestic politics.

5. Explain why Nixon widened the war as a way to end it, in the process of shifting some of the United States' defense burdens to its allies.

6. Describe the liberal and conservative elements of Richard Nixon's "New Federalism" and his appeal to the silent majority.

Review Questions

MULTIPLE CHOICE

1. The chapter introduction juxtaposes the stories of Marines in Vietnam and National Guardsmen at Kent State to make what point?
   a. Communist infiltration could harm Americans just as it did the South Vietnamese.
   b. America divided over the fundamental question of who was true friend and who real enemy.
   c. In the Vietnam War, the military was less the villain than the victim.
   d. Poorly prepared and ineptly led armed forces led to America's defeat at home and abroad.

   (pp. 1192-1195)

2. The Gulf of Tonkin resolution, as passed by
   a. the Congress, authorized President Johnson to take any measure needed to repel attacks on U.S. forces.
   b. the Congress, blocked further commitment of U.S. ground troops without Congressional approval.
   c. the U.N. Security Council, called for both U.S. and North Vietnamese forces to withdraw from South Vietnam.
   d. the U.N. General Assembly, condemned U.S. aggression against the people of Vietnam.

   (p. 1199)

3. The "Tet offensive" of 1968 was:
   a. a tactical defeat for the Communists.
   b. a political defeat for the United States.
   c. Both.
   d. Neither.

   (pp. 1207-1209)

4. The village of My Lai was the site of
   a. the largest battle of the Tet offensive.
   b. a U.S. massacre of Vietnamese civilians.
   c. a North Vietnamese harbor mined by the U.S.
   d. a Marine barracks bombed by the Vietcong.

(p. b: 1208)

5. What key segment of the American electorate did both George Wallace and Richard Nixon try to attract?
   a. individualistic-minded westerners
   b. the unemployed
   c. senior citizens
   d. the white working class

(pp. 1211-1213)

6. The Nixon-Kissinger team
   a. shared a global vision for a U.S. foreign policy with scaled back commitments overseas.
   b. paired a traditional small-town conservative with a troubled and profane easterner.
   c. showed how effective an active Vice-President could be.
   d. brought little foreign affairs expertise to the White House.

(pp. 1213-1214)

7. The term "Vietnamization" referred to the policy of:
   a. shifting the burden of actual combat to the South Vietnamese.
   b. training United States troops in the "Nine Rules" for understanding Vietnamese culture.
   c. shifting U.S. military operations from conventional tactics to guerrilla-type combat like the Viet Cong.
   d. countering anti-war propaganda by a campaign to tell the "real story" in Vietnam.

(pp. 1214-1215)

8. Nixon's slogan "the New Federalism" was supposed to mean:
   a. greater centralization of power and resources in Washington D.C., following Hamiltonian theory.
   b. the revival of the cabinet as a collective decision-making agency.
   c. restoring to Congress more voice and initiative in framing domestic and foreign policy.
   d. a reversal of the trend toward centralization of power and revenues in Washington D.C.

   (pp. 1217-1218)

9. Why did Hispanics and Indians have less success than blacks in creating unified movements?
   a. Neither group had the leadership enjoyed by the African-American civil rights organizations.
   b. The white backlash discouraged activism by other racial and ethnic minorities.
   c. Latino and native groups preferred to identify with their particular national or tribal heritage.
   d. Neither group faced prejudice and discrimination the way blacks did.

   (pp. 1220-1223)

10. How did U.S. involvement in the Vietnam War finally end?
    a. with the unilateral withdrawal of U.S. troops.
    b. with the negotiated withdrawal of U.S. troops according to a treaty with North Vietnam.
    c. with the negotiated withdrawal of U.S. troops according to a treaty with South Vietnam.
    d. with an international peace conference after the defeat of a large U.S. force.

    (pp. 1226-1227)

IDENTIFICATION QUESTIONS

You should be able to describe the following key terms, concepts, individuals and places, and explain their significance:

Terms and Concepts

Gulf of Tonkin Resolution	escalation
Rolling Thunder	body count

hawks and doves
Tet Offensive
southern strategy
SALT I
AIM
New Federalism

napalm
silent majority
détente
La Huelga
stagflation

Individuals and Places

Jackson State
Ho Chi Minh
Ho Chi Minh Trail
Pleiku
William Westmoreland
Robert McNamara
My Lai
Muhammad Ali
George Wallace
Daniel Patrick Moynihan
Spiro Agnew
César Chavez
Russell Means
Paris Peace Conference
Clark Clifford

MAP IDENTIFICATIONS

On the map on the next page, label or shade in the following places. In a sentence, note their significance to the chapter. (For reference, consult the map in *Nation of Nations* on page 1196.)

1. Pleiku
2. Ho Chi Minh Trail
3. Hue
4. Saigon
5. Haiphong

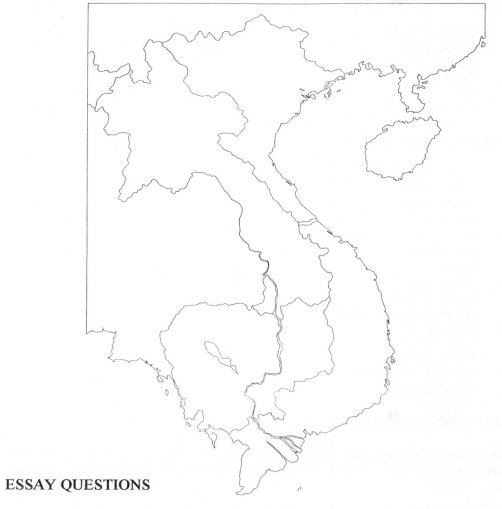

ESSAY QUESTIONS

1. What was the Domino Theory? How did it justify the American war in Vietnam?

3. Explain why you would take the position either of a hawk or dove in the debate over Vietnam.

4. Why was Vietnam sometimes called "a rich man's war and a poor man's fight"? Discuss with reference to the composition of the armed forces in Vietnam.

5. Choose four of the following events and explain why they were important turning points in the Vietnam War: Geneva accords, Tet offensive, New Hampshire primary, My Lai, Kent State.

6. It might be argued that the possibilities for change in the liberal tradition were thwarted by violence during the 1968 presidential campaign. Discuss, describing the positions of the various candidates in both the primaries and general election.

7. In what ways were Richard Nixon's domestic and foreign policies surprisingly liberal, for a traditional Republican and staunch anticommunist?

8. Both Indians and Hispanics were hardly "monolithic" ethnic groups in American life. Explain how that led to a variety of responses to the activist currents of the 1960s and 1970s, both among Hispanics and among Indians.

Critical Thinking

EVALUATING EVIDENCE (MAPS)

1. Looking at the election map of 1968 (page 1213), what assumption does Richard Nixon seem to have made about the Wallace voters when he planned his "southern strategy"?

2. What do the combined Nixon-Wallace votes, shown on the election map of 1968 (page 1213), indicate about the electorate in 1968?

3. What international complications does the route of the Ho Chi Minh trail suggest on the map of Vietnam (page 1196)?

4. On the map of Vietnam (page 1196), find the outposts of Con Thien, Song Be, Dak Tho, and Khe Sanh. According to the text, why did the Vietcong attack at these points in the months preceding the Tet offensive?

5. Looking at the map of Vietnam, what are the major geographic problems affecting the war and the conditions under which it was fought?

EVALUATING EVIDENCE (ILLUSTRATIONS AND CHARTS)

1. What does the picture on page 1193 suggest to you about the role of helicopters in the Vietnam War?

2. Suggest three different points made in the cartoon of Lyndon Johnson by David Levine (page 1206).

3. What image of Robert Kennedy is projected in the picture on page 1211? How does that affect your response to the charge that his candidacy was inspired by political opportunism? How might the picture be misleading?

4. What do you learn about César Chavez from the way he is dressed in the picture on page 1221?

5. The chart on page 1201 shows the level of American troops in Vietnam. Given those figures, what was the level of troops in Vietnam at the time of a) the Gulf of Tonkin Resolution; b) the commencement of Rolling Thunder; c) the march on the Pentagon in 1967; d) the Tet offensive; e) the proclamation of the Nixon Doctrine. How do these events each relate to the number of troops in Vietnam?

CRITICAL ANALYSIS

Read carefully the following excerpt from the text and then answer the questions that follow:

> [Nixon] thus set two fundamental requirements for his campaign: to distance himself from President Johnson on Vietnam and to turn Wallace's "average Americans" into a Republican "silent majority." The Vietnam issue was delicate, because Nixon had generally supported the president's desire to end the war. He told his aide Richard Whalen, "I've come to the conclusion that there's no way to win the war. But we can't say that, of course. In fact, we have to seem to say the opposite." For most of his campaign he hinted that he had a secret plan to end the war but steadfastly refused to disclose it. He pledged only to find an honorable solution.
>
> Nixon's managers promoted their candidate mostly through controlled television appearances. Nixon played on popular fears by promising to promote "law and order" while cracking down on "pot," pornog-

raphy, protest, and permissiveness. Hubert Humphrey had the more daunting task of surmounting the ruins of the Chicago convention. All through September antiwar protesters dogged his campaign with "Dump the Hump" posters. Finally, the vice president distanced his position on Vietnam, however slightly, from his unpopular boss. The protests then faded, Humphrey picked up momentum, and traditional blue-collar Democrats began to return to the fold. By November his rallies were enthusiastic and well-attended....

Questions

1. What was the double strategy for the Nixon campaign in 1968?

2. Why did the conflict in Vietnam cause Nixon problems in mapping his campaign strategy? How did he resolve those problems?

3. Identify the issues in Nixon's campaign that were a) substantive; b) rhetorical; c) positive; and d) negative.

4. What do you think is the authors' opinion of Nixon's campaign strategy? Identify key words or phrases that lead you to that conclusion? Do you agree with it?

5. At one point, Nixon candidly admits he intends to mislead the public. What does that tell you about Nixon? about politics in general?

PRIMARY SOURCE: Norman Mailer: The March on the Pentagon*

In the 1960s the lines between fiction and journalism began to blur as Tom Wolfe, Hunter Thompson, and Norman Mailer among others pioneered the New Journalism. Neither truly fact nor fiction, the New Journalism went beyond the traditional "objective" reporting to include the author's point of view, atmosphere, characterization, and other literary devices. In the following excerpt, Mailer describes the violence that broke out late at night during the October 1967 protest march on the Pentagon.

---

* From *Armies of the Night: History as a Novel/The Novel as History* by Norman Mailer. Copyright 1968 by Norman Mailer. Reprinted by Arrangement with New American Library, a Division of Penguin Books USA Inc. New York, New York.

The brutality by every eye witness account was not insignificant, and was made doubly unattractive by its legalistic apparatus. The line of soldiers would stamp forward until they reached the seated demonstrators, then they would kick forward with their toes until the demonstrators were sitting on their feet (or *legally* speaking, now interfering with the soldiers). Then the Marshals would leap between their legs again and pull the demonstrators out of line; he or she would then be beaten and taken away. It was a quiet rapt scene with muted curses, a spill in the dark of the most heated biles of the hottest patriotic hearts--to the Marshals and the soldiers, the enemy was finally there before them, all that Jew female legalistic stew of corruptions which would dirty the name of the nation and revile the grave of soldiers like themselves back in Vietnam, yes, the beatings went on, one by one generally of women, more women than men. Here is the most brutal description of a single beating by Harvey Mayes of the English Department at Hunter.

One soldier spilled the water from his canteen on the ground in order to add to the discomfort of the female demonstrator at his feet. She cursed him--understandably, I think--and shifted her body. She lost her balance and her shoulder hit the rifle at the soldier's side. He raised the rifle, and with its butt, came down hard on the girl's leg. The girl tried to move back but was not fast enough to avoid the billy-club of a soldier in the second row of troops. At least four times that soldier hit her with all his force, then as she lay covering her head with her arms, thrust his club swordlike between her hands into her face. Two more troops came up and began dragging the girl toward the Pentagon.... She twisted her body so we could see her face. But there was no face there: All we saw were some raw skin and blood. We couldn't see even if she was crying-- her eyes had filled with the blood pouring down her head. She vomited, and that too was blood. They rushed her away.

One wonders at the logic. There is always logic in repression, just as there is always a logic in the worst commercial. The logic is there for a reason--it will drive something into flesh.

The logic here speaks of the old misery of the professional soldier, centuries old. He is, at his most brutal, a man who managed to stay alive until the age of seven because there were men, at least his father, or his brothers, to keep him alive--his mother had drowned him in no oceans of love; his fear is therefore of the cruelty of women, he may never have another opportunity like this--to beat a woman without having to make love to her. So the Marshals went to work; so did those special soldiers saved for the hour when everyone but themselves and the Marshals was gone from the Pentagon. Now they could begin their beatings.... Yes, and they beat the women for another reason. To humiliate the demonstrators, to break them from their new resistance down to the old passive disobedience of the helpless sit-in waiting one's turn to be clubbed....

Questions

1. Identify the elements in these paragraphs you would not find in a traditional newspaper article.

2. Mailer uses the double negative in the first sentence of the excerpt, noting that the beatings were "not insignificant." He might have merely written that they were "significant." How does his choice of the double negative affect the meaning and tone of the paragraph?

3. What view does Mailer have of soldiers? Would it influence your answer to know that he was himself a veteran and author of a major war novel, on World War II?

4. What does Mailer mean when he uses the phrase "that Jew female legalistic stew of corruptions"? Whose point of view is this purported to be?

5. From reading the last sentence of the excerpt, how do you think Mailer feels about the doctrine of nonviolence?

6. Assuming that Mailer is accurate in reporting that the soldiers beat more women than men, why do you think that may have been the case? Does your answer square with Mailer's view?

33

THE AGE OF LIMITS

THE CHAPTER IN PERSPECTIVE

Chapters 29-32 all considered how economic growth and rising prosperity became central features of the post-World War II era. Growing national wealth meant increasing national power. That wealth and power sustained an interventionist foreign policy that included the ill-fated Vietnam War. The present chapter shows how the economic woes that followed Vietnam and disillusion growing out of the turmoil of political and social reform forced a reconsideration of the nation's limits. The optimism of the previous quarter century--that American power was supreme, that its prosperity might grow indefinitely--was due to receive a series of shocks in the 1970s.

OVERVIEW

In the 1970s twenty-five years of sustained economic growth came to an end, the United States recognized defeat in the Vietnam War, a President resigned in disgrace, the Soviet Union achieved nuclear parity, and the United States suffered from dependence on unstable suppliers of foreign oil. These and other problems forced Americans to confront the limits of what had recently seemed a future of infinite promise. For that reason the chapter opens by contrasting the soaring achievements of the moon landing of 1969 with the viscous reality of oil in the Santa Barbara channel during the same year.

The Limits of Reform

Reform crusades did not simply disappear as the United States passed from the turbulent 1960s into the 1970s. Rather, the sense of a "movement" splintered into more varied causes with more particular agendas. The Santa Barbara oil spill was one of many issues that advertised the importance of ecology to a healthy environment. Environmentalists also fought the Alaska pipeline, the Florida Everglades jetport, and the Supersonic Transport project (the SST). At the same time Ralph Nader sparked a consumer movement dedicated to forcing corporations to be more responsible to their customers, workers, and the public interest. Despite innovative use of tactics like the "class-action suit," the broad focus of the consumer agenda for reform dissipated its impact.

Feminists more successfully initiated a movement and sustained its high visibility. Drawing on the response to Betty Friedan's *The Feminine Mystique*, feminists incorporated gender discrimination under the 1964 Civil Rights Act and Federal affirmative action programs. Increased educational opportunities translated into new career patterns. In 1973 the Supreme Court in *Roe v. Wade* struck down restrictive abortion rules in 46 states. Yet behind that success lay divisions among women over both equal rights and abortion. And after initial progress toward ratification, the Equal Rights Amendment bogged down in conservative state legislatures. Thus, while reformers pushed on in the 1970s, they discovered the limits of the political process.

Political Limits: Watergate

Richard Nixon, too, discovered the limits of the era. He battled publicly with Congress to avoid spending funds they had appropriated; privately, he used government agencies to wage war with his perceived "enemies." During the 1972 campaign reporters Bob Woodward and Carl Bernstein discovered links between the White House and a burglary at the Democratic headquarters in the Watergate Hotel complex. In the burglary trial Judge John Sirica finally forced from defendant James McCord a confession of White House involvement in the crime and cover-up. Key Nixon aides resigned, were fired, or hired lawyers.

The Ervin Committee, in its Senate investigation of Watergate, discovered that a taping system recorded conversations in the Oval Office, setting off a battle between Special Prosecutor Archibald Cox, who sought the tapes, and the President, who refused to supply them. In the midst of this crisis, Vice President Agnew resigned under a cloud of corruption and in October 1973, Nixon fired Cox. Eventually new Special Prosecutor Leon Jaworski did receive the tapes which, despite gaps, revealed direct presidential involvement in the cover-up. Rather than face impeachment, Nixon resigned in August 1974, making Gerald Ford the first president neither elected as president or as vice president by voters. The system had worked, but not without stress.

A Ford, Not a Lincoln

Under President Ford Secretary of State Henry Kissinger pursued a policy of realism. Kissinger quietly acknowledged that American power had declined relatively, under the combined pressures of the Vietnam war and rising power blocs in Europe, Asia, and the Middle East. Inflation and falling industrial productivity, aggravated by the OPEC oil boycott, also undermined the American economy. Kissinger sought to restore strength to the western alliance by promoting stability in the Middle East in the wake of the 1973 Yom Kippur War. He also sought to strengthen key allies like the Shah of Iran. But scandals involving the CIA's covert operations and a worsening energy crisis hampered his efforts. Attempts to ease tensions through détente with the Soviet Union at summits in Vladivostok in 1974 and

Helsinki in 1975 only aroused the suspicions of Ford's conservative supporters and led him to reduce Kissinger's power.

Ford found himself more embattled on the home front. His program of amnesty for Vietnam dissenters satisfied neither conservatives nor dissenters. A public relations campaign produced no reduction in inflation. Aging industrial cities faced bankruptcy. Most controversial of all, however, Ford pardoned Richard Nixon before the nation was in a mood to forgive. In the 1976 election Washington outsider Jimmy Carter used the nation's frustrations with scandal and a weak economy to defeat Ford.

Jimmy Carter: Restoring the Faith

Carter sought to bring honesty, simplicity, and integrity to Washington. In foreign affairs, that translated into a commitment to "human rights" and some effort to reduce cold war tensions. Domestically, the idea of scaling down government ran afoul of entrenched interests and a presidency weakened by Vietnam and Watergate. Inflation and energy shortages, provoking sharp rises in the price of oil, continued to hurt the economy. Carter's responses failed to move Congress to act, and the President himself seemed to focus more on detail than on setting broad direction.

In foreign policy Carter successfully negotiated a treaty providing for an eventual transfer of the Canal Zone to Panama. He also struggled to find a way in which the United States and Soviet Union could constructively share the world stage. Conservatives opposed the move toward nuclear parity contained in the SALT II agreement of 1979. Carter responded by shifting to the hard-line policies of his National Security Adviser Zbigniew Brzezinski and a renewed military build-up. In dealing with the Middle East, Carter facilitated the signing of the Camp David Accords between traditional foes Egypt and Israel. But when Iranian fundamentalists overthrew the Shah of Iran and the deposed monarch traveled to the United States for medical treatment, militants seized the American Embassy and held 53 Americans hostage during the following year. A Soviet invasion of Afghanistan in 1980 only underscored the region's instability. By 1980 the combination of a sick economy and a foreign policy in disarray mired the nation in what Carter himself described as "a crisis of confidence."

KEY EVENTS

1962   *Silent Spring published:* Rachel Carson's warnings about pesticides and the environment

1965   *Unsafe at Any Speed published:* Ralph Nader's indictment of General Motors' Corvair

1966   *NOW:* women's rights organization established

1969   *Apollo 11:* first humans land on the moon

                    Santa Barbara oil spill: emphasizes threat to the environment

1970   *Environmental Protection Agency created*

                    Strike for Equality: feminists publicize issues

1971   *The Closing Circle published:* Barry Commoner highlights the importance of ecology

1972   *Equal Rights Amendment passed by Congress*

                    Nixon reelected: by wide margin; burglary of Democratic headquarters at Watergate causes little comment

1973   *Watergate burglars convicted:* links to the White House become more evident

                    Roe v. Wade: liberalizes restrictions on abortion

                    Ervin Committee hearings: expose Watergate abuses

                    Saturday Night Massacre: firing of Special Prosecutor Archibald Cox creates impeachment crisis

                    War Powers Act: Congress seeks to curb presidential power

                    Yom Kippur War: Egyptian attack surprises Israel

                    OPEC oil boycott: triggers U.S. recession; creates oil shortages

                    Salvador Allende overthrown in Chile: CIA helps topple democratic government

1974   *Nixon v. United States*: Supreme Court orders White House tapes released

President Nixon resigns: after House adopts articles of impeachment; Gerald Ford becomes president

Fair Campaign Practices Act: seeks to curb election abuses

Church Committee: exposes CIA and FBI abuses

1975   *Thieu government*: falls in South Vietnam

Helsinki Summit: as part of détente, U.S. recognizes Soviet position in Eastern Europe

1976   *Jimmy Carter elected president*

1977   *Panama Canal treaties signed:* effort to improve relations in Central America

1978   *Camp David meetings*: Carter mediates Egypt-Israeli accords

1979   *Three Mile Island*: nuclear reactor crisis

Peoples' Republic of China: United States extends recognition

SALT II agreement: accepts Soviet-American nuclear parity

Iran hostage crisis: militants hold American diplomats

Soviet Union invades Afghanistan: seeks to save Communist government

1980   *Sanctions against the Soviet Union*: Carter condemns Afghan invasion

1982   *Equal Rights Amendment fails*: supporters unable to get necessary approval from the states

LEARNING OBJECTIVES

When you have finished studying this chapter, you should be able to:

1. Explain how environmentalism, consumerism, and feminism reinvigorated the reform tradition.

2. Understand how the Watergate crisis taxed the Constitutional system and forced the resignation of Richard Nixon.

3. Describe Henry Kissinger's efforts to preserve American power in the face of a weak economy and presidency.

4. Explain how the backlash to Watergate and Vietnam undermined Gerald Ford and led to the election of Jimmy Carter.

5. Describe how inflation, an energy crisis, and the hostage crisis prevented Carter from creating a more efficient government and a new moral climate in politics.

6. Understand how a division between Zbigniew Brzezinski and Cyrus Vance created confusion in Carter's foreign policy.

Review Questions

MULTIPLE CHOICE

1. The chapter introduction contrasts the 1969 episodes of the Apollo II moon landing and the Santa Barbara channel oil spill to make the point that:
   a. Modern government harnesses technology for the public good, while corporations have polluted the environment.
   b. Today's technology has its successes and its failures.
   c. In the 1970s, the United States entered an era of limits.
   d. In the 1970s, space and the sea were the exciting new frontiers.

   (pp. 1230-1232)

2. What did the reform efforts of the 1970s have in common with movements of the later 1960s?
   a. a non-violent philosophy of how to achieve social change.
   b. a comprehensive concern for the quality of life as a whole.
   c. no confidence that government could effectively improve society's ills.
   d. no consensus on the pace or specific outcomes of reform.

   (pp. 1232, 1241)

3. All of the following accurately describe the troubled economy during the 1970s EXCEPT:
   a. American leadership in heavy industry, especially in automobile manufacturing, suffered from management and labor inefficiencies as well as foreign competition.
   b. Hardest hit were the older industrial cities of Northeast and Midwest.
   c. Economic trends changed from high inflation and high unemployment to the opposite.
   d. Political, economic and environmental crises undermined the American faith in limitless growth and technological solutions.

   (pp. 1232, 1247-1248, 1251-1257)

4. The 1960s are remembered as a decade of crisis. But your text stresses that the 1970s were also a time of a "crisis of confidence" regarding the future in general and American government in particular. What during the Nixon years was most important in initiating this crisis of authority?
   a. political scandal and economic "stagflation"
   b. the President's personal style and the petty politics of the Congress
   c. defeat in Vietnam and the end of the space program
   d. Supreme Court rulings and bureaucratic ineffectiveness in the executive branch

   (pp. 1241-1246; also ch. 32, p. 1219)

5. As a result of the Watergate scandal, President Richard Nixon was forced to resign. But a separate scandal had earlier forced the resignation of another high government official. Who?
   a. a famous Senator
   b. a high-ranking Nixon aide
   c. the Secretary of Defense
   d. the Vice-President

   (p. 1244)

6. The most dramatic consequence of the Middle East ("Yom Kippur") War in 1973
   was:
   a. a shift in U.S. Middle East policy from neutral to pro-Israel.
   b. an Arab oil embargo.
   c. Israeli occupation of Egyptian, Jordanian, Syrian, and Lebanese territory.
   d. overwhelming Jewish support for Nixon in the 1972 election.
   (pp. 1248, 1251)

7. What act of President Ford led to a quick end to his "honeymoon" with Congress
   and the American people?
   a. manipulations of the CIA and FBI.
   b. a pardon of former President Nixon.
   c. imposition of wage and price controls.
   d. signing a treaty returning the canal to Panama.
   (pp. 1250-1251)

8. All of the following explain Carter's defeat of Ford in 1976 EXCEPT:
   a. Voters felt satisfaction with Carter as a well-known political insider.
   b. Most voted for their own party's candidate.
   c. Southerner Carter's support from southern blacks overcame Ford's lead in the
      West.
   d. Economic troubles, as usual, hurt the incumbent.
   (pp. 1252-1253)

9. Significant features of U.S. foreign policy in Carter's early years included all EX-
   CEPT:
   a. repudiating the SALT process.
   b. signing a treaty to return the Canal Zone to Panama.
   c. using economic pressure to promote human rights in other countries.
   d. facilitating an agreement between Israel and Egypt.
   (pp. 1257-1260)

10. In November 1979, Iranian militants took over the United States embassy in
    Teheran and held hostage fifty-three embassy personnel for more than a year.
    What provoked their action was the fact that the United States:
    a. refused to recognize the new Khomeini regime in Iran.
    b. began supporting Iraq in its war against Iran.
    c. attempted to restore the pro-American shah to power in Iran.
    d. allowed the exiled ex-shah of Iran to enter the United States.
    (pp. 1260-1261)

IDENTIFICATION QUESTIONS

You should be able to describe the following key terms, concepts, individuals and places, and explain their significance:

Terms and Concepts

OPEC
ecology
sexism
Roe v. Wade
impoundment
SALT II
meltdown
MIRV missiles

Earth Day
class-action suit
The Feminine Mystique
Equal Rights Amendment
executive privilege
human rights
Camp David accords

Individuals and Places

Barry Commoner
Ralph Nader
the Plumbers
John W. Dean III
Angola
"rust belt" cities
the Ayatollah Khomeini

Betty Friedan
Santa Barbara
Bob Woodward and Carl Bernstein
Archibald Cox
Anwar Sadat
Three-Mile Island
Moscow Olympics

MAP IDENTIFICATIONS

On the map on the next page, label or shade in the following places. In a sentence, note their significance to the chapter. (For reference, consult the map in *Nation of Nations* on page 1249.)

1. Suez Canal
2. Teheran
3. Israel
4. Persian Gulf
5. Sinai Peninsula

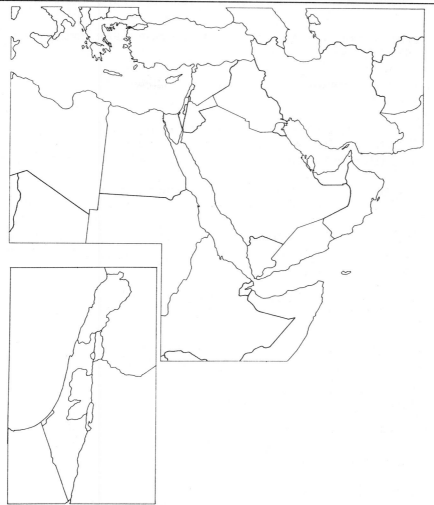

ESSAY QUESTIONS

1. Explain one major achievement for each of the environmental, feminist and consumer movements.

2. How did each of the environmental, feminist and consumer movements experience limits to their reform efforts? To what degree did they make progress?

3. What were the primary reasons Richard Nixon faced impeachment?

4. How did Henry Kissinger seek to develop a more realistic foreign policy for the 1970s? Give specific examples.

5. What role did energy resources play in placing limits on both American domestic and foreign policy?

6. "The environmental movement became compelling enough that even relative conservatives like Richard Nixon embraced it." Present the arguments for defending such a statement. In what ways did Nixon *not* press for environmental protection?

7. "At bottom, the Watergate crisis revolved around a presidency that had become too imperial." Do you agree? Support your arguments with a discussion of Watergate.

8. "Foreign policy always pits the values of idealism and hope against realism and stability." Discuss this statement by contrasting the foreign policies of Henry Kissinger and Jimmy Carter.

9. Describe the Supreme Court's decision in *Roe v. Wade*; then defend or criticize it.

Critical Thinking

EVALUATING EVIDENCE (MAPS)

1. Locate the following features on the map of the Middle East (page 1249): straits of Hormuz, Jordan River, Gulf of Aqaba, Golan Heights. In what ways are each of these strategic locations?

2. Looking at the map of the Middle East (page 1251), describe the relationship between the location of major oil fields and areas of political unrest. What does that suggest to you about Western dependence on oil from the region?

3. On the Middle East map (page 1249) what strategic problem does Israel face in defending itself?

4. What does the Middle East map (page 1249) suggest to you about the strategic importance of Iran? Discuss by referring to specific geographic features.

EVALUATING EVIDENCE (ILLUSTRATIONS)

1. In what ways does the photograph of John Dean (page 1244) reinforce the description of him in the text? Examine the other features of the picture. What do they suggest about the setting in which congressional committees hold their hearings?

2. Photographs are often "ceremonial" in nature: posed deliberately and designed to convey certain kinds of information. Examine the photographs in this chapter and identify those that are ceremonial in nature. What is the "message" being communicated in each one?

3. The picture of the Santa Barbara oil spill that opens the chapter (page 1231) is not a ceremonial photograph, but it is symbolic. What message is it effective at conveying? What aspects of the environmental crisis or the spill itself are such dramatic pictures *not* well suited for conveying?

4. What does the graph on "Income Projections" (page 1257) suggest about average incomes from 1970 to 1980? What does it mean to say that the figures have been given in "constant dollars" or that they have been adjusted for inflation? Does the graph confirm or refute the authors' claim that the 1970s brought an "era of limits"? How do those numbers suggest one reason for the decline in the savings rate that alarmed economists in the 1980s?

5. What does the graph of "OPEC Oil Prices" (page 1252) show were the years of highest oil prices? In what ways would the price of oil contribute to the rate of inflation? In what ways might the graph suggest one reason why Ronald Reagan would prove more successful than Jimmy Carter in fighting inflation?

CRITICAL ANALYSIS

Read carefully the following excerpt from the text and then answer the questions that follow:

> As Nixon's star fell, that of his Secretary of State Henry Kissinger rapidly rose. Kissinger cultivated reporters, who relished his witty quips, intellectual breadth, and willingness to feed stories to the press. Kissinger viewed himself as a realist, a man for whom order and stability were more important than principle. In that way he offended idealists on the political left and right. Quoting the German philosopher Goethe, Kissinger acknowledged, "If I had to choose between justice and disor-

der, on the one hand, and injustice and order on the other, I would always choose the latter."

Kissinger had struggled to prevent Vietnam and Watergate from eroding the president's power to conduct an independent foreign policy. He believed Congress was too sensitive to public opinion and special interest pressure groups to pursue consistent long-term policies. But after Vietnam congressional leaders were eager to curtail presidential powers. The War Powers Act of 1973 required the president to consult Congress whenever possible before committing troops, to send an explanation for his actions within 2 days, and to withdraw any troops after 60 days unless Congress voted to retain them. Such limits often led Kissinger to take a covert approach, as he did in an attempt to quell political ferment in Chile.

In 1970 Chile ranked as one of South America's few viable democracies. When a coalition of Socialists, Communists, and radicals elected Salvador Allende Gossens as president, the Central Intelligence Agency determined that his victory created a danger to the United States. Kissinger pressed the CIA to bribe the Chilean Congress and to promote a military coup against Allende. When those attempts failed, Kissinger resorted to economic warfare between the United States and the Allende government. By 1973 a conservative Chilean coalition with CIA backing had joined to drive the Socialists from power. On September 17 the Chilean military attacked the presidential palace and killed Allende. The United States immediately recognized the new government, which over the next decade deteriorated into a brutally repressive dictatorship. Kissinger argued that the United States had the right to destroy this democracy because Communists themselves threatened an even longer-term dictatorship.

Questions

1. What does the passage suggest were the major problems Kissinger confronted in the making of foreign policy?

2. Explain Kissinger's theory of foreign affairs. How did he perceive Congress to be a hindrance to the conduct of foreign affairs? Do you agree with him? Do you agree with his judgment about the quotation from Goethe?

3. What words or phrases do the authors use that suggest their opinion of Kissinger? How does that compare with your opinion? If you disagree with the authors, what approach might you take in rewriting the passage?

4 Explain why you would support or oppose Kissinger's argument that the United States could destroy a democracy because Communists would create a dictatorship. Would it change your view of Kissinger and the Chile coup d'etat if Allende had not been a Communist?

5. Kissinger felt Congress did not have the vision to adequately consider long-term issues of foreign policy. The same argument could be made for domestic issues. Could you justify giving the president greater powers in the domestic arena as well as in foreign affairs? To what degree would you agree that his quotation of Goethe should apply to domestic as well as foreign affairs?

PRIMARY SOURCE: Ralph Nader Takes on Pollution*

Ralph Nader is best known as an advocate for consumer rights. But Nader by 1970 was also addressing environmental issues. He was concerned that corporate greed, which could saddle the public with shoddy goods, also imposed enormous hidden expenses on the environment. His solution in almost every case was an aroused public willing to force government to impose needed rules and regulations in the public interest.

Three additional points deserve the attention of concerned citizens:

First, a major corporate strategy in combating anti-pollution measures is to engage workers on the company side by leading them to believe that such measures would threaten their livelihood. This kind of industrial extortion in a community--especially a company town--has worked before and will work again unless citizens anticipate and confront it squarely.

Second, both industry spokesmen and their governmental allies (such as the President's Science Adviser, Lee DuBridge) insist that consumers will have to pay the price of pollution control. While this point of view may be an unintended manifestation of the economy's administered price structure, it cannot go unchallenged. Pollution control must

---

* From Ralph Nader, "The Profits of Pollution." Reprinted by permission from *The Progressive*, (XXXIV, 1970) 409 East Main Street, Madison, WI 53703.

not become another lever to lift up excess profits and fuel the fires of inflation. The costs of pollution control technology should come from corporate profits which have been enhanced by the use of the public's environment as industry's private sewer. The sooner industry realizes that it must bear the costs of cleanups, the more likely it will be to employ the quickest and most efficient techniques.

Finally, those who believe deeply in a humane ecology must act in accordance with their beliefs. They must so order their consumption and disposal habits that they can, in good conscience, preach what they actually practice. In brief, they must exercise a personal discipline as they advocate the discipline of governments and corporations.

The battle of the environmentalists is to preserve the physiological integrity of land, air, and water. The planet earth is a seamless structure with a thin slice of sustaining air, water, and soil that supports almost four billion people. This thin slice belongs to all of us, and we use it and hold it in trust for future earthlings. Here we must take our stand.

Questions

1. In the 1970s a popular bumper sticker declared "Out of work? Hungry? Eat an environmentalist." How does Nader's first point reflect on that sentiment?

2. In Nader's second point, what are the two alternatives he describes for absorbing the costs of controlling pollution? Which one does he favor? Why?

3. What does Nader seem to assume is the primary motivator of corporate behavior? Do you agree? What might more conservative economists suggest is the primary motivator of corporate behavior?

4. What does Nader see as the relationship between the government and corporations?

5. Why does Nader believe that the burden of environmental clean-up costs will spur more environmentally responsible behavior from corporations?

6. What life style changes does Nader propose for environmentally concerned citizens?

7. In what ways is Nader an idealist and what ways a realist in his approach to the environment?

34

A NATION STILL DIVISIBLE

THE CHAPTER IN PERSPECTIVE

This chapter brings us to the present--and yet it is linked in innumerable ways to all those that come before it. The trends discussed so far--the rise of the United States as an industrial nation and as an international power, the growth of a consumer-driven economy, the debate over the meaning of equality and freedom, the role of government in regulating the economy and maintaining the welfare of its citizens--all these issues remain central to the nation at the end of the twentieth century. More narrowly, this chapter reveals a reaction to the events of the Vietnam Era and the Age of Limits (Chapters 32 and 33). Ronald Reagan was one of the most visible leaders of the reaction: he wanted to rein in the programs of the Great Society and recommit the United States to an interventionist foreign policy. Further, he and his advisers believed that less government, not more, would reverse the economic slide that weakened the nation in the 1970s. Conservatives generally objected to the liberal bias they saw in the Courts, the media, and the schools. These became areas of conflict that Bill Clinton inherited after his victory in 1992.

OVERVIEW

In the 1970s the majority of Americans turned away from the reform movements associated with the 1960s. What currents of social perfectionism that did exist were concentrated in evangelical religious movements, conservative groups, and self-help therapies. Most people were content to vent their frustrations through more traditional channels or to turn their backs on the larger public arena. "When the going gets tough, the tough go shopping," one popular T-shirt stated. In San Diego, shoppers headed for Horton Mall, the subject of the chapter introduction, which in many ways epitomized the temper of the 1980s.

The Conservative Rebellion

Inspiring the conservative call for a return to fundamentals was a revival of evangelical religion. Despite significant divisions within evangelical ranks, most opposed the liberal rulings of the Supreme Court on pornography, criminal rights, and, above all, abortion. To get their message across, traditionally minded religious leaders often adopted sophisticated media technologies. Catholics and Jews experienced their own movements for conservative renewal. Most religious traditionalists found the mass media, especially network television, too preoccupied with sex and violence. Many found in M*A*S*H and other sitcoms a liberal bias and an attack on traditional values. Parent groups objected to television's impact on children, while feminists and minorities found it treated them unfairly. Yet it was skill in mastering television that gave Ronald Reagan a decisive edge in his debates with Jimmy Carter during the 1980 presidential campaign.

Prime Time with Ronald Reagan

As president, Reagan used his formidable media skills to communicate his message to the nation. He declared his intention to get government off peoples' backs by reducing federal spending, federal regulation, and inflation. At the same time he was determined that the United States would shake off the unhappy heritage of the Vietnam war and stand tall again. He sought to accomplish that with an aggressive anti-Soviet foreign policy and a sharp increase in defense spending.

Reagan quickly set the public agenda. He dramatized his opposition to labor by breaking a strike by air traffic controllers. His Secretary of Interior James Watt and EPA Director Anne Gorsuch set out to dismantle or undermine environmental regulations. And the cornerstone of the Reagan revolution was a significant tax cut under the Economic Recovery Tax Act of 1981. But for several years tight money policies designed to reduce inflation put the economy into recession. The combination of tax cuts, high unemployment, and cuts in government social programs led to a transfer of wealth from the poor to the rich. At the same time the Defense Department conducted a substantial build-up in all categories of weapons, led by the Strategic Defense Initiative (SDI). Neither Reagan nor Congress could agree on a plan to ease growing budget deficits. That did not dampen Reagan's reelection prospects in 1984, as he overwhelmed Democratic candidate Walter Mondale and Geraldine Ferraro, the first female vice presidential candidate.

Second Term Blues

Increasingly, however, Reagan encountered problems that did not yield easy solutions. In foreign policy, efforts to stabilize Lebanon were jolted by a terrorist attack on a Marine barracks and the withdrawal of American forces. A rescue operation on the island of Grenada and the bombing of Libya were public relations successes, though hardly a solution to unrest in the Caribbean and terrorism in the Middle East. In Central America, Reagan's support for right-wing terrorists in El Salvador proved unpopular and his efforts to topple the Sandinista government in Nicaragua met repeated resistance from Congress.

By 1985 the Reaganites were frustrated on two fronts: terrorists still held American hostages in Lebanon and the Sandinistas had survived the attacks of American-supported Contra rebels. Officials in the National Security Council began to implement a scheme, first to secretly trade arms to Iranian moderates for release of hostages, and then to use the secret profits from those arms sales to raise money for the Contras. Selling arms to Iran contradicted Reagan's firm public pledges never to deal with terrorists. Aid to the Contras violated the explicit prohibitions of the Boland Amendment, passed by Congress in 1984. But the actions went undetected, since they were carried out in great secrecy from Congress, from responsible executive agencies, and, possibly, even from the president himself. When the activities of Robert McFarlane, John Poindexter, and Oliver North became known, Congress investigated what was popularly called "Irangate." While the public seemed relatively uninterested in the scandal, the concept of secret government pursuing illegal policies raised profound Constitutional questions.

Reagan retrieved much of his popularity through a series of dramatic meetings in Iceland and Moscow with the new and charismatic Soviet Premier Mikhail Gorbachev. The two eventually agreed to a treaty that reduced intermediate-range missiles in Europe.

Beyond his public personality the key to Reagan's electoral success lay in his promise to advance the conservative social agenda aimed at restoring traditional family values. His appointments to the Supreme Court did shift it in a more conservative direction. But on issues like abortion, school prayer, and drugs Reagan delivered little more than rhetorical support. For much of his second term his administration was bogged down in scandals and Congress proved unwilling to take leadership on issues like the huge federal deficit. Most of the high-paying jobs created during the economic expansion of the 1980s went either to young professionals or offered the poor deadend jobs in fast-food chains or other unskilled areas. Still, the economy was robust enough and Republican policies popular enough to assure victory in 1988 for Reagan's vice president, George Bush.

An End to the Cold War

George Bush much preferred to lead in foreign than in domestic affairs. At first that strengthened his presidency, as world events dominated the headlines. Most startling was the rapid break-up of the Soviet bloc. In Eastern Europe, nation after nation threw off Communist rule. In 1889 the ultimate Cold War symbol, the Berlin Wall, came tumbling down. Events seemed to race out of control. By 1991 the Soviet Union disbanded. Gorbachev had to yield power in Russia to Boris Yeltsin.

President Bush's response was a cautious one. He supported the changes, but made no major commitments. When China's hard-line leaders crushed a popular rebellion, he protested only mildly. Against weaker regional leaders he was more forceful. When Panama's Manuel Noriega became an embarrassment, Bush sent U.S. forces to topple his government and arrest him. A more threatening crisis arose when Iraqi dictator Saddam Hussein sent his troops to conquer oil-rich Kuwait. Bush responded forcefully. He organized America's allies into a coalition that saddled Iraq with a tight economic boycott. Since Saddam refused to leave Kuwait, Bush finally used a UN resolution as authority to launch operation Desert Storm in January 1991. Massive air raids devastated Saddam's forces and prepared the way for a smashing invasion. Still, the war ended with Saddam Hussein in power, though much weakened.

Popular acclaim from Desert Storm seemed to assure Bush reelection in 1992. But his popularity quickly eroded as the economy soured and the president failed to respond effectively to domestic issues. He outraged environmentalists by weakening the Clean Air Act of 1991 and opposing the agenda of the "Earth Summit" that met in 1992 in Rio de Janiero. Scandals shook the Housing and Education Departments. The appointment of Clarence Thomas to the Supreme Court raised troublesome issues about the administration's sensitivity to women.

More trouble came with the economy in recession. Growing budget deficits raised questions about the Republican party's financial strategies. In an effort to ease a budget crisis in 1990 Bush agreed to tax increases. Conservative Republicans felt betrayed by a president who in 1988 had loudly promised, "No new taxes." And in 1991 a violent riot ripped Los Angeles, calling attention to the problems of decayed urban areas that had gone largely unaddressed during the Reagan-Bush years. Even worse for Bush, middle-class voters were hurt by a recession that refused to end. By 1992 voters had turned angry. Some of the anger buoyed the campaign of a Texas maverick, Ross Perot. But many more "Reagan Democrats" returned to the fold to vote for candidate Bill Clinton as a moderate who nonetheless promised activism and change.

A Nation of Nations in the Twenty-First Century

If anything, America society was more diverse at the end of the twentieth century than ever before. Social and political stability thus hinged, as in the past, on giving all groups access to the mainstream of American life.

That access was complicated because immigration continued to alter the face of the nation. Hispanic and Asian immigrants constituted the largest groups of newcomers. Under the reforms of the Immigration Act of 1965, Asians had surpassed Hispanics by the 1980s, in supplying the largest number of legal immigrants, who concentrated heavily in California, Hawaii, and New York City. To deal with a flood of illegal aliens, largely from Central America and Mexico, Congress passed the Immigration Reform and Control Act of 1986. Friction with older groups sometimes resulted in violence. The issues of race prejudice and minority poverty still troubled the nation. The Supreme Court had limited the use of affirmative action quotas in the *Bakke* case, though still allowing them in some cases. Incidents of violence and racism troubled even normally tolerant college campuses.

The election of Bill Clinton brought to the White House a president likely to revive the activist traditions of Woodrow Wilson, Franklin Roosevelt, and Lyndon Johnson. To Clinton fell the task of shaping a government that represented all the groups in this nation of nations.

KEY EVENTS

1978   *Regents of California v. Bakke*: Court rules against fixed quotas

1979   *Moral Majority*: Rev. Jerry Falwell establishes advocacy group for fundamentalists

               Sandinistas: radicals overthrow Somoza in Nicaragua

1980   *Ronald Reagan elected president*

1981   *Reagan military buildup:* massive increase in defense spending

               Reagan ends air traffic controllers' strike

               Economic Recovery Tax Act: tax cut legislation passed

1982   *Attack on U.S. Marine barracks*: terrorists kill 239 Marines in Lebanon

1983   *Invasion of Grenada*: U.S. forces topple leftist government

1984   *Boland Amendment*: forbids U.S. aid to Contras

               Geraldine Ferraro becomes first woman nominated for vice president

1985   *Gramm-Rudman Act*: sets mandatory budget cuts

               U.S. bombing raid on Libya: Reagan fights terrorism

1986   *Space shuttle Challenger explodes*

               Tax Reform Act: bipartisan effort to reform tax codes

               Reykjavik summit: Reagan and Gorbachev discuss broad nuclear arms cuts

Iran-Contra scandal: story breaks on illegal arms transfers

1987   *Iran-Contra hearings*: reveal details of illegal arms policies

INF Treaty: United States and Soviet Union agree on limiting some missiles

Immigration Reform Act: seeks to ease problem of illegal aliens

Stock market plunge: Dow-Jones average drops sharply

1988   *George Bush elected president*

1989   *Revolutions in Communist-bloc nations:* Berlin Wall falls

Panama invasion: Noriega arrested

1990   *Kuwait invasion*: Saddam Hussein threatens Middle East oil

1991   *Operation Desert Storm*: Allied forces crush Iraq, liberate Kuwait

1992   *Bill Clinton elected president*

LEARNING OBJECTIVES

When you have finished studying this chapter, you should be able to:

1. Explain the rising influence of evangelical religious groups and the conservative backlash against the liberal media.

2. Describe Ronald Reagan's first-term success in establishing a conservative political agenda.

3. Discuss the three major areas of Reagan's foreign policy.

4. Explain the origins of the Iran-Contra scandals.

5. Discuss the major social, economic, and moral problems facing the nation at the end of the Reagan administration.

6. Analyze the ways in which new patterns of minority relations and immigration are reshaping the social fabric of America.

Review Questions

MULTIPLE CHOICE

1. The chapter introduction tells the story of San Diego's Horton Plaza to make the point that
    a. malls like Horton Plaza caused the decline of downtown business districts.
    b. Ronald Reagan's successful Presidential campaign focused on California-style shopping malls.
    c. religious activists began to relocate Sunday services from traditional churches to the new retail malls.
    d. malls, as centers of consumer culture, symbolized the private quest for personal fulfillment typical of the 1980s.

(pp. 1264-1266)

2. The conservative revival:
    a. affected Catholics as well as Protestants.
    b. reflected rural ignorance about sophisticated modern technology.
    c. stressed the rights of individuals to make social and economic choices free of government regulation.
    d. opposed the Presidential candidacy of the divorced movie actor, Ronald Reagan.

(pp. 1267-1273)

3. Demonstrating a desire to curb the power of organized labor, the Reagan administration took a hard line against an illegal strike by
    a. the Teamsters.
    b. air traffic controllers.
    c. FBI agents.
    d. the Labor Department.

(p. 1274)

4. Conservative Protestants ("evangelicals") shared with conservative Catholics certain concerns about trends in American society. Which is NOT an accurate statement of beliefs they held in common?
   a. Non-public, religious-oriented schools provide a more morally acceptable education than the increasingly secular public schools.
   b. Mass entertainment promotes permissive social behavior and a liberal political agenda.
   c. A major moral failure of contemporary society is the persistence of racism.
   d. Abortion should be legally restricted because it amounts to killing an unborn human being.

   (pp. 1268-1270)

5. What is meant by "supply-side economics"--the new Reagan approach to economic policy in the early 1980s?
   a. the attempt to increase domestic oil supplies
   b. cutting back welfare and other programs for the poor, to force them to supply their own needs
   c. encouraging, through tax cuts, private sector investment that would create new jobs, thus promoting economic growth and increasing net tax revenues
   d. keeping interest rates high, to increase the money supply

   (p. 1273)

6. What was unique about the Democratic ticket in 1984?
   a. A Greek immigrant headed the ticket.
   b. Both Presidential and Vice Presidential candidates came from the same state.
   c. Both Presidential and Vice Presidential candidates were Southerners.
   d. The Vice-Presidential candidate was a woman.

   (pp. 1277-1278)

7. The text suggests that Reagan's "second term blues" stemmed from two characteristic aspects of his administration:
   a. awkwardness with the media and hatred of his enemies.
   b. anti-communism and a hands-off management style.
   c. religious conservatism and ignorance about the Middle East.
   d. militarism and Congressional opposition.

   (p. 1279)

8. The Reagan administration focused on three priorities in foreign policy. Which of the following accurately states an initiative in one of the three areas?
   a. Central America: an invasion of Panama to rescue American students and prevent a Marxist takeover
   b. Middle East: successful retaliation against Libya and Lebanon for terrorist attacks
   c. Far East: public rhetoric critical of China's suppression of democratic reform
   d. Soviet Union: both a sharp military build-up and a new arms control treaty
   (pp. 1279-1285)

9. The Reagan and Bush administrations sent American invasion forces abroad in all of the following cases EXCEPT:
   a. to a Caribbean island to protect Americans and topple a leftist government.
   b. to Panama to capture the country's dictator-President.
   c. to Nicaragua to fight alongside the contra rebels.
   d. to the Persian Gulf to expel Iraqis from Kuwait.
   (pp. 1279, 1291-1292)

10. Which statement best explains Bill Clinton's victory in 1992?
   a. As a southerner and liberal, Clinton rebuilt the traditional Democratic coalition and won a solid majority of both popular and electoral votes.
   b. Voters, in an upbeat mood, rejected the sour criticisms of Bush and Perot and embraced Clinton's optimistic vision for change.
   c. Worried about growing instability around the world, voters opted for the candidate with experience in foreign affairs.
   d. Many one-time supporters of President Bush voted against him this time on either ideological or economic grounds.
   (pp. 1296-1297)

IDENTIFICATION QUESTIONS

You should be able to describe the following key terms, concepts, individuals and places, and explain their significance:

Terms and Concepts

Pentecostal	Moral Majority
sitcoms	tight money
supply-side economics	nuclear winter

Gramm-Rudman Act

Strategic Defense Initiative

Contadora Group

Iran-Contra connection

INF Treaty

gay rights

Rainbow Coalition

affirmative action

Individuals and Places

The Rev. Jerry Falwell
Father Robert Drinan
Archie Bunker
James Watt
Caspar Weinberger
Geraldine Ferraro
Sandra Day O'Connor
William Rehnquist
Beirut, Lebanon
Edward Boland
Robert McFarlane
Oliver North
John Poindexter
Reykjavik
Edwin Meese
Allan Bakke
Michael Dukakis

MAP IDENTIFICATIONS

On the map on the next page, label or shade in the following places. In a sentence, note their significance to the chapter. (For reference, consult the map in *Nation of Nations* on page 1281.)

1. Nicaragua
2. El Salvador
3. Colombia
4. Venezuela
5. Grenada

ESSAY QUESTIONS

1. How did the swing toward more conservative politics reflect views about the following: abortion, television, films, family life, textbooks?

2. What factors led to the economic prosperity of the Reagan years? To what extent do you believe the president's economic policies helped to solve underlying economic problems?

3. Ronald Reagan hoped to execute a foreign policy that made America "stand tall." Discuss how he attempted to implement that goal in the following areas: Grenada, Lebanon, Libya, Iran.

4. Explain the major features of Reagan and Gorbachev's negotiations on strategic arms.

5. Explain which you think was worse--Irangate or Watergate.

6. What were the major features of immigration in the 1980s? Discuss both the conti-
   nuities with previous immigration trends and changes. How did government policy
   help, hinder or shape these patterns?

Critical Thinking

EVALUATING EVIDENCE (MAPS)

1. Which nations of Central and South America (map, page 1281) are the principal
   producers of cocaine? Which nations have the most serious debt crises? Which nations are the primary sources of immigrants to the United States?

2. Why would Honduras be a pivotal nation in the Reagan administration's campaign
   against the Sandinistas? (Map, page 1281.) Where were rebel groups fighting established governments during the 1980s?

3. What three major areas of concern does the map of Central America point up for
   American foreign policy? Which area gave the Reagan administration the most
   concern? Which area seems most threatening, in your opinion?

4. In the maps of Hispanic and Asian populations (page 1298) what geographic
   similarities are evident on both maps? How would you explain them? What factors
   mentioned in the text might account for the distribution of Hispanics and Asian
   immigrants?

5. Comparing the map of Operation Desert Storm (page 1293) with the Geography
   feature on Vietnam (page 1196-97) explain why airpower was more effective
   against Iraq.

EVALUATING EVIDENCE (ILLUSTRATIONS AND CHARTS)

1. What does the photograph showing Right to Life protesters (page 1267) suggest to
   you about civil rights politics in the 1980s?

2. What economic strategies have Asian-American immigrants adopted, based on the photograph (page 1300)? What evidence would indicate that they maintain ties with their homelands?

3. What does the graph "Poverty in America, 1970-1990" (page 1275) suggest about the distribution of poverty, especially during the Reagan years? How does it reflect Michael Harrington's view that the elderly are no longer the major victims of poverty?

4. What does the graph on the federal deficit (page 1276) suggest about Reagan's commitment to a balanced budget? Has the deficit increased only in absolute numbers or as a percentage of the Federal budget as well?

CRITICAL ANALYSIS

Read carefully the following excerpt from the text and then answer the questions that follow:

> Reagan's skill as an actor obscured contradictions between his rhetoric and reality. With his jaunty wave and jutting jaw, he projected the physical vitality and charismatic good looks of John Kennedy. Yet at 69, he was the oldest President to take office, and none since Calvin Coolidge slept as soundly or as much. Reagan had begun his political life as a New Deal Democrat, but over the next two decades he moved increasingly to the right. By the 1950s he had become an ardent anticommunist, earning a reputation among conservatives as an engaging after-dinner speaker and corporate spokesperson for General Electric. In 1966 he began two terms as governor of California with a promise to pare down government programs and balance budgets. In fact, spending jumped sharply during his term in office. Similarly he continued to champion family values, although he was divorced and estranged from some of his children.
>
> Similar inconsistencies marked Reagan's leadership as president. Outsiders applauded Reagan's "hands-off" management: less management, not more was what the nation needed after a succession of activist presidents from Kennedy to Carter. Reagan set the tone and direction, letting his advisers take care of the details. On the other hand, many within the administration, like Secretary of the Treasury Donald Regan, were shocked to find the new president remarkably ignorant and

uninterested about important matters of policy. "The Presidential mind was not cluttered with facts," Regan lamented.

Then, too, Reagan disliked personal confrontation. Outsiders viewed that quality as loyalty; some insiders saw it as an inability to control his advisers and staff. Nancy Reagan (aided by an astrologer) often dictated his schedule, helped select his advisers, and even sometimes determined the major issues the president addressed. Yet the public believed he was firmly in charge and, until the Iran arms scandal in 1986, consistently approved his conduct. His capacity for deflecting responsibility for mistakes earned him the reputation as the "Teflon president," since no criticism seemed to stick.

Questions

1. How did Reagan's experience as an actor help him in office? Is that a positive or negative quality for a politician?

2. Identify any language the authors use that reflects bias rather than objective analysis. Do the authors respect Reagan? Do they provide information that would permit readers to come to a different conclusion than they may have reached?

3. Why do you think the authors make reference to Nancy Reagan's contacts with an astrologer? In what way does that affect your view of Reagan as President?

4. Do you think from reading this passage that Reagan was sufficiently in charge as President? To what degree did he need to be, given the precedent of more activist presidents?

5. On the basis of your knowledge in this course, how would you rank Ronald Reagan compared with past presidents? Would he be in the top, middle, or bottom third in terms of accomplishments? Justify your choice.

PRIMARY SOURCE: The Spiritual State of Americans in the 1980s*

From 1979 to 1984 Robert Bellah, a historian of religion, set out with a team of researchers to explore the state of the American character. Their primary focus was on the

---

* From Robert Bellah et al., *Habits of the Heart*, Copyright 1985 by The Regents of the University of California.

concept of individualism and the ways in which Americans found meaning in their private and public lives. What they seem to have discovered is that after Vietnam, "The Me Generation," and the era of limits, Americans were no longer so buoyantly optimistic about the future.

There was a time when, under the battle cry of "freedom," separation and individuation were embraced as the key to a marvelous future of unlimited possibility. It is true that there were always those ...who viewed the past with nostalgia and the present with apprehension and who warned that we were entering unknown and dangerous waters. It is also true that there are still those who maintain their enthusiasm for modernity, who speak of the third wave or the Aquarian Age or the new paradigm in which a dissociated individuation will reach a final fulfillment. Perhaps most common today, however, is a note of uncertainty, not a desire to turn back to the past but an anxiety about where we seem to be headed. In this view, modernity seems to be a period of enormously rapid change, a transition from something relatively fixed toward something not clear. Many might find still applicable Matthew Arnold's assertion that we are

Wandering between two worlds, one dead,
The other powerless to be born.

There is a widespread feeling that the promise of the modern era is slipping away from us. A movement of enlightenment and liberation that was to have freed us from superstition and tyranny has led in the twentieth century to a world in which ideological fanaticism and political oppression have reached extremes unknown in previous history. Science, which was to have unlocked the bounties of nature, has given us the power to destroy all life on earth. Progress, modernity's master idea, seems less compelling when it appears it may be progress into the abyss. And the globe today is divided between a liberal world so incoherent that it seems to be losing the significance of its own ideals, an oppressive and archaic communist statism, and a poor, often tyrannical Third World reaching for the very first rungs of modernity. In the liberal world, the state which was supposed to be a neutral watchman that would maintain order while individuals pursued their various interests, has become so overgrown and militarized that it threatens to become a universal policeman.

Yet in spite of those daunting considerations, many of those we talked to are still hopeful. They realize that though the process of separation and individuation were necessary to free us from the tyrannical structures of the past, they must be balanced by a renewal of commitment and community if they are not to end in self-destruction or turn into their opposites. Such a renewal is indeed a world waiting to be born if we only had the courage to see it.

Questions

1. What are the two worlds Arnold refers to in the line quoted in the excerpt?

2. What do you think Bellah means by the terms separation and individuation? How have they been historically linked to freedom?

3. Give examples of the liberal, communist, and Third World states that support Bellah's point of view.

4. Give historical examples of what Bellah means by ideological fanaticism and political oppression "unknown in previous history."

5. Explain why you agree or disagree with Bellah's view of science as a two-edged sword.

6. Explain why you agree or disagree with the idea that the United States government has "become so overgrown and militarized that it threatens to become a universal policeman."

7. To what degree does Bellah seem to have caught the temper of the 1980s? Could what he says be applied to earlier decades in American history? If so, are his sentiments too general to be a useful description of the era? What defining moods and temperaments do you believe have characterized the 1980s?